Jan. 26, 2012

World Exploration from Ancient Times

Compton's by Britannica®

ENCYCLOPÆDIA
Britannica®

CHICAGO   LONDON   NEW DELHI   PARIS   SEOUL   SYDNEY   TAIPEI   TOKYO

Learn & Explore series
World Exploration from Ancient Times
Compton's by Britannica

Library of Congress Control Number: 2010938152
International Standard Book Number: 978-1-61535-454-2

Printed in Malaysia/Times Offset
01-012011

Britannica may be accessed at http://www.britannica.com on the Internet.

Cover (background): iStockphoto/Thinkstock; front cover (top left): L. Prang and Company, Library of Congress,
Washington, D.C. (neg. no. LC-USZC2-1687); (top right, center): Photos.com/Jupiterimages; (bottom right):
© Getty Images; back cover (left, center, right): Photos.com/Jupiterimages; (top): NASA

www.britannica.com

EDITOR'S PREFACE

Whether it be land, sea, or space, what lies beyond one's physical limitations has always piqued the interest of the human race. This book takes a look at exploration of Earth's land masses from early times. Although the primary motivation for different exploratory missions may have varied throughout the years, one recurring theme has always been curiosity. Venturing out to find what lies beyond is a part of human nature.

The story of world exploration is often a compelling one. *World Exploration from Ancient Times* organizes this material by region (Eurasia [Europe and Asia], the Americas, Australia and the Pacific Islands, Africa, and the Polar Regions) and employs the use of 140 maps and photos to aid in illustrating the story. In addition, quotations from several key explorers are sprinkled throughout the text. Sidebars and several pages of mini-biographies (World Explorers at a Glance) round out the body of the book. The introduction, opposite the editor's overview, was contributed by Stephen P. Davis, geography contributor for several articles in *Compton's Encyclopedia* and graduate instructor at the University of Illinois at Chicago. His article on Australia in *Compton's* served as the jumping off point for the section on Australia and the Pacific Islands. Begin your journey by reading Davis' introduction on page vi and the editor's overview on page 1.

As a previous editor in chief of *Compton's Encyclopedia* once said of the set, "whether the incentive to open the books came from the suggestion of parents, from the requirements of schoolwork, or from the child's own natural curiosity, upon these pages would rest a responsibility greater than merely offering bare answers to isolated questions. They must arouse interest, they must give color and significance and due emphasis to the facts, they must relate them to other essential facts; in short, they must give more than the young reader has the experience to ask for." This is true not only of *Compton's Encyclopedia* today, but of the *Learn & Explore* series as well.

TABLE OF CONTENTS

INTRODUCTION

This introduction was contributed by Stephen P. Davis, former Associate Editor, Encyclopædia Britannica; *Graduate Instructor in the Department of Anthropology and Geography, University of Illinois at Chicago; and author of popular and scholarly articles on geography, history, sociology of religion, and cultural anthropology.*

Why do we seem driven to explore? Is exploration a gift of "the human condition" that raises us above the animals? Or does it instead link us with the biological world and other wandering, migrating, and mobile species to a degree that some would not care to admit? Our common ancestors became bipedal millions of years ago, and *Homo sapiens* explored within, and beyond, Africa 150,000 to 50,000 years ago. What drove them as far as Australia, Hawaii, and the southern tip of South America? Instinct? The sublime? Or a matrix that we can barely imagine? Whatever the reason, we seem compelled to honor those sharing their spirit. Many of our films, novels, and hearthside tales focus on risk-takers, bringers of knowledge, and "discoverers," regardless of the chaos and lamentation that can follow in their wakes—whether the diseases carried by Columbus to the Americas in 1492, the abuses wrought on Australia's Aborigines in the 1800s, or the slavery and warfare that European incursions sparked in Africa.

We may wish to emulate explorers, to attain their heights of ability and self-reliance. Or, just maybe, we share a suspicion that history could not have unfolded without their intrusions (though we hope that is not the guiding light of our fate). We thrill to Balboa's "discovery" of the Pacific Ocean (which was already known to local peoples) though it contributed to Pizarro's conquest of the Inca Empire. Likewise, we marvel at the Chinese travelers who contributed to imperial expansion, with mixed results. In our science fiction, the beloved Star Trek character Captain James Kirk is an echo of the explorer Captain James Cook, who boldly went "farther than any other man has been before" across the void-like Pacific Ocean. Yet we often ignore the colonial, cultural, and biological abuses unleashed after the captains' logs reached home. Today, we grant explorers sizable space in our popular histories, especially in the histories of nations anxious to solidify control over their claimed lands.

Exploration has contributed to greater scientific knowledge, and yet misinformation has gone hand in hand with many a voyage. Greek and Roman scholars repeated tales of giant, gold-mining ants in the east. Columbus recorded accounts of "one-eyed men, and others, with snouts of dogs, who ate men." Many expected to encounter Patagonian giants, antipodes (people with feet pointed backward), and Amazons. Arctic explorers in the 1800s believed that a warm zone encircled the North Pole. Cartographers would fill in the blank spaces on maps with sea monsters.

As we survey the good and the bad that these wanderings have wrought, we should acknowledge an error of omission—namely, that most of the talented and courageous women who have contributed to these events, in all times and places, have been lost to history. It is true, of course, that explorers' roles have often been restricted to men by the commands of nations, navies, and the societies of their times, but we also need to read between the lines. In a similar vein, we should not give credence to a "big man" version of history that would depict only the solitary, triumphant ship captain, the general, or the king—the only person whose name *was* recorded in many histories. None of these leaders could have succeeded without supporters at home and, more vital still, strangers on the road, gracious hosts, and indigenous guides. The Muslim scholar Ibn Battutah could never have covered 75,000 miles (more than 120,000 kilometers) of Asia, Africa, and the Indian Ocean in the 1300s were it not for the unnamed fishers and traders before him. In 1804–06 Lewis and Clark depended heavily on Native American guides and chiefs who sketched maps for them in the sand. The monikers of explorers persist today because of those whose names were never written down or have been lost to history.

WORLD EXPLORATION FROM ANCIENT TIMES

The explorers who appear in this book sailed across vast open seas and crossed mountains, deserts, jungles, rivers, and even great sheets of polar ice. They journeyed into the unknown, connecting cultures and adding new places to the map. The risks were often great. Many explorers died while investigating new territory or while trying to return home again.

The motives for exploration were varied. Many explorers sought wealth for themselves and their sponsors, hoping to find new lands rich in gold, silver, and jewels. Others searched for new and shorter trade routes, which could lead to greater commercial profits for trading companies. Some explorers hoped to gain fame and glory by becoming the first to set foot on a strange land. Others traveled for religious reasons. Pilgrims visited the great centers of Buddhism or Islam, and missionaries traveled to spread Christianity. Many explorers set out in search of adventure or for the sheer thrill of discovery.

Curiosity about the world was a major motive. Explorers wanted to travel farther than anyone else had before in order to find out what was there. They sought to reveal the geography of unknown places, to chart uncharted territories and seas. Scientists often accompanied exploring expeditions. They journeyed to study the plants, animals, rocks, climates, and other aspects of new lands.

Many explorers found new territory for their people to settle. From the ancient Phoenicians and Greeks setting up outposts in the Mediterranean to the European powers carving up Africa into territories in the 19th century, exploration often went together with colonization and conquest. Societies expanded into empires by establishing far-flung colonies. They wanted to gain new living space, farmland, precious metals, and other economic resources for their people, as well as increased political power. In some cases, the colonists settled land that was unoccupied. Often, however, they took control of land where other people already lived.

It is important to note that most of the new lands that the great explorers found were already populated. To say, then, that Christopher Columbus "discovered" America or that Willem Jansz "discovered" Australia should not be taken to mean that they were the first people to set foot in these places. A great number of people already lived there. Instead, these explorers discovered places wholly unknown to their own cultures—important achievements, nevertheless, that literally broadened their cultures' horizons. Their explorations also led to profound and often devastating changes in the societies they "discovered."

This book focuses on voyages of exploration and discovery made in the world's great land areas. Sections cover the exploration of Eurasia (Europe and Asia), the Americas, Australia and the Pacific Islands, Africa, and the polar regions. For the major explorers, additional biographical details, including birth and death dates, can be found at the back of the book, in the section "World Explorers at a Glance." Some explorers were active in more than one continent and so are discussed in more than one section. The index is the best place to start if one is looking for information on a specific explorer, expedition, or geographic feature.

EURASIA

In ancient times several major civilizations arose in Eurasia, or Europe and Asia. Western civilization traces its roots to the peoples of Mesopotamia, in the land between the Tigris and Euphrates rivers, in what is now Iraq. Western knowledge of the world expanded from this valley to the lands around the Mediterranean Sea. Exploration of the Mediterranean region went hand in hand with its colonization. The ancient Greeks and a seafaring people known as the Phoenicians established settlements throughout the Mediterranean world. Ancient Egypt, in northern Africa bordering the Mediterranean, also developed an advanced society. Meanwhile, important civilizations developed in the East, in the lands that are today China and India and Pakistan. The Chinese were active explorers of what are now China and Central Asia.

EARLY EUROPEAN EXPLORATION

Shores of the Mediterranean and the Atlantic

The first phase in European exploration centered on the Mediterranean region. In the 1st millennium BC Phoenicia and the Greek city-states rapidly colonized the shores of the Mediterranean and Black seas. This widespread expansion must have been accompanied by exploration of the adjacent inland areas by countless unknown soldiers and traders. In the 5th century BC the ancient Greek writer Herodotus prefaced his *History* with a geographic description of what was then the known world. This introduction reveals that the coastlines of the Mediterranean and the Black seas had already been explored by then. Much of Europe, however, remained uncharted. Herodotus concludes by saying, "Whether the sea girds Europe round on the north none can tell."

The Phoenicians were notable merchants, colonizers, and sailors. Fearless and patient navigators, they ventured into regions where no one else dared to go. They are credited with the discovery and use of the North Star for navigation. The Phoenicians sought to dominate trade and exclude all their rivals. For this reason, they carefully guarded the secrets of their trade routes and discoveries and their knowledge of winds and currents.

The homeland of the Phoenicians was located mainly in what is now Lebanon. From there, they established colonies along the coasts of Syria, Israel, Cyprus, Sicily, Sardinia, southern Spain, and northern Africa. Their great colony of Carthage (now in Tunisia), produced two notable explorers in the 5th century BC. Hanno sailed along the coast of western Africa (*see* Africa, "Phoenicians and Greeks"). Himilco sailed to the north on a four-month journey. The purpose of his voyage was apparently to consolidate control of the trade in tin along the Atlantic coast of Europe. From Carthage, he sailed to the Phoenician colony of Gades (now Cádiz, Spain). After visiting the coasts of Spain and Portugal, he reached northwestern France. Some historians believe that Himilco may also have visited Great Britain.

In ancient Greece, as in Phoenicia, knowledge of other lands came with overseas settlement. Organized Greek colonization began in the 8th century BC. Commercial interests, greed, and sheer curiosity seem to be the forces that drove the Greek city-states to expand and explore. At its height, ancient Greece comprised settlements in Asia Minor, the Greek islands, southern Italy, Sicily, and North Africa.

The Phoenicians long controlled the Strait of Gibraltar, at the western end of the Mediterranean Sea. They

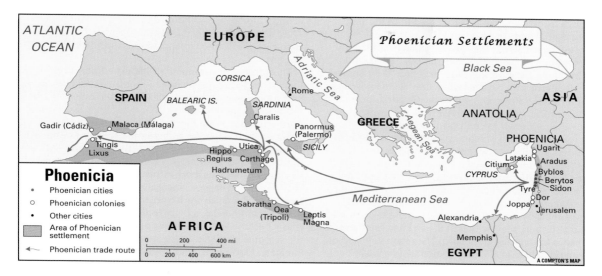

allowed no one else to pass through this channel to the Atlantic Ocean. In about 300 BC, however, Carthage became embroiled in a struggle with a Greek city in Sicily. As a result, Phoenician power at the gate of the Mediterranean temporarily weakened. This lapse allowed the Greek explorer Pytheas to sail right through.

Pytheas was a navigator, geographer, and astronomer from the Greek colony of Massalia (now Marseille, France). He became the first Greek to visit and describe the British Isles and the Atlantic coast of Europe. Sailing from the Mediterranean Sea into the Atlantic, Pytheas stopped at southern Spain. He then probably followed the European shoreline to the tip of northwestern France. He eventually reached the southwestern tip of England, in what is now Cornwall. There he may have visited the tin mines, which were famous in the ancient world. Pytheas claimed to have explored a large part of

Great Britain on foot. He may have sailed around the island; he accurately estimated its circumference at 4,000 miles (6,400 kilometers). Pytheas visited some northern European countries and may have reached the mouth of the Vistula River on the Baltic Sea. He also told of Thule, "the northernmost of the British Isles, six days sail from Britain." The place he visited may have been Iceland or Norway.

Pytheas made a number of scientific observations during his voyage of exploration. He made calculations with a sundial at the summer solstice and noted the lengthening days as he traveled northward. He also observed that the North Star is not at the true North Pole and that the Moon affects the tides.

Exploration of the North Atlantic was not carried farther until several centuries later. This exploration was undertaken not by Mediterranean peoples but by

A relief carving from the 1st century AD shows the kind of ship that the Phoenicians used on the Mediterranean Sea.

Viking longships were exceptionally sturdy in heavy seas. They carried a single square sail and were also propelled by oars. From 40 to 60 oarsmen sat on the rowers' benches.

Vikings from Scandinavia. From the 8th to the 11th century AD, bands of Swedish Vikings traded southeastward across the Russian plains. At the same time, groups of Danish Vikings raided, traded, and settled along the coasts of the North Sea. They arrived in the Mediterranean region, where they were known as the Normans. However, neither the Swedes nor the Danes traveling in these regions were exploring lands that were unknown to civilized Europeans.

It was the Vikings of Norway who were the true explorers. In about AD 890 the Viking Ohthere of Norway was "desirous to try how far that country extended north." He sailed around Norway's North Cape, along the coast of Lapland to the White Sea. By contrast, most other Vikings sailing in high latitudes explored not eastward but westward. Sweeping down the outer edge of Great Britain, they settled in the Orkney, Shetland, and Hebrides islands and in Ireland. They then voyaged on to Iceland, where in 870 they settled among Irish colonists who had preceded them by some two centuries. The Vikings may well have arrived piloted by Irish sailors. Norwegian Vikings later explored farther west in the Atlantic, reaching Greenland and Newfoundland in North America (see The Americas).

Shores of the Indian Ocean and the China Sea

From very early times, people pursued trade across the land bridges and through the gulfs linking the parts of Asia, Africa, and Europe that lie between the Mediterranean and Arabian seas. It is therefore not surprising that exploratory voyages early revealed the coastlines of the Indian Ocean.

The first Western observer to give an account of India was Scylax of Caria (an ancient district of Anatolia, in Turkey). In about 510 BC, Darius the Great, the king of Persia (Iran), sent Scylax to explore the course of the Indus River. Scylax traveled overland to the Kabul River, in Afghanistan. He reached the Indus River and followed it through India to its mouth at the Arabian Sea, which is the northwestern part of the Indian Ocean. He then sailed westward. Passing by the Persian Gulf (which was already well known to the Western world), he explored the Red Sea. Scylax finished his voyage in northern Egypt. His journey had taken two and a half years to complete.

The expeditions in the 4th century BC of the famous conqueror Alexander the Great of Macedonia brought much new geographic knowledge to the Greek world, as well as control of vast new territory. They also carried the influence of Mediterranean culture to the East and of Eastern culture to the Mediterranean.

Most of Alexander's campaigns were journeys of military exploration. His earlier expeditions were to regions already familiar to the Greeks—Babylonia (in Iraq) and Persia. The later ones, however, brought the Greeks a great deal of new information. These campaigns took him through the enormous tract of land from the south of the Caspian Sea to the mountains of the Hindu Kush of Central Asia. Alexander and his army crossed these mountains to the Indus River valley. They then marched westward through the desolate country along the southern edge of the Iranian plateau. They ultimately reached Susa (now Shush, Iran), the capital of Darius the Great, and overthrew the Persian Empire.

The admiral in command of the expedition's naval forces was Nearchus. He waited for the favorable monsoon winds and then sailed from the mouth of the Indus to the mouth of the Euphrates. He explored the northern coast of the Persian Gulf on his way.

The Roman Republic and later the Roman Empire succeeded the Greek city-states as the great power of the Western world. The empire eventually included most of western Europe, northern Africa, and the Middle East. As Roman power grew, increasing wealth brought increasing demands for luxuries from the East. This led to great commercial activity in the eastern seas. As the coasts became well known, Roman sailors skillfully used the seasonal character of the monsoon winds to navigate. During the reign of the Roman emperor Hadrian in the 1st century BC, Western traders reached what are now Thailand, Cambodia, and Indonesia. A few also seem to have reached the coast of China. In the late 2nd century AD, according to Chinese records, an "embassy" came from the Roman emperor Marcus Aurelius to the Chinese emperor Huandi.

CHINESE EXPLORATION

The Chinese developed an advanced civilization in early times and were energetic explorers. From their ancient homeland in the basin of the Huang He (Yellow River), they spread out widely, ultimately creating a vast empire. Early explorations centered on the courses of the rivers that provided the growing state with water for agriculture as well as transportation routes. The state built many canals and dikes. The search for land routes through the mountains and deserts to the northwest and west also became important. Expansion was a major spur to exploration. Chinese farmers ventured out to settle new lands. State-sponsored missions also sent out parties to conquer and colonize territory, to survey and administer the conquered lands, and to maintain state security.

Zhang Qian and the Silk Road

During the Han Dynasty (206 BC–AD 220), the expanding Chinese Empire was threatened by raiders from the north. People who led a nomadic, or wandering, life in the northern steppe land would invade settled agricultural communities to the south to solve periodic food shortages. The Great Wall of China had been built to defend Chinese territory against northern nomads, especially the Xiongnu. The Xiongnu may have been the same people known as the Huns in Europe. Starting in the reign of the Han emperor Wudi, the Chinese carried out long and costly military campaigns along the northern and northwestern borders.

Wudi also dispatched an envoy, Zhang Qian, to try to forge a military alliance with another nomadic people against the Xiongnu. Zhang became a pioneering explorer. He was the first person to bring back a reliable account of the lands of Central Asia to the court of

China. He set off in 138 BC to try to establish relations with a nomadic people called the Yuezhi. He traveled through what is now the Chinese province of Gansu, but he was captured by the Xiongnu. They kept him prisoner for 10 years in the Altai Mountains before he finally managed to escape. He then proceeded on his mission, reaching the Yuezhi in what is now Afghanistan. On his return voyage via Tibet, he was again captured by the Xiongnu, but he escaped about a year later. He returned to China after an absence of some 13 years. Seven years later Zhang was sent on another mission, this time to the Wusun, a people living in the Ili River valley (in what is now northwestern China).

Although Zhang was not able to establish an alliance with the Yuezhi or the Wusun, he made important diplomatic contacts and collected much useful information. In addition to traveling himself, he sent his assistant to visit parts of what are now Uzbekistan and Afghanistan. Zhang gathered information on Parthia (now in Iran), India, and other states in the area. His missions opened the way for exchanges of envoys between these Central Asian states and China. His voyages also brought the Chinese into contact with the outposts of Greek culture established by Alexander the Great. As a result of Zhang's missions, new items were introduced in China, including a superior breed of horses and new plants, such as grapes and alfalfa.

Commerce as well as conquest inspired Chinese travel. Zhang Qian had encountered a series of trade routes that skirted the great Takla Makan Desert of Central Asia. Trade began to flourish along these caravan routes. The routes are now known collectively as the Silk Road, because Chinese silk was a major and valuable product traded along them. The Silk Road ultimately extended from China through Central Asia to the Middle East. From there, goods were shipped to Europe. Another branch of the Silk Road led to India. In addition to being a commercial thoroughfare, the Silk Road became a

Silk Road

In ancient and medieval times the Silk Road was a major thoroughfare for trade and travel between Asia, the Middle East, and Europe. The route carried goods and ideas between the great civilizations of Rome and China. Caravans carried highly prized Chinese silk westward and wools, gold, and silver eastward. Though mainly a trade route, the Silk Road was also used by conquering armies, Buddhist missionaries, and Muslim clerics. Inventions, works of literature, and languages likewise followed its path.

When the European explorer Marco Polo traveled from Venice, Italy, to China via the Silk Road in the 1270s, the road was already about 1,500 years old. It came into partial existence in about 300 BC. At that time, the road was used to bring jade from Khotan (now Hotan, China) to China. By 200 BC the Silk Road was linked to the West, and by 100 BC it was carrying active trade between the East and the West. At its height in AD 200, this route and its western connections over the Roman system constituted the longest road system on Earth. Few persons traveled the entire route. Instead, goods were handled in a staggered progression by middlemen.

The Silk Road stretched for some 4,000 miles (6,400 kilometers). It crossed a wide range of climates and cultures, from the lush, temperate region of eastern China to the deserts and mountains of Muslim Central Asia. It originated at Xi'an, China, but was linked to the Pacific Ocean on the east. From Xi'an, the route followed the Great Wall of China to the northwest. It then skirted the Takla Makan Desert, climbed the Pamirs (mountains), crossed Afghanistan, and continued to the eastern Mediterranean Sea. From there, merchandise was shipped across the sea to Europe. A southern branch of the Silk Road led from Persia (Iran) to the Bay of Bengal in India.

Today, part of the route exists in the form of a paved highway connecting Pakistan and northwestern China. The Silk Road has also been the impetus behind the building of the Asian Highway network. In 1999 the road inspired cellist Yo Yo Ma to found the Silk Road Project, which has explored cultural traditions along its route.

major route for travel and cultural exchange between the East and the West.

In the 1st century AD Chinese envoys were frustrated in an attempt to visit the western part of the world. However, as already mentioned, a mission from Rome reached China by ship in the 2nd century. The first record of official visitors arriving at the Han court from Japan is for the year AD 57.

Buddhist Pilgrimages to India

Chinese knowledge of India was expanded by the voyages of Chinese Buddhist monks to study there, in the "Holy Land" of Buddhism. The first known Chinese monk to undertake such a pilgrimage was Faxian. He set out in AD 399 in order to

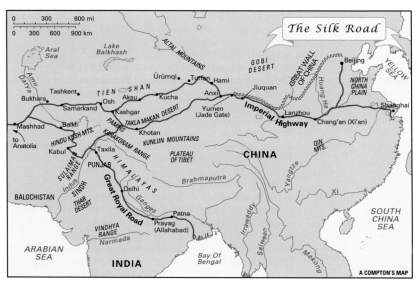

The Silk Road

A COMPTON'S MAP

bring back Buddhist texts from India that were unavailable in China. His trip took him across the trackless desert wastes of Central Asia to Khotan (now Hotan, China), an oasis center for caravans on the Silk Road. He then crossed the mountain area known as the Pamirs along a treacherously narrow and steep path. In 402 he arrived in India. There he visited the most important seats of Buddhist learning and the holiest Buddhist places. He stayed for a long time at what is now the city of Patna, transcribing Buddhist texts.

" In the desert were numerous evil spirits and scorching winds, causing death to anyone who would meet them. Above there were no birds, while on the ground there were no animals. One looked as far as one could in all directions for a path to cross, but there was none to choose. Only the dried bones of the dead served as indications."

—Faxian, a Chinese Buddhist monk, describing his trek through Central Asia in the 5th century AD

On the way home, Faxian sailed to Ceylon (now Sri Lanka), where he collected additional Buddhist writings. After setting sail for China, a violent storm drove his ship onto an island that was probably Java (now in Indonesia). He took another boat, but it too was driven astray before finally being blown to a Chinese port. In all, Faxian spent more than 200 days at sea. After returning to his homeland, Faxian translated into Chinese the Buddhist texts he had taken so much trouble to bring back. He also wrote a detailed account of his pioneering journeys.

The Chinese Buddhist monk Xuanzang returns from his pilgrimage to India in AD 645.
© Lebrecht Music and Arts
Photo Library/Alamy

After Faxian, many other Chinese monks went on pilgrimages to India. Among them was Xuanzang in the 7th century. He was unable to obtain a travel permit, so he left Chang'an, China, by stealth in 629. He traveled north of the Takla Makan Desert and across the mountains known as the Hindu Kush to northwestern India. From there he sailed down the Ganges River, arriving at its eastern reaches in 633. After visiting many holy places and studying at a Buddhist monastery for several years, he returned home in 645. He had been gone 16 years. Like Faxian, he brought back numerous religious texts. Xuanzang's record of his travels, with its wealth of precise data, has been of great value to modern historians and archaeologists.

Zheng He Sails the Indian Ocean

The greatest Chinese naval explorer was probably the admiral and diplomat Zheng He. His seven major expeditions in the early 15th century helped to extend Chinese maritime and commercial influence throughout the regions bordering the Indian Ocean. Zheng was the son of Chinese Muslims. As a youth, he was among the boys whom the Chinese government captured, castrated, and sent into the army. He distinguished himself as a junior officer, skilled in war and diplomacy. He also made influential friends at the Chinese court. Eunuchs (castrated men) had long functioned as political advisers to the emperors.

During the Ming Dynasty (1368–1644), the Chinese court sought to display its naval power to bring the maritime states of South and Southeast Asia in line. For 300 years the Chinese had been extending their power out to sea. An extensive seaborne commerce had developed to meet China's desire for spices and raw materials for industry. Chinese travelers abroad, as well as Indian and Muslim visitors to China, widened the geographic horizon of the Chinese. Technological developments in shipbuilding and in the arts of seafaring reached new heights by the beginning of the Ming Dynasty.

The emperor selected Zheng to be the commander in chief of new missions to the Indian Ocean. Zheng first set sail in 1405, commanding 62 ships and 27,800 men. The fleet visited what are now southern Vietnam, Thailand, Malaysia, and Java, Indonesia. It then sailed to southwestern India and Ceylon (Sri Lanka). Zheng returned to China in 1407.

On his second voyage, in 1409, he encountered treachery from the king of Ceylon. Zheng defeated the king's forces and took him back to China as a captive. In 1411 Zheng set out on his third voyage. This time, traveling beyond the seaports of India, he sailed to Hormuz on the Persian Gulf. On his return he touched at the northern tip of Sumatra (now in Indonesia).

Zheng left on his fourth voyage in 1413. After stopping at the principal ports of Asia, he proceeded westward from India to Hormuz. Part of the fleet cruised southward down the Arabian coast and dispatched a Chinese mission to visit Mecca (now in Saudi Arabia) and Egypt. The fleet visited coastal towns

Zheng He's Fourth Voyage, 1413–15

— Main fleet
···· Secondary fleet

A COMPTON'S MAP

in what are now Somalia and Kenya and almost reached the Mozambique Channel. On his return to China in 1415, Zheng brought the envoys of more than 30 states of South and Southeast Asia to pay homage to the Chinese emperor.

On Zheng's fifth voyage (1417–19), the fleet revisited the Persian Gulf and the east coast of Africa. A sixth voyage was launched in 1421 to take the foreign emissaries back home from China. Zheng again visited Southeast Asia, India, Arabia, and Africa. In 1424 the emperor died. His successor shifted policy and suspended naval expeditions abroad. One final expedition, which was Zheng's seventh voyage, was sent out. The fleet left China in the winter of 1431, visiting the states of Southeast Asia, the coast of India, the Persian Gulf, the Red Sea, and the east coast of Africa. Zheng died in India in the spring of 1433, and the fleet returned to China that summer.

MEDIEVAL EUROPEAN TRAVELERS

The period of intense European exploration and colonization of the Americas known as the Age of Discovery took place in the 15th and 16th centuries. The foundation for this period was laid in the Middle Ages, as Europeans traveled to the Middle East and China. Contacts with the East introduced new ideas and goods to Europe and inspired further exploration.

The Crusades

During the military expeditions known as the Crusades, Europeans traveled to the Middle East to wage war, not to explore new territory. Nevertheless, the Crusades brought Europeans in greater contact with the Muslim world. From the late 11th century to the 16th century, European Christians mounted a series of military campaigns to attempt to recapture the Holy Land (Palestine) from the Muslims. The Crusades ultimately failed to regain the Holy Land but played an important role in the expansion of Europe.

The Crusades opened up trade contact with the East, and new foods and textiles began to appear in Europe. The new products included cane sugar, buckwheat, rice, apricots, watermelons, oranges, limes, lemons, cotton, damask, satin, velvet, and dyestuffs. The Crusades also introduced western Europe to the great cities and cultures of the Islamic world. Contact with the Christian Byzantine Empire, in southern Europe and western Asia, provided access to ancient Greek learning.

European Travelers to China

European knowledge of China increased greatly in the late Middle Ages, when Christian European missionaries and merchants journeyed by land to Central and East Asia. Goods had passed between East and West along the Silk Road since ancient times. However, traders did not travel the entire road. Goods usually changed hands at many different marts along the way.

In the 13th century the political geography changed. Under their leader Genghis Khan, the Mongols took control of northern China. They then turned their conquering armies westward, building up an enormous empire. By the late 13th century, the Mongol emperor Kublai Khan reigned supreme from the Black Sea to the Yellow Sea. Astute Europeans saw the opportunities that friendship with the Mongol state might bring. If Europeans could convert the Mongols to Christianity,

The Legend of Prester John

Starting in the Middle Ages, European rulers sent out many expeditions to find Prester John, a Christian priest and king. Explorers searched for his kingdom first in Asia, then later in northern Africa. Prester John never existed, however; he was merely a legend. John was purportedly a Nestorian Christian, a member of an independent Eastern Christian church. The title Prester is short for *presbyter*, which means "elder" or "priest."

The myth of Prester John arose in the 12th century during the Crusades, when European Christians were fighting to regain the Holy Land from the Muslims. Prester John was said to be a wealthy and powerful ruler who was fighting against the Muslims. His kingdom was supposedly located somewhere "in the Far East beyond Persia and Armenia." European rulers hoped to form an alliance with him against the Muslims. His legend thus arose partly from wishful thinking.

In 1165 several Christian rulers in Europe received a letter that claimed to be from Prester John. It is not known who actually wrote the letter, which was a fiction. In the letter, the realm of Prester John is described as a land of natural riches, marvels, peace, and justice. Prester John declared in the letter that he intended to come to Palestine with his armies to battle the Muslims and to regain the Holy Sepulchre, the burial place of Jesus. Pope Alexander III sent a letter to Prester John in 1177.

In the 13th and 14th centuries various missionaries and travelers searched for Prester John's kingdom in Asia. Among them were Giovanni da Pian del Carpini, Giovanni da Montecorvino, and Marco Polo. As European knowledge of Asia increased, the search moved elsewhere.

After the mid-14th century Ethiopia was the center of the quest, as Prester John became identified with the emperor of that African Christian state. The Portuguese, who began actively exploring Africa, hoped to find the king. In 1482 the Portuguese navigator Diogo Cão encountered the mouth of the Congo River, which he believed to be a strait providing access to the realm of Prester John. In 1486 rumor arose of a great ruler far to the east who was thought to be Prester John. The Portuguese king sent the explorers Pêro da Covilhã and Afonso Paiva overland to search for the mythical ruler and to locate India and Ethiopia. They, of course, never found him.

the balance of power would be tipped against the Muslims and in favor of the Christians. Forming an alliance with the Mongols would also be beneficial to trade. Christian merchants would be provided with political protection along the trade routes to the legendary sources of wealth in China. With these opportunities in mind, Pope Innocent IV sent friars to "diligently search out all things" concerning the Mongol Empire and to try to convert the Mongols.

Giovanni and Willem. Among the Franciscan friars who went forth to follow these instructions were Giovanni da Pian del Carpini of Italy and Willem van Ruysbroeck of France. They traveled the great caravan routes from southern Russia, north of the Caspian and Aral seas and north of the Tien Shan (Tien Mountains). Both Giovanni and Willem eventually reached the court of the Mongol emperor at Karakorum.

Giovanni set out from France in 1245, when he was more than 60 years old. A year later, he and his companions had reached the camp of Batu, the Mongol conqueror of eastern Europe, on the Volga River. With Batu's permission, the friars proceeded to Karakorum. They arrived just over 106 days later, after a journey on horseback of about 3,000 miles (4,800 kilometers). Giovanni and his companions were present to witness the coronation of a new Mongol emperor. More than 3,000 envoys and deputies from all parts of the empire had gathered there for the event. The friars remained at the new emperor's court for a few months. They were then sent back home to deliver a letter from the emperor to the pope. The friars suffered greatly on their long winter journey homeward. By the time they reached Europe in the summer of 1247, they had been taken for dead.

Immediately upon his return, Giovanni recorded his observations of the Mongols and the regions he had traversed. His work discredited many of the fables concerning the Mongols. Its account of Mongol customs and history is one of the best treatments of the subject by any medieval Christian writer. Only on geographic and personal detail is it inferior to the one written a few years later by Willem.

Willem and his companions set out by sea in 1253 from what is now Turkey. They crossed the Black Sea to the Crimean Peninsula, in what is now Ukraine. On land, they acquired oxen and carts for their five-week trek across the steppes to Batu's camp. From there, they set off on horseback, reaching Karakoram in January 1254. They were received courteously by the emperor and remained at his court until the summer. Upon his return, Willem wrote about his Mongolian experiences for the French king. His narrative is free from legend and shows him to have been an intelligent and honest observer.

The Polo family. The greatest of the 13th-century European travelers in Asia were the Polos, wealthy merchants of Venice. In 1260 the brothers Niccolò and Maffeo Polo set out on a trading expedition to the Crimean Peninsula. After two years they were ready to return to Venice. Finding the way home blocked by war, however, they traveled eastward to Bukhara (now in Uzbekistan), where they spent another three years. The Polos then accepted an invitation to accompany a party of Mongol envoys returning to the court of Kublai Khan at Dadu (now Beijing). The emperor received them well. They eventually returned to Europe as his ambassadors, carrying letters asking the pope to send him 100 Christian scholars. The Polos finally arrived back home three years later.

In 1271 the Polos set off for China again, accompanied by Niccolò's son, Marco Polo, then a youth of 17. This time the Polos took a different route. From Venice they sailed to Acre (now 'Akko, Israel), where they received letters for Kublai from a representative of the pope. The Polos crossed the deserts of Iran and Afghanistan. Northeastern Afghanistan, in particular, pleased the travelers. They seem to have remained there for a year.

Setting off again, the Polos mounted the heights of the Pamirs. They descended from the mountains to the trading city of Kashgar (Kashi), which is now in Xinjiang, China. By then, they were traveling on the

Marco Polo sets sail from Venice in 1271, in a painting from an illuminated manuscript from about the 15th century.
© Photos.com/Jupiterimages

main part of the Silk Road. They continued eastward, crossing the Takla Makan Desert to what is now the Chinese province of Gansu. Prior to this, the Polos had traveled primarily among Muslim peoples. In Gansu an entirely different civilization—mainly Buddhist in religion but partly Chinese in culture—prevailed.

> "All these pieces of paper are issued with as much solemnity and authority as if they were of pure gold or silver … [With them the emperor] causes all payments on his own account to be made; and he makes them to pass current universally over all his kingdoms and provinces and territories … And nobody, however important he may think himself, dares to refuse them on pain of death … And all the while they are so light … "
>
> —Marco Polo, a 13th-century Italian traveler, describing the use in China of paper money, which was then unknown in Europe

Sometime in 1274 or 1275 the Polos arrived at Kublai's court at his summer capital, Shangdu (now Duolun, in northern China). They remained in Kublai's empire for some 16 or 17 years. They may have moved with the court to the emperor's winter residence at Dadu. The elder Polos were probably employed by the empire in some technical capacity.

Marco quickly became a favorite of Kublai's. Although Marco knew little or no Chinese, he did speak some of the many languages then used in East Asia. Kublai took great delight in hearing of strange countries. He repeatedly sent Marco on fact-finding missions to far places in the empire, including Hangzhou in the southeast, Yunnan in the southwest, and perhaps also what is now Myanmar (Burma). From these lands Marco brought back stories of the people and their lives. He may also have had other official responsibilities, such as inspecting taxes. In any event, Marco seems to have considered himself an adoptive son of his new country.

The Polos became wealthy in China. They began to fear, however, that jealous men in the court would destroy them when the elderly emperor died. In about 1290 or 1292, Kublai was preparing to send a Mongol princess to Iran to become a consort of the ruler there. The Polos asked to accompany her on the voyage and, from Iran, to return to Venice. Kublai at first refused but then reluctantly agreed.

Since there was danger from robbers and enemies of the emperor along the overland trade routes, they went by sea. They sailed in a fleet of 14 ships, which carried the Polos, the princess, and 600 courtiers and sailors. The fleet traveled southward along the coast of what is now Vietnam and the Malay Peninsula to Sumatra (now in Indonesia), where the voyage was delayed for several months. The ships then turned westward and visited Ceylon (Sri Lanka) and India before reaching their destination in Iran. The Polos set off by land for Venice. They were robbed along the way of most of their earnings from China. When they arrived in Venice in 1295, they had been gone 24 years.

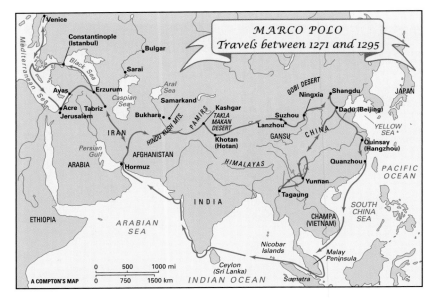

MARCO POLO
Travels between 1271 and 1295

A COMPTON'S MAP

1328. Another Franciscan missionary, the Italian friar Odoric of Pordenone, journeyed throughout the greater part of Asia between 1316 and 1330. He reached Beijing by way of India and Malaysia. He then traveled by sea to Guangzhou, China. Odoric returned to Europe by way of Central Asia. His account of his journeys had considerable influence in his day. It was from Odoric's work that the English writer Sir John Mandeville plagiarized most of his travel stories.

MUSLIM TRAVELERS

Starting in what were the Middle Ages in Europe, the study of geography was nurtured in the Arab world, along with other scholarly pursuits. Arab scholars produced a number of geographic works, including encyclopedias, descriptive geographies and histories, and maps of the world. The Arabs were great seafarers. They dominated trade in the Indian Ocean from the 3rd to the 15th century. Interest in geography was also kindled in part by the great political and military expansion of the Arabs in the 7th and 8th centuries. Islam was established by Muhammad in Arabia, the homeland of the Arabs, in the early 7th century. The new religion spread rapidly. Within a century, the Arabs had conquered most of the Middle East, North Africa, and Spain.

Travel was an important part of Islamic culture. Muslims were (and still are) required to undertake a pilgrimage to Mecca (now in Saudi Arabia) once in their life. It was also common for Muslims to visit great scholars and centers of learning throughout the Islamic world. Many travelers wrote accounts of their journeys, and the travel narrative became a well-established genre in Arabic literature.

One of the earliest notable Islamic travelers was the 9th-century geographer known as al-Yaʿqubi. For many years he lived in Armenia and Khorasan (now part of Iran), under the patronage of the Iranian dynasty of the Tahirids. After the fall of the Tahirids, he traveled to India and the Maghrib (North Africa) and died in Egypt. Al-Yaʿqubi wrote a world history and a geography based on his travels. In the geography, he describes the larger cities of Iraq, Iran, Arabia, Syria, Egypt, the Maghrib, India, China, and the Byzantine Empire. Much of this work is now lost.

The fame of the 10th-century geographer al-Hamdani rests mainly on his authoritative writings on South Arabian history and geography. He was born in Yemen and spent most of his life in the Arabian Peninsula. He traveled extensively, acquiring a broad knowledge of his country. He was also a poet, historian, and astronomer.

Soon after his return, Marco sailed aboard a ship in the Mediterranean. It was captured by forces of the trading city of Genoa, a rival of Venice, during a skirmish. Marco was thrown into a Genoese prison. There he recorded observations from his travel to Asia, with the help of another prisoner, Rustichello, who was a writer of romances. The result was Marco's famous and fascinating book, which became known as *Il milione* (The Million). Its name most likely came from his nickname, "Il Milione," from his tendency to describe the millions of things he saw in the Mongol Empire. In English, the book is known as the *Travels of Marco Polo*.

Polo's book contains vivid descriptions of China and other parts of Asia. Rather than being a collection of personal recollections, it was intended to provide an overview of the region. The narrative often branches off into descriptions of places that Marco probably never visited. Instead, he gathered information about these places from his relatives or other people he knew. Typical digressions are those on Mesopotamia, Samarkand, Siberia, India, Japan, Ethiopia, and Madagascar.

His most detailed descriptions and the highest praise were reserved for the Mongol capital of Dadu, whose splendors were beyond compare. To this city, he said, "everything that is most rare and valuable in all parts of the world finds its way: . . . for not fewer than 1,000 carriages and pack-horses loaded with raw silk make their daily entry; and gold tissues and silks of various kinds are manufactured to an immense extent."

It is no wonder that when Europe learned of these things it became enthralled. Marco's book was an instant success and was translated into many languages. Fellow Europeans read his accounts of the riches of Asia and became eager to find sea routes to China, Japan, and the East Indies.

A few travelers followed the Polos. Giovanni da Montecorvino, a Franciscan friar from Italy, became archbishop of Beijing. He lived in China from 1294 to

His encyclopedia *Al-Iklil* (The Crown) and his other writings are a major source of information on medieval Arabia.

The geographer al-Maqdisi also traveled widely in the 10th century. He wrote a notable work based on his personal observations of the populations, manners, and economic life of the various peoples of the Islamic world.

Al-Mas'udi was the first Arab to combine history and scientific geography in a large-scale work. This work, a world history, was called *Muruj adh-dhahab wa ma'adin al-jawahir* (The Meadows of Gold and Mines of Gems). It appeared in the mid-10th century.

As a child, al-Mas'udi showed an extraordinary love of learning, an excellent memory, and a boundless curiosity. His main interests were history and geography, but he also studied such subjects as comparative religion and science. Al-Mas'udi was not content to learn merely from books and teachers but traveled widely to gain firsthand knowledge of the countries about which he wrote. His travels extended to Syria, Iran, Armenia, the shores of the Caspian Sea, the Indus Valley, Ceylon (now Sri Lanka), Oman, and the east coast of Africa as far south as Zanzibar, at least, and, possibly, Madagascar.

Al-Mas'udi is believed to have written more than 20 books, including several about Islamic beliefs and even one about poisons. Unfortunately, most of his writings have been lost. His book of world history became famous. It includes chapters describing the history, geography, social life, and religious customs of non-Islamic lands, such as India, Greece, and Rome. The book also provides accounts of climates, the oceans, the hazards of navigation, and the calendars of various nations. Among the particularly interesting sections are those on pearl diving in the Persian Gulf, amber found in East Africa, Hindu burial customs, and the land route to China.

Al-Mas'udi's approach to his task was original. He gave as much weight to social, economic, religious, and cultural matters as to politics. He also displayed interest in all religions. Moreover, he used information obtained from sources not previously regarded as reliable. These sources included merchants, local writers (including non-Muslims), and others he met on his travels.

Another great work of medieval geography was written by ash-Sharif al-Idrisi in the 12th century. He spent much of his early life traveling in North Africa and Spain, where his ancestors had lived. Apparently his travels also took him to many other parts of western Europe besides Spain, including Portugal, the French Atlantic coast, and southern England. He visited Asia Minor when he was barely 16 years old.

In about 1145 al-Idrisi entered the service of Roger II, the king of Sicily, who was Christian. For the king, al-Idrisi completed maps of the world and his great geographic book. This book is called *Kitab nuzhat al-mushtaq fi ikhtiraq al-afaq* (The Pleasure Excursion of One Who Is Eager to Traverse the Regions of the World). It is also known in English as "The Book of Roger." In compiling it, he combined material from Arabic and Greek geographic works with information obtained

World History Archive/Alamy

The geographer ash-Sharif al-Idrisi completed a map of the world in the 12th century. A later copy of the map is shown. South is at top, and north is at bottom. Africa thus appears above Eurasia. The extent of Africa was not known. The Americas and Australia, which were then unknown in Eurasia, are not shown.

through firsthand observation and eyewitness reports. The king and al-Idrisi sent a number of persons, including men skilled in drawing, to various countries to observe and record what they saw. Al-Idrisi completed the book in January 1154.

The greatest medieval Arab traveler was Ibn Battutah. He visited nearly all the Muslim countries and journeyed as far as China and Sumatra (now in Indonesia). He was the author of one of the most famous of all travel books, the *Rihlah* (Travels).

Ibn Battutah was born in Morocco. He began his travels in 1325, at the age of 21, by undertaking the pilgrimage to Mecca. On this voyage he also sought to study under famous scholars in Egypt and Syria. It was during his trip to Egypt that he became enthusiastic about traveling, vowing to visit as many parts of the world as possible. He established as a rule for himself "never to travel any road a second time." Other travelers of the time journeyed for practical reasons, such as for trade, pilgrimage, and education. Ibn Battutah, however, traveled for its own sake, for the reward of learning about new countries and new peoples. As he became increasingly famous as a traveler and scholar, he also made a living from his travels. Numerous rulers and other powerful people were generous toward him, enabling him to secure an income and to continue his wanderings.

From Egypt, Ibn Battutah traveled to Syria and completed his pilgrimage to Mecca in 1326. He then crossed the Arabian Desert to Iraq, southern Iran, and Azerbaijan. From 1327 to 1330 he studied in Mecca and Medina (now in Saudi Arabia), but such a long stay did not suit his temperament. He set off again, sailing down both shores of the Red Sea to Yemen. He later visited

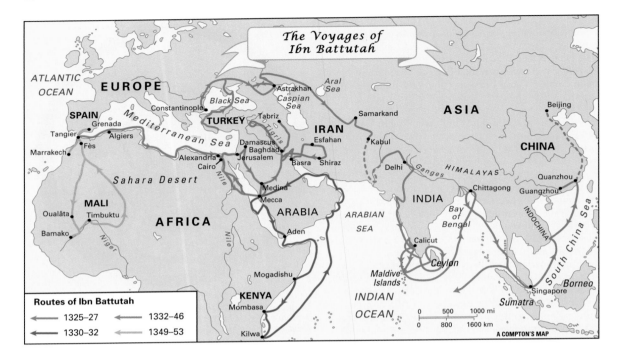

The Voyages of Ibn Battutah

Routes of Ibn Battutah

← 1325–27   ← 1332–46
← 1330–32   ← 1349–53

trading city-states along the eastern African coast. His return journey took him to southern Arabia, southern Iran, and across the Persian Gulf back to Mecca in 1332.

There he developed a new, ambitious plan. He heard that the sultan of Delhi, the Islamic ruler of northern India, was very generous to Muslim scholars. Ibn Battutah decided to try his luck at the sultan's court. He traveled to Syria, where he boarded a ship for Asia Minor. He crisscrossed this "land of the Turks" in many directions and met many local rulers.

His journey continued across the Black Sea to the Crimea, then to the northern Caucasus. He reached Saray, on the lower Volga, which was the capital of the ruler of the western part of the Mongol Empire. This ruler's wife was a Byzantine princess. Ibn Battutah accompanied the princess and her attendants on a visit to Constantinople, the capital of the Byzantine Empire, which was Christian. (Today, this city is named Istanbul and is part of Turkey.) Although Ibn Battutah shared the strong opinions of his fellow Muslims toward non-Muslims, his vivid accounts of the capital show him as a rather tolerant man with a lively curiosity. Nevertheless, he always felt happier in Muslim rather than non-Muslim lands.

After his return from Constantinople through the Russian steppes, he traveled with a caravan to Central Asia. He then took rather complicated routes through Khorasan and Afghanistan. After crossing the Hindu Kush (mountains), he arrived at the frontiers of India.

India and its sultan lived up to Ibn Battutah's expectations of wealth and generosity. He was received with honors and gifts and was appointed a judge in Delhi, a post that he held for several years. In 1342 the sultan made Ibn Battutah his envoy to the Chinese emperor.

After Ibn Battutah left Delhi, his party was soon waylaid by Hindu insurgents. He barely escaped with his life. On the southwest coast of India he became involved in local wars and was finally shipwrecked there. He lost all his property and the presents he was carrying for the Chinese emperor. Fearing the wrath of the sultan, Ibn Battutah chose to go to the Maldive Islands south of India, where he spent nearly two years. He then visited Ceylon. After a new shipwreck on the southeast coast of India, he took part in a war led by his brother-in-law. He later visited northeastern India. Deciding to resume his mission to China, he sailed for Sumatra. There he was given a new ship by the island's Muslim ruler and started for China.

Ibn Battutah landed at the great Chinese port Zaytun (now Quanzhou) in the southeast. He then traveled on inland waterways as far as Beijing and back. This part of his narrative is rather brief, and problems with it lead modern historians to wonder whether it is really true. He returned via Sumatra and the Persian Gulf to Baghdad, Syria, and Egypt. In Syria he witnessed the ravages of the plague of 1348. He also performed his final pilgrimage to Mecca. At last he returned home to Morocco.

But there still remained two Muslim countries not yet known to him. Shortly after his return he went to the kingdom of Granada, the last remnant of Moorish Spain. In 1352, he set out on a journey to the western Sudan. This last journey, across the desert known as the Sahara to western Africa, was taken unwillingly at the command of the sultan of Morocco. Crossing the Sahara, Ibn Battutah spent a year in the empire of Mali. Toward the end of 1353, he returned back home to Morocco. There, he dictated an account of his travels to a scholar, who wrote them down. Over the course of his more than 20 years of traveling, he had journeyed some 75,000 miles (more than 120,000 kilometers). He had met at least 60 rulers and many more dignitaries. His book is valued for its insights on many aspects of the social, cultural, and political history of a great part of the Muslim world.

THE SEA ROUTE TO INDIA

Before the 16th century, little was known in Europe about the interior and east coast of India. Europeans had been in contact with India since ancient times. Trade between Europe and India came to a halt, however, with the fall of the Roman Empire in the 4th century AD. Trade with the East then passed into Arab hands. The only physical contact with Europe came from occasional travelers, such as Marco Polo and, in the 15th century, the Italian Niccolò dei Conti and the Russian Afanasy Nikitin. In the 15th century Europeans eagerly searched for a sea route from western Europe to India and China. They wanted to profit from the trade in valuable spices from the East. At the end of the century, the Portuguese navigator Vasco da Gama successfully sailed from Europe to India. He thereby restored a link between Europe and the East that had existed many centuries previously. A series of European expeditions to southern Asia followed, ultimately leading to its colonization.

The direct routes for trade between Europe and India involved traveling via the Red Sea and Egypt or across Iran, Iraq, Syria, and Anatolia (now in Turkey). In the 15th century these routes became increasingly blocked to Europeans, mainly because of the activities of the Turkish Ottoman Empire. In addition, the Venetians and later the Ottomans held a near-monopoly on trade in the eastern Mediterranean. For these reasons, western Europeans began searching for another route. (The Suez Canal, which now links the Mediterranean Sea to the Red Sea, was not built until the late 19th century.)

The search for a sea route to the East initiated the Age of Discovery. Christopher Columbus sought to reach China by traveling west, and thereby accidentally reached the Americas (see The Americas, "The Age of Discovery"). Other explorers tried the long and hazardous eastern route, via the Atlantic and Indian Oceans. First, a ship had to sail south along the west coast of Africa. It then had to round the continent's southern tip and head north in the Indian Ocean along Africa's east coast. It was not known if this was possible, however; some Europeans thought that the Indian Ocean might be entirely surrounded by land. Europeans also did not know how far south the African continent extended. In addition, sailing around the southern tip of the continent—near the land now known as the Cape of Good Hope—proved to be difficult. The seas are rough, the weather is stormy, and the winds are strong.

Portugal took the lead in the search for the eastern sea route. Throughout the 15th century, the Portuguese sent forth expedition after expedition to explore the west coast of Africa. The king also sent the Portuguese explorer Pêro da Covilhã on a mission to India via a land and sea route in 1487. Pêro traveled through Egypt and Ethiopia to the Red Sea and the Indian Ocean. He arrived in India, visiting the towns of Cannanore (now Kannur), Calicut (now Kozhikode), and Goa on the west coast. He then journeyed in Africa (see Africa, "The Portuguese").

Also in 1487, the king sent the Portuguese explorer Bartolomeu Dias on a mission to search for the eastern sea route. Dias and his crew became the first Europeans to see the stormy Cape of Good Hope. With two light, quick sailing ships called caravels plus a supply ship, Dias left Lisbon, Portugal, in August. He sailed down the entire west coast of Africa, farther than any other European before him. Early in January 1488, a gale hit his ships and blew them southward, past the southernmost tip of land. After 13

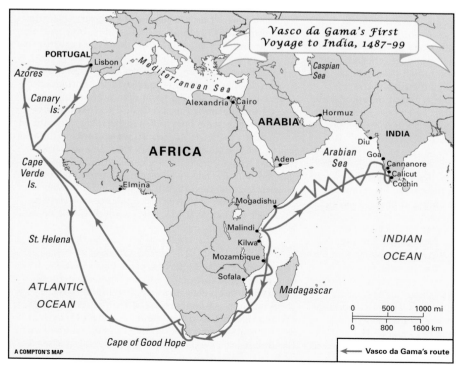

Vasco da Gama's First Voyage to India, 1487-99

A COMPTON'S MAP

← Vasco da Gama's route

Marine Museum Lisbon—Gianni Dagli Orti/The Art Archive

The Portuguese navigator Bartolomeu Dias holds an astrolabe, a navigational instrument used to determine latitude (north-south position).

days of sailing out of sight of land, he managed to turn east but found no sheltering shore. Turning north, he sighted Mossel Bay, beyond the Cape of Good Hope. He had thus rounded the cape without having seen it.

Almost at the entrance to the Indian Ocean, Dias' crew, weary and afraid, virtually forced him to turn back. On the return voyage, Dias charted the southern waters. In May 1488 he saw the Cape of Good Hope for the first time. Dias was welcomed home in December 1488. The task that he had begun was completed 10 years later by Vasco da Gama.

Da Gama set off from Lisbon for India on July 8, 1497. He sailed with four ships: two medium-sized three-masted sailing ships, one smaller caravel, and one supply ship. After months of sailing, the crew reached the Cape Verde islands off the west coast of Africa on July 26. Then, to avoid the currents of the Gulf of Guinea, da Gama undertook a long detour through the South Atlantic rather than hugging the coast. The ship sailed out of sight of land for three months before reaching St. Helena Bay (in what is now South Africa) on November 7. Unfavorable winds and the adverse current delayed the rounding of the Cape of Good Hope until November 22. Da Gama reached what is now Mozambique, on the east coast, in January 1498.

The expedition visited trading cities as it sailed up the east coast of Africa. Relations between the Portuguese and the local people were often mutually hostile. The expedition arrived at Malindi (now in Kenya) on April 14. There da Gama acquired an Indian pilot who helped him navigate eastward across the Indian Ocean to Calicut, on the southwest coast of India. The expedition reached Calicut, which was then an important trading center, on May 20. Da Gama failed to conclude a commercial treaty with the Hindu ruler of the city. Influenced by Muslim traders who feared competition, the ruler was suspicious of the Europeans. He was also insulted by the rude behavior of the Portuguese and the cheap gifts they gave him.

Da Gama secured samples of valuable spices, however, and began the homeward journey. He also took with him five or six Hindus so that the Portuguese king might learn about their customs. Ignorance and indifference to local knowledge had led da Gama to choose the worst possible time of year for his departure. As a result, he had to sail against the strong winds of the monsoon. It took him nearly three months to cross the Arabian Sea, and many of the crew members became sick with scurvy. Da Gama finally reached Lisbon on September 9, 1499. Out of his original crew of 170 men, only 55 had survived. Most of the rest had died of scurvy.

In February 1502 da Gama set sail a second time for India, this time with a fleet of 20 ships. This time he formed alliances with the rulers of Cannanore and Cochin (now Kochi). He also sought to ruin Calicut's trade and to punish its ruler for not having signed a trading treaty with the Portuguese. The expedition bombarded the port of Calicut and seized and massacred 38 hostages. He returned home in October 1503 with the first tribute of gold from the East. Da Gama's voyages brought his country immense wealth. As a result of his exploration, Portugal had become one of the foremost powers of Europe because it controlled the sea route to the East.

Da Gama's successors—Francisco de Almeida and Afonso de Albuquerque—established the Portuguese empire in the East. Almeida set up a number of fortified posts. Albuquerque captured Goa in western India in 1510, Malacca in the East Indies in 1511, and Hormuz in the Persian Gulf in 1515. He also set up posts in the East Indian Spice Islands (Indonesia). Da Gama was sent back to India a third time as viceroy in 1524. He was charged with the task of reforming abuses in the colonial government. He died within a few months, however, in Cochin. Portuguese power in South and Southeastern Asia later waned, as the Dutch and English took control of the region.

THE HIMALAYAS AND TIBET

The mountain system known as the Himalayas stretches in a massive arc through southern Asia. The earliest journeys through these towering mountains were undertaken by Asian traders, shepherds, and pilgrims. The pilgrims believed that the harder the journey was, the nearer it brought them to salvation or enlightenment. The traders and shepherds accepted crossing passes as high as 19,000 feet (5,800 meters) as a way of life. For all others, however, the Himalayas constituted a formidable and fearsome barrier.

The adjacent Plateau of Tibet was also very difficult for outsiders to reach. It is the highest of the world's highlands and is surrounded by enormous and often snowy mountains on three sides. In addition to the considerable physical difficulties in traveling to Tibet, it was also isolated by policy. Europeans were long forbidden to enter the Tibetan capital of Lhasa, which ultimately became an irresistible draw to several European explorers. The first European visitor to Lhasa may have been the friar Odoric of Pordenone in the 14th century.

Christian missionaries were the first Europeans to travel in the region. The earliest-known reasonably accurate map of the Himalayas was drawn up in 1590 by the Spanish missionary Antonio Monserrate. He never crossed the mountains himself but used information obtained by others.

The Portuguese Jesuits Bento de Goes and Antonio de Andrade traveled through the region in the 17th century. (Andrade may have been Spanish.) Goes disguised himself as a Muslim trader, while Andrade traveled as a Hindu pilgrim. Goes set out in 1603. From northern India, he journeyed to Afghanistan, and then crossed the mountains of the Hindu Kush and the Pamirs. He ultimately reached Suzhou, China, in 1605. Andrade departed from India in 1624. He crossed the Himalayas—becoming the first European to do so—and reached western Tibet. He later established the first Christian mission there.

In 1661–62 two Jesuits reached Tibet from the east. The Austrian missionary John Grueber and the Belgian priest Albert d'Orville met in Bejing, China. From there, they trekked south to Xian, China, and then west and south, arriving in Lhasa in October 1661. They remained in the city for several weeks and then crossed the Himalayas into Nepal. They ended their journey in India. Grueber and d'Orville were either the first Europeans to reach Lhasa or the first to do so after Odoric. The first European woman to visit Lhasa was the French traveler Alexandra David-Neel, in 1924.

The first map of Tibet and the Himalayas that was based on systematic exploration dates to 1733. It was compiled by the French geographer Jean-Baptiste Bourguignon d'Arville.

In the 19th century European exploration of south-central Asia increased. Both Russia and Britain sought to control Tibet, and maps of the region would be useful to their militaries. The Russians surveyed Central Asia, while the British conducted their Great Survey of India and the surrounding areas. The British survey included a systematic program to measure correctly the heights of the Himalayan peaks. Mount Everest is named after the British surveyor general George Everest.

The British also wanted to survey and map Tibet, but at the time Europeans were not allowed there. Instead, they hired a series of Indians—notably Nain Singh and Kishen Singh—to act as their secret agents starting in the 1860s. These Indians were remarkable for their physical stamina, mental quickness, courage, and loyalty. The

British trained these men, nicknamed the "pundits," as surveyors. To perform their hazardous work, the pundits had to assume a number of disguises, especially that of Buddhist pilgrims. They had to memorize much of their data, though they also had scrolls of paper concealed in their Buddhist prayer wheels, along with a compass. They hid other surveying instruments in their walking sticks and in trunks with false bottoms. The pundits learned to walk taking steps of precisely the same length. Along their trek, they used their prayer beads to help them count their steps, in order to measure distance. The intrepid pundits successfully surveyed the mountainous, desolate, and cold lands of Tibet and many of the surrounding areas.

"*Because it's there.*"

—British mountaineer George Mallory famously replying in 1924 to the question of why climbers struggle to scale Mount Everest

In addition to the surveying expeditions, various scientific studies of the area were conducted in the 19th century. In 1848–49 the British botanist Joseph Dalton Hooker made a pioneering study of the plant life of the eastern Himalayas. In the 1870s and 1880s the Russian explorer Nikolay Mikhaylovich Przhevalsky collected specimens of plants and animals on four trips in east-central Asia. His natural history discoveries include the wild camel and the wild horse, which is now named Przewalski's horse in his honor (using a variant spelling of his name). Although all his attempts to reach Lhasa failed, he added vastly to geographic knowledge of the region. The Swedish explorer Sven Hedin led a series of expeditions through Central Asia that resulted in

George Mallory, seated at far left, participated in the first expedition to Mount Everest, in 1921. The other mountaineers shown are, clockwise from top left, A.F.R. Wollaston, Charles Howard-Bury, Alexander Heron, Harold Raeburn, Henry T. Morshead, Guy Bullock, and Oliver Wheeler.

Climbing Mount Everest

The highest point on Earth is the peak of Mount Everest, at an elevation of 29,035 feet (8,850 meters). It lies in the Himalayas on the border between Nepal and Tibet. Numerous mountaineers have undertaken the very great challenge of climbing the peak. Many have died trying. Mount Everest is difficult to get to and more difficult to climb, even with modern equipment. The mountain itself lies in a highly isolated location. There are no roads in the region on the Nepalese side. Before an airstrip was built in the 1960s, all goods and supplies had to be carried long distances by humans and pack animals. In addition, there are only two brief time periods when the weather is more hospitable for an ascent. At other times, the mountain is too stormy or the snow is too soft and prone to avalanches. Frostbite and falling are, of course, always risks.

In addition, the effects of high altitudes on the human body are extreme. The region of the Himalayas above about 25,000 feet (7,600 meters) is known as the "death zone." Climbers at such high altitudes have breathing and pulse rates that are much faster than normal. They are not able to digest food well, they sleep poorly, and their thinking is often confused. These symptoms are manifestations of oxygen deprivation, or hypoxia, in the body tissues. It makes any effort difficult and can lead a climber to make poor decisions in an already dangerous environment. Bottled oxygen breathed through a mask can partially alleviate the effects of hypoxia.

The Granger Collection, New York

Edmund Hillary, left, and Tenzing Norgay reached the summit of Mount Everest on May 29, 1953.

In the traditional method of ascending Everest, a large team of climbers establishes a series of tented camps farther and farther up the mountain's side. The climbers establish a camp farther up the route, then come down to sleep at night at the camp below it. This practice allows climbers to adjust to the high altitude. Finally, a last camp is set up close enough to the summit—usually about 3,000 feet (900 meters) below—to allow a small group to reach the peak. Expeditions usually employ local people called Sherpas as porters to carry their gear and provisions.

Some climbers have felt that ascending with oxygen, support from Sherpas, and a large party is "unsporting" or that it misses the point of mountain climbing. These climbers favor an approach in which perhaps three or four climbers go up and down the mountain as quickly as possible, without bottled oxygen and carrying all their own supplies.

EARLIEST ATTEMPTS

Two British exploring organizations—the Royal Geographical Society and the Alpine Club—became instrumental in fostering interest in exploring the mountain. They organized and financed several expeditions, including the first one, in 1921. This expedition was mainly for reconnaissance. The team of nine climbers, plus Sherpas, had to first locate the mountain. They thoroughly explored the northern approaches and then attempted to climb Everest, but high winds forced them to turn back.

important archaeological and geographic findings. In the early 20th century the British naturalist Richard W.G. Hingston wrote valuable accounts of the natural history of animals living at high elevations in the Himalayas.

ARABIA

The Arabian Peninsula was among the last parts of Asia to be explored by outsiders. As in Tibet, the difficulties were both physical and political. The interior of Arabia consists of the vast and inhospitable Arabian Desert. The heat is intense there in summer, often reaching temperatures as high as 130° F (55° C). During parts of the year, strong winds blow huge amounts of sand and dust across the desolate terrain. The southern part of the desert consists of the Rubʿ al-Khali (Empty Quarter), the largest continuous expanse of sand on Earth. A decade may pass there without any precipitation at all. In addition, much of Arabia was off-limits to European exploration, especially official expeditions. The rulers of Arabia feared that European countries wanted to explore the peninsula in order to take control of it. It was thus largely individual travelers who were the first outsiders to explore the interior.

Before the 18th century many Arabs but few Europeans had succeeded in penetrating the Arabian Desert. Few authors had written about it. Travel literature concentrated on the routes taken by Muslim pilgrims to Mecca. Non-Muslims are not allowed to enter this city, which is the holiest in Islam. Some European adventurers did not respect this ban but sought to enter Mecca, like Lhasa, precisely because it was forbidden. To reach the city, European travelers had to wear Arabian clothing and to pretend to be Muslim pilgrims. They also had to study local customs and learn Arabic—they risked death if they were found out.

One of the early non-Muslim European visitors was the Portuguese explorer Pêro da Covilhã, who entered Mecca in the late 15th century. He also visited Medina, the second holiest city in Islam. Lodovico de Varthema, an intrepid Italian traveler, visited Mecca in 1503. He remained in the sacred city for about three weeks. Afterward, he joined a group of Indian pilgrims on their way to India. He was arrested as a Christian spy, however, at Aden, Yemen, and imprisoned for two months. He was sent to the palace of the sultan, where one of the sultan's wives pled his case. By this means, and by feigning madness, he was set free. He then made

A second expedition set out in 1922. Some of the climbers tried using bottled oxygen for the first time. The team made a couple of attempts to reach the summit, reaching a height of 27,300 feet (8,230 meters). A third attempt ended in disaster, as an avalanche swept nine Sherpas over an ice cliff. Seven were killed.

GEORGE MALLORY

The third attempt on Everest, in 1924, ended with the death of the British climber George Mallory, who had also been a member of the first two expeditions. The third expedition had a difficult time with high winds and deep snows. On June 6 Mallory and a less-experienced climber, Andrew Irvine, set off for an attempt on the summit. The two started out from their last camp at 26,800 feet (8,170 meters) on the morning of June 8. Another member of the expedition claimed to have caught a glimpse of the men climbing in the early afternoon when the mists briefly cleared. They would have been only some 500 feet (150 meters) below the summit at that point. Mallory and Irvine were never seen again.

The mystery of Mallory and Irvine's fateful climb has been debated since that day. Some people think that the pair successfully made it to the top that day. It is not known if they were ascending or descending the mountain when they were last seen. Irvine's body was never found. Mallory's body was located 75 years later, in 1999, by an expedition led by the American climber Eric Simonson. It was found at an elevation of 26,760 feet (8,155 meters), and it was determined that Mallory had died because of a bad fall.

SUCCESS: EDMUND HILLARY AND TENZING NORGAY

Several teams tried to climb Everest between 1933 and 1952. A well-organized British expedition led by Col. John Hunt finally succeeded in 1953. After a pair of climbers failed to reach the top on May 27, Edmund Hillary of New Zealand and Tenzing Norgay, a Sherpa, set out for the top on May 29. At 11:30 AM they reached the summit of Mount Everest, becoming the first people known to have done so. They spent about 15 minutes at the top of the world before they began their descent. The expedition was received in Britain with great fanfare and acclaim, and Hillary and Hunt were knighted.

LATER CLIMBS

Hillary and Tenzing had taken the southern route up the mountain. This is the route most commonly taken by climbers today. The northern route, attempted unsuccessfully by seven British expeditions in the 1920s and '30s, is also climbed. A Chinese expedition is thought to have made the first successful ascent via the northern approach, in 1960. Wang Fuzhou, Qu Yinhua, Liu Lianman, and a Tibetan, Konbu, reached the summit. The East Face, Everest's biggest, is rarely climbed. An American team made the first ascent of it in 1983, and Carlos Buhler, Kim Momb, and Lou Reichardt reached the summit.

The first woman to reach the top of Everest was the Japanese climber Tabei Junko, in 1975. She was part of the first all-woman expedition to Everest (though male Sherpas were used as porters). In 1978 two men became the first to reach the summit without using bottled oxygen. They were the Italian climber Reinhold Messner and the Austrian climber Peter Habeler. Two years later Messner completed the first successful solo ascent. He did not use bottled oxygen for that climb, either. In 1980 a Polish expedition made the first successful climb during the winter, and Leszek Cichy and Krzysztof Wielicki reached the summit. In 2001 the American Erik Weihenmayer became the first blind person to reach the top.

Climbing Mount Everest has become a big business. It has become increasingly common for many expeditions to set out each season. By the 2003 season, a half century after the historic climb by Hillary and Tenzing, more than 1,200 people had reached the summit. More than 200 of them had reached the top more than once. In 2010 the Sherpa mountaineer Apa Sherpa made his 20th successful ascent.

a walking tour of about 600 miles (965 kilometers) through the mountainous southwestern corner of the Arabian Peninsula, visiting Sanaa, Yemen. Varthema later traveled in Iran, India, and parts of Southeast Asia. His book about his travels was widely read throughout Europe and earned him great fame. He made significant discoveries in Arabia and made many valuable observations of the peoples he visited.

The Swiss traveler Johann Ludwig Burckhardt visited Mecca and Medina in the early 19th century. Burckhardt is more famous for having been the first European in modern times to visit the ruins of Petra, an ancient city carved out of pink sandstone cliffs in southwestern Jordan. He also visited the great ancient Egyptian temple at Abu Simbel.

Richard Burton, the famous British explorer and scholar, also visited the sacred cities of Arabia. Disguising himself as a Muslim from Afghanistan, he traveled to Medina in 1853. He then traversed the bandit-ridden route to Mecca. His book *Pilgrimage to El-Medinah and Mecca* (1855–56) is a great adventure narrative. It is also a classic commentary on Muslim life and manners, especially on the annual pilgrimage. After his journeys in Arabia, he searched for the source of the Nile River in eastern Africa (*see* Africa, "Burton and Speke").

Meanwhile, the first scientific study of Arabia had taken place in 1762. A Danish expedition surveyed the southwestern portion of the peninsula and studied the animal and plant life there. The explorers faced many hardships, including malaria. The German surveyor Carsten Niebuhr was the only member of the six-man expedition to survive.

In 1819 George Sadlier, a British soldier, crossed the Arabian Desert. He may have been the first European to do so. He traveled from east to west, from Al-Qatif on the Persian Gulf to Yanbuʻ on the Red Sea.

The first important modern work on the geography of Arabia was *Travels in Arabia Deserta* (1888) by the British traveler Charles M. Doughty. He began his journey to northwestern Arabia at Damascus, Syria, in 1876. He proceeded southward with pilgrims headed for Mecca as far as Madaʼin Salih. There he studied inscriptions left by the ancient Nabataean civilization. He made his most important geographic, geologic, and anthropological observations on the later part of his journey, which included visits to Taymaʼ, Haʼil, ʻUnayzah, al-Taʼif, and Jiddah.

Women Travelers in Arabia

Starting in the late 19th century, the ranks of European travelers in the Middle East included some notable women, mainly from the upper classes. The British traveler Lady Anne Blunt was the first European woman to visit Arabia, in 1878–79. She was a granddaughter of the famous poet and adventurer George Gordon, Lord Byron. Lady Anne accompanied her husband, Wilfrid Scawen Blunt, on his travels in the Middle East. Wilfrid was a poet, diplomat, and anti-imperialist political activist as well as a traveler. Having already visited what are now Turkey, Algeria, Egypt, and Syria, the Blunts traveled with Bedouin tribes in Iraq in 1878. They then set off on a long trek through the desert of central Arabia. Lady Anne wrote two books about their travels.

Gertrude Bell of England traveled extensively in the Middle East in the late 19th and early 20th centuries. She set off on her travels after graduating with high honors from Oxford in 1887. She became a mountaineer, climbing several peaks in the Alps of southern Europe, including the Matterhorn. She later visited what are now Iran, Israel, Lebanon, Jordan, Syria, Turkey, and Iraq. Bell set off

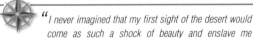

Mediacolor's/Alamy

Lady Anne Blunt, right, and her husband, Wilfrid Scawen Blunt, traveled through the Arabian Desert in the late 19th century.

for central Arabia in 1913. During World War I she worked for the British intelligence agency in Egypt. After the war she became an administrator in the British colonial government of what is now Iraq. She helped to draw the modern boundaries of that country and to place the ruler Faysal I on the Iraqi throne in 1921. Her last years were spent in founding and directing the National Museum of Iraq. She promoted the new idea that excavated antiquities should stay in their country of origin, rather than being taken by Western archaeologists. She wrote several books about her travels.

The British travel writer Freya Stark took many trips in the 20th century to remote areas in the Middle East where few Europeans, particularly women, had traveled before. She also visited Asia, notably Afghanistan and Nepal. Stark wrote two dozen highly personal books in which she combined practical traveling tips with descriptions of the people, places, customs, and history of the countries she visited. Her extensive travels included long journeys by donkey through southern Arabia.

At the turn of the 20th century, the Czech explorer Alois Musil traveled through northern and western Arabia, mapping the topography as he went. The first European to cross the Rubʿ al-Khali was the British traveler Bertram Thomas, in 1930–31. The next to do so

> " I never imagined that my first sight of the desert would come as such a shock of beauty and enslave me right away. "
>
> —Freya Stark, 20th-century British travel writer, describing her love of the Arabian Desert

The British explorer Wilfred Thesiger traveled through the Rubʿ al-Khali, part of the vast Arabian Desert, in 1948. European explorers in the area typically wore Arabian clothing.

The Granger Collection, New York

was the British explorer H. St. John Philby, who crossed the peninsula from east to west. In 1917, as an official of the British Foreign Office, he visited a sultan who later became Ibn Saʿud, the king of Saudi Arabia. Philby later became a Muslim, settled in Riyadh as a counselor to Ibn Saʿud, and explored the Arabian Desert. He wrote detailed and accurate accounts of his travels. Another British official, T.E. Lawrence ("Lawrence of Arabia") was an adviser to the Arabs during their World War I revolt. Lawrence gained fame for his romantic writings about his exploits in the region. Many other individuals traveled in limited parts of the desert. The most notable among them was the British traveler Wilfred Thesiger, who crossed the Rubʿ al-Khali twice after World War II.

After World War II geographic and geologic exploration intensified. It was accompanied by vast aerial photographic surveys, from which the first accurate maps of the peninsula were prepared and published between 1956 and 1965. The countries of the region subsequently have undertaken other surveys of the land and its mineral resources.

THE AMERICAS

The first peoples to explore the Americas—North and South America—were the ancestors of the American Indians. These early explorers were members of nomadic hunter-gatherer cultural groups. They moved from Asia to North America during the last ice age, when thick ice sheets covered much of northern North America. As the ice sheets absorbed water, the sea levels dropped and a land bridge emerged along what is now the Bering Strait. From about 30,000 to 12,000 years ago, this land bridge connected northeastern Asia to what is now Alaska. Some peoples came to North America by following the Pacific coast southward. They may have combined walking with boat travel. Others walked across a glacier-free area through the center of what is now Canada.

Continued melting of the ice gradually opened up the land, allowing people to spread out across North America and down through Central America into South America. No single person made any large part of the long journey; one group after another continued the march over many centuries. The first Europeans did not arrive in the Americas until many thousands of years later. By that time, the Indians had explored and settled all portions of the "New World."

EARLY EUROPEAN EXPLORERS

It is not known for certain when the first Europeans reached the Americas. Legends tell of early visitors from Ireland and Wales. According to an epic tale, St. Brendan and other Irish monks made an astonishing journey westward through the Atlantic Ocean in the 6th century AD. They are said to have reached a large landmass. It has been speculated that this land could have been North America or the Canary Islands. Although St.

Brendan was a real person, the tale of his Atlantic journey was likely fiction.

Another legendary traveler, Madog Ab Owain Gwynedd of Wales, was said to have reached North America in the 12th century AD. He supposedly sailed to Ireland and then westward. Some people have believed that Madog and his party became the ancestors of a group of American Indians who were said to speak Welsh. However, most anthropologists believe that the story of Madog is not true.

In the 9th century AD the Vikings of Norway, or the Norsemen, arrived in Iceland, which had already been settled by Irish colonists. Irish refugees from Iceland, fleeing before the advance of the Vikings, may have been the first Europeans to arrive in Greenland and Newfoundland (now in northeastern Canada), though this is mere surmise. Greenland, a large island in the North Atlantic Ocean, is part of North America.

The Vikings of Norway are the first Europeans known to have visited North America. A Viking named Gunnbjörn Ulfsson sailed near Greenland in the 10th century AD. The Viking known as Erik the Red (because of his red hair and beard) was the first to colonize the island. In about 980 Erik was banished from Iceland after he killed a neighbor in a quarrel. He decided to spend his exile exploring Greenland. Erik sailed in 982 with his household and livestock and established a colony on the southwest coast of Greenland. During Erik's three-year exile, the settlers encountered no other people, though they explored to the north.

Erik returned to Iceland in 986. He wanted to persuade the Norse people there to help him colonize the land he had explored, so he gave the icy island a favorable name—Greenland. His descriptions of the

The Viking expedition led by Leif Eriksson lands on Vinland in about 1000. Vinland was probably located in what is now eastern Canada or the eastern United States.

territory convinced many people to join a return expedition. By the year 1000 there were an estimated 1,000 Scandinavian settlers in the colony.

The first Europeans to land on the mainland of North America were the Viking explorer Leif Eriksson and his party. Leif was one of Erik the Red's sons and had accompanied him to Greenland. The exploits of Erik and Leif are the subjects of Norse sagas, which are stories or histories in prose. According to one of the sagas, a man named Bjarni Herjulfsson was blown off course while sailing from Iceland to Greenland in about the year 1000. He was carried far to the southwest, where he saw an unknown shore, and then returned to tell his tale. Leif Eriksson and about 30 other people set out in 1001 to explore this land. They probably reached the coasts of Newfoundland and Labrador (now in northeastern Canada). Modern archaeologists have found evidence of Viking settlements there from about Leif's time.

The expedition continued southward, reaching a warmer wooded land where "wine berries," or grapes, grew. They named this place Vinland, meaning "Wine Land," though the fruit they found may actually have been cranberries. Vinland may have been in what is now Maryland or Virginia, in the southern United States, or perhaps the lands around the Gulf of St. Lawrence, in southeastern Canada.

Leif and the other members of the expedition built houses in Vinland and explored the region before returning to Greenland. Later Viking expeditions tried to establish colonies, but within a few years their trade with the local Indians had turned to warfare. The colonists gave up and returned to Greenland. In about 1013 Erik the Red's daughter Freydis led an unsuccessful expedition to Vinland. So ended the Norse visits to the Americas as far as the historical record is concerned. Little knowledge of these first discoveries came down to the next European explorers to reach the Americas, hundreds of years later.

THE AGE OF DISCOVERY

Europeans "rediscovered" the Americas during the great period of maritime exploration known as the Age of Discovery, in the 15th and 16th centuries. During this period, Europeans also explored the coasts of Africa, sent ships directly to India and Southeast Asia, and sailed completely around the globe. They found the New World by mistake; they were not looking to find new continents but new sea routes.

Europeans mainly wanted to find better trade routes to China, India, and Southeast Asia. They valued many products from Asia, including cloves, pepper, and other spices that were used to make food taste good and to keep it from spoiling. Also in demand were such luxuries as sheer, colorful silken cloths, rich carpets, and sparkling jewelry. The wealth of the East had been trickling into western Europe mainly by overland routes. Asian merchandise was thus both scarce and expensive in Europe. Goods changed hands many times before they reached the consumer, and at each exchange the cost increased. The merchandise was transported by camel or horse caravans, with each animal carrying only a comparatively small load. Ships could carry goods more cheaply and in greater quantity. The Italian port cities were satisfied with their monopoly of the old trading routes. On the other hand, Portugal, Spain, England, and France wanted to find new sea routes to Asia in order to import goods directly.

The older trading routes were also becoming less useful. While the Mongols controlled a vast empire in China and Central Asia, traders had been able to travel the overland routes safely. Toward the end of the 14th century the empire began to break apart, and Western merchants were no longer assured of safe-conduct along the land routes. In addition, the Ottoman Turks, who were hostile to Christians, were gaining power. They blocked the outlets to the Mediterranean Sea and thus to the ancient sea routes from the East. The Ottomans also effectively closed the land routes.

The Portuguese Find the Eastern Route

Henry the Navigator, prince of Portugal, initiated the first great enterprise of the Age of Discovery—the search for an eastern sea route to China. Although Henry is called "the Navigator," he did not sail on voyages of discovery; he sponsored them. He had several reasons for promoting exploration. He was curious about the world. He was also interested in new navigational aids and better ship design and was eager to test them. Moreover, Christian Europe was still fighting the wars known as the Crusades against Islamic powers. Henry hoped to challenge Arab power in North Africa. The desire to establish profitable trade was yet another motive.

The eastern sea route to China involved first sailing south along the west coast of Africa. In the 15th century Portuguese sea captains made ever-lengthening voyages of discovery down this coast. Bartolomeu Dias first reached the cliffs of the Cape of Good Hope at Africa's southern tip in 1488. In 1497–98 Vasco da Gama rounded

(continued on page 22)

Ships and Navigation in the Age of Discovery

The Age of Discovery was accompanied by improvements in European shipbuilding and navigational technology. Europe had made some progress in discovery before the main age of exploration.

SHIP TECHNOLOGY

In the 14th century Genoese seamen had discovered the Madeira and Azores islands in the North Atlantic. These discoveries could not, however, be followed up immediately. These voyages had been made in vessels called galleys that were built to be used in the Mediterranean Sea and were ill suited to ocean travel. Galleys were propelled primarily by oars, so they required numerous crew members to act as rowers. They also lacked substantial holds to store sufficient provisions and cargo for a long voyage. Traders of the time sailed the Mediterranean in a type of vessel called a buss, a full-bodied, rounded two-masted sailing ship.

Vessels called caravels largely superseded galleys for Atlantic travel in the early 15th century. The caravels were small, light, and quick ships. They were propelled entirely by sails and steered with a rudder. The design of caravels underwent changes over the years, but a typical caravel of the late 15th century was a broad-beamed vessel of 50 or 60 tons. Some were as large as 160 tons. They were typically about 75 feet (23 meters) long.

Caravels were often equipped with lateen (triangular) sails, rather than square sails. The ancient square sail permitted sailing only before the wind—that is, with the wind generally behind the ship. The lateen sail was a major advance, because it allowed the ship to sail close to the direction from which the wind blew. The lateen was the earliest "fore-and-aft" sail, one that extends in the direction from stem to stern, parallel to the keel. The caravel had two or three masts. Later versions added a fourth mast with a square sail for running before the wind.

Photos, The Granger Collection, New York

A 16th-century engraving (bottom) shows three Spanish caravels in a harbor. A Portuguese bronze astrolabe (top) dates to 1555.

The early 15th century also saw the rise of the full-rigged ship, which had three masts and five or six sails. There was no way to enlarge the propulsive force of ships except by increasing the area of sail. To pack more square yards of canvas on a hull required multiple masts and more and larger sails on each mast.

Some caravels had full rigging. However, when longer voyages began, the carrack (or *nao*) proved better than the caravel. The carrack was a rounder, heavier ship, more fitted to cope with ocean winds. Full-rigged, it had three masts. Most of its sails were square sails, which provided a larger sail area. The carrack also had more room to store provisions for longer voyages as well as spices and other trade goods the explorers acquired.

NAVIGATIONAL TECHNOLOGY

The arts of navigation were also improving. Pilots began to rely on "portolan charts." These charts had lines radiating from the center in the direction of the wind or compass points. Pilots used the charts to lay courses from one harbor to another. Of course, voyages of exploration took the ships into uncharted waters.

Compasses were used for direction-finding. The compass was probably imported to Europe in primitive form from China. It was gradually developed until, by the 15th century, European pilots were using an iron pin that pivoted in a round box. They realized that the pin did not point to the true north, though no one at that time knew of the magnetic pole. Navigators learned approximately how to correct the readings.

Navigators also used the cross-staff or the astrolabe, two devices that measured the altitudes of celestial bodies. From these measurements it was possible to determine the vessel's approximate latitude—its north-south position. The measurements also allowed one to calculate the approximate local time. The simplest version of the cross-staff was a stick, or staff, about one yard (0.9 meter) long. A shorter sliding stick was set at right angles to the staff. The navigator pointed the staff at a spot about halfway between the horizon and the Sun or other star. The crosspiece was then moved until the sights at its ends were in line with both the observed body and the horizon. A scale along the staff showed the altitude, or angle above the horizon, of the body.

The astrolabe was a disk of brass or bronze, from 4 to 20 inches (10 to 50 centimeters) in diameter. A pointer, called an alidade, was pivoted at the center of the disk. One person held the astrolabe by a small ring at the top while another person knelt facing the rim of the instrument. The person kneeling pointed the alidade at the Sun or other star and read the angle from the markings on the disk. The astrolabe had been known since ancient times, but its use by seafarers was rare, even as late as 1300. It became more common during the next 50 years. The sextant, an instrument that allowed more accurate determination of latitude, came into use in the 18th century.

Determining a ship's longitude—its east-west position—remained a serious problem during the Age of Discovery, and for many years after. The only method available was dead reckoning, or keeping a running record of estimates of the distances and directions traveled. Dead reckoning could be reasonably accurate, however, when done by experts.

It was long known that one could determine longitude by comparing the local time with the reading of a clock that reliably kept the time of a known meridian. Because Earth's revolution rate was known, it was possible to figure out how far east or west a ship had traveled. But no accurate marine timekeeper was then available. It was not until the mid-18th century that the first practical marine chronometers were invented. They were essentially very accurate pocket watches. These instruments finally allowed navigators to accurately determine longitude.

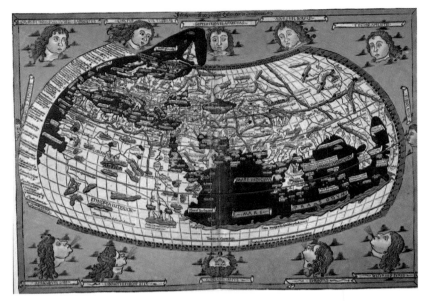

A copy of an ancient world map by Ptolemy shows only Europe, Asia, and northern Africa. In 1482, when the copy of the map was made, the Americas, southern Africa, Australia, the Pacific islands, and Antarctica were still unknown to Europeans.

The Granger Collection, New York

(continued from page 20)

the Cape and reached India by sea, successfully finding the eastern route. He brought back a cargo of spices that netted a huge profit. Portugal occupied key cities on the sea lanes between China and the Red Sea. Its wealth became the envy of western Europe. (*See also* Eurasia; Africa.)

Columbus Sails West

On the morning of Oct. 12, 1492, the master navigator Christopher Columbus stepped ashore on an island in the Americas. The arrival of his ships in the Western Hemisphere was one of the pivotal events in world history. Columbus' voyages opened the way for European exploration, exploitation, and colonization of the Americas. They also led to the near total annihilation of numerous American Indian cultures. Ironically, Columbus had landed in the New World by accident. He was seeking a western sea route from Europe to Asia. When he sighted land, he believed that he had reached his goal. To the day he died, he still believed that he had reached Asia. Although Columbus was mistaken, he still ranks as a highly skilled navigator and a courageous and persistent explorer. Few other navigators of his time would have dared to sail far west into the unknown, without proof that the winds would allow them to return.

It is not known when the idea originated of sailing west to reach China. Many sailors searched for islands in the west. Educated people knew that the world was round and that the east could be reached by sailing west. To believe, however, that it would be practical to make such a voyage was an entirely different matter. Columbus was one of the most optimistic advocates of the western route. His studies led him to believe that Earth's circumference was much smaller than it actually is and that Asia extended much farther east than it does. He believed that Asia lay only a few thousand miles west of Europe, across the open sea.

Columbus was probably originally from Genoa, Italy. In about 1476 he settled in Lisbon, Portugal. He and his brother worked as mapmakers there, but Columbus was mainly a seagoing businessman. He sailed to Ireland, Iceland, and a Portuguese settlement in West Africa, gaining knowledge of Portuguese navigation and the Atlantic wind systems.

In 1484 Columbus first began seeking support from King John II of Portugal for a voyage west to Asia. He was not able to convince the king that his idea was worth

Christopher Columbus' fleet of three ships sets sail from Spain in 1492.

Kean Collection/Hulton Archive/Getty Images

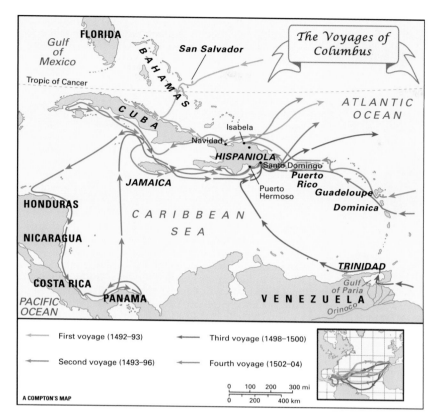

The Voyages of Columbus

First voyage (1492–93)   Third voyage (1498–1500)

Second voyage (1493–96)   Fourth voyage (1502–04)

A COMPTON'S MAP

0   100   200   300 mi
0   200   400 km

Niña, while his brother Martín Pinzón was captain of the *Pinta.* Columbus commanded the *Santa María,* the flagship. At about 117 feet (36 meters) long, it was more than twice the size of the caravels. The *Santa María* was probably a type of rounder, heavier ship called a *nao* or carrack. Some of the funding for the voyage came from the Spanish monarchs. A group of Italian bankers in Seville, Spain, also contributed a large sum of money.

The little fleet set sail from Palos, Spain, on Aug. 3, 1492. Columbus' navigational genius showed itself immediately. The fleet sailed southward to the Canary Islands, off the northwest African mainland, rather than sailing due west to the islands of the Azores. The westerlies (winds blowing from the west) prevail in the Azores. These winds had defeated previous attempts to sail to the west. In the Canaries the three ships could pick up the northeast trade winds. Supposedly, they could trust to the westerlies for their return.

Only three days out of Palos, the *Pinta* lost its rudder. The Spaniards repaired the ship in the Canary Islands and set sail again on September 9. Steady trade winds from the northeast drove them on their course due west. As they sailed westward, Columbus kept two records of progress. One was the distance he thought they had actually traveled. The other was a much shorter estimate that he showed the crew to quiet their fears at being so far from home.

For the most part the passage was smooth and the winds were steady. As the days passed, however, the men could not see how they could sail home against winds that had blown them steadily west. On October 8 and 9 the men were ready to rebel. Columbus said that he would turn back if land was not sighted within three days. They found land just in time. On the night of October 11, Columbus thought he saw lights in the distance. At 2 AM on October 12, Rodrigo de Triana, a seaman aboard the *Pinta,* cried loudly the first sight of land. The voyage from the Canaries had taken 33 days.

The small Spanish fleet had unknowingly reached not Asia but the Caribbean islands that are now The Bahamas. The islands are part of North America, lying between Florida on the U.S. mainland and the island of Cuba. Columbus named the first land that the expedition sighted San Salvador. This island may have been the one now called San Salvador or perhaps Samana Cay. The expedition landed and was met by a

backing. Columbus next tried to obtain sponsorship from France and England. By 1486 he was in Spain, asking for patronage from King Ferdinand and Queen Isabella. After at least two rejections, he at last obtained their support in January 1492. They probably argued that the cost of equipping the expedition would not be very great. If it failed, the loss could be borne. If the expedition should succeed, however, the gain would be enormous—it might divert to Spain all the wealth of Asia.

Ferdinand and Isabella also hoped that such an enterprise would gain them greater status in Europe, especially against their main rival, Portugal. Then, in alliance with the pope, they might hope to take the lead in the Christian war against Islamic powers. Spanish soldiers had just recaptured the last foothold of the Muslim Moors in Spain earlier that month. Columbus himself hoped to amass riches for his family and to join the ranks of the nobility of Spain. Ferdinand and Isabella promised that if he succeeded, he would be made "Admiral of the Ocean Sea" and that he would receive 10 percent of any profit. Columbus and later his descendants would be appointed the governor of any lands he discovered. Columbus was also a devout Christian, and he hoped that his voyage would lead to the conversion of the Chinese to Christianity.

The historic first voyage. On his first voyage, Columbus took three ships and a total crew of about 90 Spaniards. The *Niña* and the *Pinta* were small, speedy ships called caravels. Vicente Pinzón commanded the

L. Prang and Company/Library of Congress,
Washington, D.C. (neg. no. LC-USZC2-1687)

Christopher Columbus, kneeling, claims the island of San Salvador for Spain in 1492. San Salvador was the first place the Spaniards landed in the New World.

group of Taino people. Carrying the royal banners of Ferdinand and Isabella, the Spaniards took possession of San Salvador for Spain.

The Taino were friendly and helpful to the Spaniards. Columbus believed that he had reached the "Indies"— East and Southeast Asia. He thus called the people he encountered there Indians. The Caribbean islands are today known as the West Indies, to distinguish them from the East Indies of Asia.

"Soon many of the islanders gathered round us. I could see that they were people who would be more easily converted to our Holy Faith by love than by coercion ... I gave some of them red bonnets and glass beads which they hung round their necks, and many other things of small value, at which they were so delighted and so eager to please us that we could not believe it. Later they swam out to the boats to bring us parrots and balls of cotton thread and darts ..."

—Christopher Columbus, describing the Spaniards' first encounter with Indians, on San Salvador on Oct. 12, 1492

Sailing on with Indian guides, Columbus stopped at islands he named Santa María de la Concepción (now Rum Cay), Fernandina (Long Island), and Isabela (Crooked Island). He then sailed south to Cuba, reaching its north coast on October 28. He thought that Cuba might be Japan, but he later convinced himself that it was actually the Chinese mainland.

Everywhere the Spaniards asked the Indians where gold could be found. On Dec. 6, 1492, the explorers reached an island called Ayti (Haiti) by its Taino inhabitants. On December 6, Columbus renamed the island Hispaniola (now divided politically into Haiti and the Dominican Republic). Previously he had found small trinkets of gold, but on Hispaniola he found at least enough gold and prosperity to save him from ridicule on his return to Spain.

On December 25 the *Santa María* ran aground off the north coast of Hispaniola and had to be abandoned. From its timber Columbus built a small fort, La Navidad, with the help of a Taino chief named Guacanagarí. The Spaniards left 39 crewmen behind at La Navidad as colonists.

On Jan. 16, 1493, the *Niña* and the *Pinta* began the return voyage. They carried gold, colorful parrots, other strange animals and plants, spices, and some Indian cloth and ornaments. They also carried several Indians, whom they had captured to show to Ferdinand and Isabella. The journey back was a nightmare. The westerlies did indeed direct the ships homeward. In mid-February, however, a terrible storm engulfed the fleet, and the ships were separated. Columbus, on the damaged *Niña,* eventually limped to port in Lisbon for repairs. The *Pinta* made port at the Spanish town of Bayona, to the north of Portugal. With repairs completed, Columbus set sail, reaching Palos on March 15, 1493. Ferdinand and Isabella welcomed Columbus at Barcelona, Spain, with great honor. All the titles and privileges promised to him were confirmed.

Later voyages. The wealth and human captives that Columbus displayed for the Spanish rulers convinced all of the need for a rapid second voyage. Columbus, now an admiral, was at the height of his glory. He led at least 17 ships out from Cádiz, Spain, on Sept. 25, 1493. The ships carried about 1,500 men and supplies to enable them to found permanent colonies. The expedition also included a group of friars, who hoped to convert the Indians to Christianity.

Sailing again via the Canary Islands, the fleet took a more southerly course than on the first voyage. The Spaniards reached Dominica in the Lesser Antilles on November 3. After sighting the Virgin Islands, they arrived at Hispaniola on November 23. There they found that La Navidad had been burned and the 39 men slain. The Spaniards started a new colony, named La Isabela for the queen. Columbus then explored the coasts of Jamaica, Cuba, and Hispaniola. Doubts seem to have arisen among some of the Spaniards as to the identity of the islands. In June 1494 Columbus forced his men to swear a declaration that Cuba was indeed the Chinese mainland. The following year he began to conquer Hispaniola, spreading devastation among the Taino. The Spaniards forced many of them to work in gold mines and shipped others to Spain as slaves. Columbus left his brothers in charge of La Isabela and returned to Spain, arriving at Cádiz on June 11, 1496.

Columbus set out on his third voyage with a smaller fleet of six ships on May 30, 1498. He planned to explore to the south of his earlier discoveries and hoped to find a strait from Cuba to India. After stopping at Trinidad, he entered the Gulf of Paria and planted the Spanish flag on what is now Venezuela, in South America. He realized that the great torrents of freshwater flowing into the Gulf of Paria meant that he had discovered another continent. But of course he did not find a strait to India.

When Columbus returned to Hispaniola, he discovered that both the Taino and the European colonists resented the rule of his brothers. Dissatisfied colonists had complained to the Spanish rulers. A new governor was sent to replace Columbus. He arrested Columbus and his brothers and shipped them back to Spain in chains. Ferdinand and Isabella released the brothers but did not reappoint Columbus governor.

Columbus' fourth and final expedition was the most disappointing and unlucky of all his voyages. He set sail on May 9, 1502, with only a small fleet of four ships. The Spanish rulers had by then lost much of their confidence in him. He explored the coast of Jamaica, the southern shore of Cuba, and the east coast of Central America, searching for gold and a strait to India. The fleet had lost two ships. The two remaining ships, in poor condition, ran aground on Jamaica in June 1503. Columbus sent messengers by canoe to Hispaniola, but the governor was in no hurry to send help. Meanwhile, Columbus correctly predicted an eclipse of the Moon from his astronomical tables, thereby frightening the local peoples into providing food for the Spaniards. Rescue ships from Hispaniola finally arrived in June 1504.

The admiral returned to Spain broken in health and spirit. He was not received at court, and the king refused to restore his privileges and honors. He was, however, far from poor.

Over the hundreds of years since Columbus sailed to the Americas, there has been a major shift in how he has been perceived. In the older perspective, Columbus has been celebrated by people of European descent as a hero for "discovering" the Americas. His four voyages to the New World were the means of bringing great wealth to Spain and other European countries and of opening up the Americas to European settlement. More recent approaches have emphasized the destructive effects of his voyages. They stress the disastrous impact of the slave trade and the ravages of the diseases the Europeans accidentally brought with them on the peoples of the Americas.

Spain and Portugal Divide Up the New World

When Columbus first returned to Spain, the Portuguese claimed that he had merely visited a part of their dominion of Guinea in Africa. Spain and Portugal asked the pope to settle the dispute. He complied in 1493 by drawing an arbitrary north-south Line of Demarcation. This imaginary line lay about 320 miles (515 kilometers) west of the Cape Verde Islands. Spain was given exclusive rights to all newly discovered and undiscovered lands in the region west of the line. Portuguese expeditions were to keep to the east of the line. Neither power was to occupy any territory already in the hands of a Christian ruler.

King John II of Portugal was dissatisfied with the pope's decision. Under the new rule, the Portuguese would not even have sufficient room at sea for their African voyages. In 1494 Spain and Portugal negotiated a treaty that moved the Line of Demarcation to about

1,185 miles (1,900 kilometers) west of the Cape Verde Islands. The pope eventually sanctioned the change. However, no other European country facing the Atlantic ever accepted this line.

The new Line of Demarcation allowed Portugal to claim a significant prize in the New World—Brazil. On March 9, 1500, the Portuguese navigator Pedro Álvares Cabral set sail from Lisbon for India, intending to follow the route around Africa taken by Vasco da Gama. To avoid the calms off the Gulf of Guinea, Cabral bore so far to the west that on April 22, 1500, he sighted the Brazilian coast. He took formal possession of the land for Portugal and then set off for India.

News of Cabral's landing in Brazil aroused great enthusiasm among the Portuguese. The king began to sponsor major transatlantic explorations, including that of the Italian navigator Amerigo Vespucci. Vespucci had already completed an expedition in 1499–1500 for Spain, as navigator of a fleet under the command of Alonso de Ojeda. On that mission, Vespucci arrived in Guyana and then turned south to Brazil. He is believed to have discovered the mouth of the Amazon River. On the way back he reached Trinidad, sighted the mouth of the Orinoco River, and then made for Haiti. Vespucci thought that he had sailed along the coast of an eastern peninsula of Asia.

Vespucci led an expedition for Portugal in 1501–02. His small fleet sailed along the coast of Brazil and for the first time estimated the extent of the land. Calendar in hand, he named different points on the coast after the Christian saints on whose days they were discovered. The extent of this voyage is disputed, but Vespucci claimed to have continued southward. He may have discovered the Río de la Plata, an estuary between what are now Uruguay and Argentina.

Vespucci and also scholars became convinced for the first time that the newly discovered lands were not part of Asia but a "New World." Vespucci wrote a lively and embellished description of this New World that became quite popular. In 1507 Martin Waldseemüller, a German scholar, suggested in a pamphlet that the new land be named America after him. (His name in Latin is Americus Vespucius.) The name caught on and brought Vespucci an honor that many feel he did not deserve. The name America originally was applied only to South America, but the term soon was extended to include North America.

Magellan's Ship Circles the Globe

Spain claimed that the Line of Demarcation extended around the globe, but no one knew where it fell in the Eastern Hemisphere. A Portuguese captain named Ferdinand Magellan believed there might be a water passage through South America that would lead to Asia. He presented his idea to the king of Spain, Charles I (later the Holy Roman emperor Charles V). Magellan convinced the king that the richest lands in the East—including the Spice Islands (now the Moluccas of Indonesia)—lay in the region reserved for Spain by the Line of Demarcation. The king commissioned Magellan to find a western route to Asia.

The five ships of Ferdinand Magellan's expedition depart from Spain in 1519. One of these ships would become the first to circle the globe.

Spanish officials furnished five small ships for the expedition. Magellan's flagship, the *Trinidad*, had as consorts the *San Antonio*, the *Concepción*, the *Victoria*, and the *Santiago*. The ships were old ones, not in the best condition or fitted as Magellan would have liked. They carried a crew of about 250 men, mostly Spaniards. The fleet left Sanlúcar de Barrameda, in southwestern Spain, on Sept. 20, 1519.

The ships reached the Canary Islands on Sept. 26, 1519, and set sail on October 3 for Brazil. They then sailed southward along the east coast of South America. The expedition explored the estuary of the Río de la

Plata in the vain hope that it might prove to be a strait leading to the Pacific Ocean. The ships continued southward along the coast of Patagonia, in what is now Argentina, in search of a strait.

Eventually, with the weather worsening, Magellan decided that the expedition would spend the winter on land. Winter quarters were established at Port St. Julian, in southern Argentina. There, Spanish captains led a serious mutiny against the Portuguese commander. With resolution, ruthlessness, and daring, Magellan quelled it. He executed one of the rebellious captains. He left another of the captains ashore when, on Aug. 24, 1520, the fleet left St. Julian.

On October 21, Magellan at last found a strait leading westward. This channel, which is now named the Strait of Magellan, lies between the southern tip of mainland South America and the island of Tierra del Fuego. The strait proved to be an extremely difficult one: it was long, deep, tortuous, rock-walled, and bedeviled by icy squalls and dense fogs. It was a miracle that three of the five ships got through its 325-mile (525-kilometer) length. After 38 days, they sailed out into the open ocean. At the news that the ocean had been sighted, the iron-willed Magellan reportedly broke down and cried with joy.

Once away from land, the ocean seemed calm enough. Magellan consequently named it the Pacific, meaning "peaceable." The Pacific, however, proved to be of vast extent. For 14 weeks the little ships sailed on a northwesterly course without encountering land. Short of food and water, the sailors ate sawdust mixed with putrid ship's biscuits and what few rats they could catch. They finally resorted to chewing the leather parts of their gear to keep themselves alive. Many of the men fell seriously ill with scurvy. At last, on March 6, 1521, exhausted and in poor health, they landed at the island of Guam. They were the first Europeans to have crossed the Pacific.

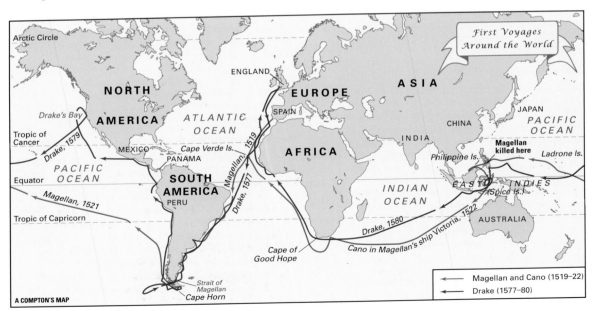

Scurvy, the Sailors' Scourge

Toward the end of the 15th century, scurvy became the major cause of disability and death among explorers and other sailors on long sea voyages. Scurvy is a disorder characterized by swollen and bleeding gums, loosened teeth, and sore, stiff joints. It also causes internal bleeding, slow wound healing, and profound weakness. Sailors suffering from scurvy had trouble eating, and they often starved. Scurvy is now known to be caused by a lack of vitamin C in the diet. Vitamin C is found in many fresh fruits and vegetables, particularly citrus fruits, but sailors often lacked access to fresh produce for long periods.

In the 16th century the Dutch and Spanish discovered the benefits of citrus fruits and juices to sailors on long voyages. In 1753 the Scottish naval surgeon James Lind conducted an early example of a clinical trial. He compared the effects of citrus fruits on patients with scurvy against five alternative remedies. The fruit was noticeably better than vinegar, cider, seawater, and other treatments. Lind recommended that sailors eat citrus. When this dietary practice was finally adopted by the British Royal Navy in 1795, scurvy disappeared from the ranks "as if by magic." Lime juice and other citrus juices became so common aboard ship that British sailors were referred to as "limeys."

In Guam they obtained fresh food for the first time in 99 days. They left a few days later, steering west-southwestward to the Philippines. There, Magellan secured the first alliance for Spain with a leader in the Pacific. At Cebu Island the expedition converted the island's ruler to Christianity. Weeks later, however, Magellan was killed in a fight with the people of nearby Mactan Island.

The survivors, in two ships, sailed on to the Moluccas, where the expedition obtained large amounts of valuable spices. One ship attempted, but failed, to return across the Pacific. The remaining ship, the *Victoria*, sailed alone across the Indian Ocean. It was commanded by the Spanish navigator Juan Sebastián del Cano. The ship rounded the Cape of Good Hope and arrived at Seville on Sept. 9, 1522. After a voyage of slightly more than three years, it had circled the globe. Besides Cano, the surviving crew consisted of only 17 Europeans and a small number of Moluccans. The spices they brought back more than paid for the expenses of the voyage.

Magellan was undoubtedly one of the most skilled sailors of the great age of European maritime discoveries. Although he died before the completion of the voyage, he did circumnavigate, or sail round, the world. He did not encompass the globe on a single trip, however. On a previous eastbound voyage to the East Indies, he had gone farther east than the Philippines. Thus, at the time he was killed, he had already overlapped his earlier course.

It is fitting to consider Magellan and Cano's circumnavigation as marking the close of the Age of Discovery. Magellan and his men proved that Columbus had discovered a New World and not the route to China. They also demonstrated that this New World was separated from Asia by a vast ocean.

LATIN AMERICA

According to the Line of Demarcation, Spain was left in control of most of the New World. Spanish conquerors, known as conquistadores, soon began to explore and take control of the region that is now Latin America. This region includes Mexico, Central America, South America, and the islands of the West Indies in the Caribbean. Because the Spaniards colonized much of this vast region, most of its people today speak Spanish.

The earliest Spanish settlements were in the West Indies. With Columbus' arrival there, the Caribbean Sea was essentially transformed into a Spanish lake. Settlement by the Spanish concentrated on the islands of Cuba, Jamaica, Puerto Rico, and above all Hispaniola. The first permanent Spanish settlement in the Americas was established at Santo Domingo, on Hispaniola, in 1496. Santo Domingo rapidly became the "mother of settlement" in Latin America. From this city, major Spanish expeditions of conquest and settlement set out. The Spaniards found gold, silver, and precious stones and enslaved the Indians. Ambitious men became governors of conquered lands. Missionaries brought a new religion to the Indians.

Balboa Reaches the Pacific

The first European to look upon the Pacific Ocean from the shores of the New World was Vasco Núñez de Balboa. The Spanish adventurer and explorer sailed for

Sword in hand, the Spanish explorer Vasco Núñez de Balboa claims the Pacific Ocean for Spain in 1513.

North Wind Picture Archives/Alamy

America in 1500 and settled in Santo Domingo. There his unsuccessful attempts at farming led him into debt. In 1510, hoping to escape his creditors, he stowed away on a ship. The ship carried an expedition bound for the new colony of San Sebastián on the mainland of South America, in what is now Colombia.

When the expedition arrived at San Sebastián, it was discovered that the colony's founder had fled and abandoned the survivors. Balboa persuaded his superiors to transfer the colony to the region of Darién, in the Isthmus of Panama. There they founded Santa María de la Antigua, the first stable European settlement in Central America. Balboa eventually gained command of the colony.

Balboa meanwhile had organized a series of expeditions into the Indian chiefdoms of the area to hunt for gold and slaves. From the Indians, he learned of a great ocean beyond the mountains and of a province rich in gold. The gold was perhaps a reference to the riches of the Inca Empire. Balboa sent word to Spain that he needed reinforcements to explore the area. In Spain an expedition was organized, but Balboa was not given command. The king instead sent Pedro Arias Dávila as commander and as governor of Darién.

Balboa had already set out, however, without waiting for reinforcements. On Sept. 1, 1513, he sailed to the narrowest part of the isthmus. It took about 25 days for his party of 190 Spaniards and hundreds of Indians to cross 45 miles (70 kilometers) of dense jungle. On Sept. 25 (or 27), 1513, Balboa climbed to the peak of a mountain, from which he first sighted the Pacific Ocean. A few days later, the expedition reached the shores of the Pacific, which Balboa called the South Sea. He took possession of the ocean and all lands washed by it in the name of the Spanish monarch.

Cortés Conquers the Aztec of Mexico

The Spanish dream of finding great riches in America was realized when Hernán Cortés (or Cortéz) conquered the Aztec Empire in 1519–21. The Aztec ruled a great civilization of some 5 to 6 million people in what is now central and southern Mexico. Their capital, Tenochtitlán, was one of the largest cities in the world. The Spaniards were impressed by the city's grandeur. Nevertheless, they methodically destroyed Tenochtitlán. On its ruins they built Mexico City.

Cortés arrived in the New World when he was about 19. For several years he worked as a farmer and a public official in Hispaniola. In 1511 he sailed under Diego Velázquez to help conquer Cuba.

In 1518 Velázquez sent his nephew Juan de Grijalba to explore the Yucatán Peninsula. Setting sail from Cuba with four ships and about 200 men, Grijalba became the first European to set foot on what is now Mexican soil. He and his men mapped rivers and discovered Cozumel Island. During their explorations, the men heard tales of a rich civilization in the interior. They eventually met with representatives of the Aztec.

Grijalba returned to Cuba with news of the cities and precious metals of the Aztec. Velázquez was furious that his nephew had made no attempt at settlement, though

Grijalba's orders had been to explore only. As a result, Grijalba was passed over and the job of colonization was given to Cortés.

Velázquez soon suspected Cortés of ambitions beyond his orders, however, and canceled his expedition. Cortés nevertheless assembled men and equipment and set out without permission. He sailed for the coast of Yucatán on Feb. 18, 1519, with 11 ships, 508 soldiers, about 100 sailors, and 16 horses. In March he landed at what is now the Mexican state of Tabasco. Cortés stayed for a time in order to gain intelligence from the local Indians. He won them over and received presents from them, including 20 women. Among them was Malintzin, to whom he gave the Spanish name Marina. She became his lover, interpreter, and adviser. The success of his ventures was often directly due to her guidance.

Cortés sailed to another spot on the southeastern Mexican coast and founded Veracruz there. Then, to prevent all thought of retreat, he burned his ships. Leaving a small force on the coast, Cortés led the remainder of his men into the interior. In his dealings with the local Indians, he relied sometimes on force and sometimes on establishing friendly relations. The key to his subsequent conquests lay in the political crisis within the Aztec Empire. Many of the people who had been subjugated by the Aztec bitterly resented them.

The Spanish conqueror Hernán Cortés, left, meets the Aztec emperor Montezuma II in 1519.

Chocolate from the New World

Beloved around the world today, chocolate was first made by American Indians. It is produced from cocoa beans, the fruit of the cacao tree, which is native to the tropical regions of the Americas. The cacao tree was cultivated more than 3,000 years ago by the Maya, Toltec, and Aztec of what is now Mexico. They prepared a beverage from the bean, sometimes using it as a ceremonial drink. The cocoa bean was so valuable that they also used it as a currency.

Christopher Columbus took cocoa beans back to Spain after his fourth voyage in 1502. However, chocolate did not yet become popular there. In 1519 the Spanish explorer Hernán Cortés and his men were served a bitter chocolate beverage at the court of Montezuma II, the Aztec emperor. The Aztec beverage was made from sun-dried shelled cocoa beans, which were probably fermented in their pods. The broken kernels, or nibs, were roasted in earthen pots and then ground to a paste over a small fire. Vanilla and various herbs and spices such as chili peppers were added. Corn (maize) was sometimes used to produce a milder flavor. The paste was formed into small cakes, cooled, and hardened. The cakes were then broken up, mixed with hot water, and beaten to a foamy consistency with a small wooden beater. This produced a drink called *xocoatl* (from Nahuatl words meaning "bitter water").

Cortés introduced chocolate to the Spanish court, where it became fashionable. The Spaniards added sugar to their chocolate drink. They also flavored it with cinnamon and vanilla and served it hot. This beverage remained a Spanish secret for almost a hundred years before its introduction to Italy and France. It was later brought to other European countries and the American Colonies. For a long time, however, chocolate remained an expensive luxury drink that only the wealthy could afford. After factories began the mass production of chocolate in the 18th century, the price dropped, and it became widely popular. Chocolate candy was not produced until the 19th century.

Chocolate is only one of many foods cultivated by the Indians that European explorers brought back from the Americas. Corn (maize) and cassava are now staple crops in many parts of the globe. Europeans also brought back such foods as tomatoes, potatoes, sweet potatoes, chili peppers, pineapples, peanuts (groundnuts), and cashews.

The Aztec made a bitter chocolate drink. A 17th-century illustration shows an Aztec man with containers of chocolate, above, and cocoa beans from the cacao tree, below.

Taking advantage of this situation, Cortés began making allies with Indians who wanted the Aztec to fall. He ultimately made more than 200,000 Indian allies.

On Nov. 8, 1519, Cortés reached Tenochtitlán with his small Spanish force and about 1,000 Indian allies. In accordance with the diplomatic customs of the region, the Aztec ruler, Montezuma II, received him graciously. However, the Spaniards soon seized Montezuma.

Meanwhile Velázquez had sent soldiers to arrest Cortés and bring him back to Cuba. Cortés defeated this army at Veracruz and enlisted most of the survivors under his banner. He returned to the Aztec capital in December 1520. After subduing the neighboring territories, he laid siege to the city itself, conquering it street by street. Its capture was completed on Aug. 13, 1521. This victory marked the fall of the Aztec Empire. Cortés had become the absolute ruler of a huge territory extending from the Caribbean Sea to the Pacific Ocean.

Pizarro Conquers the Inca of Peru

The Spaniards soon conquered another great Indian empire, that of the Inca. The Inca ruled a vast area that extended along the Pacific coast and Andean highlands from what is now northern Ecuador, through Peru and Bolivia, to central Chile. Their capital was at Cuzco (now in Peru). The conquest of the fabulously wealthy Inca Empire by the Spanish adventurer Francisco Pizarro is one of the most dramatic episodes in the history of the New World.

Pizarro was one of the first Spanish captains on the American mainland. After traveling to Hispaniola in 1502, he took part in an expedition to what is now Colombia in 1510. Three years later, he accompanied Balboa on the journey that ended in the discovery of the Pacific Ocean. Pizarro accumulated a small fortune as mayor and magistrate of the town of Panamá.

Hearing of a large and wealthy Indian empire to the south, Pizarro enlisted the help of two friends to form an

Remains of the great Inca fortress of Sacsahuamán still stand near Cuzco, Peru. Many of its stones are the size of boulders, weighing as much as 100–300 tons. The stone walls extend outward for more than 1,000 feet (305 meters). Spanish forces destroyed the defensive towers and other structures on the hill behind the walls.
© Jarno Gonzalez Zarraonandia/Shutterstock.com

The Granger Collection, New York

Francisco Pizarro conquered the Inca Empire, rich in gold and silver, for Spain in 1533.

expedition to explore and conquer the land. A soldier named Diego de Almagro provided the equipment and helped lead the expedition. Hernando de Luque, a priest, furnished the funds.

Their first expedition resulted in disaster after two years of suffering and hardship. Only about a third of the men survived. When a second expedition in 1526 fared little better, Pizarro sent Almagro back to Panama for reinforcements. Instead of sending help, however, the governor of Panama sent vessels to bring back the explorers. Pizarro refused to return. He is said to have drawn a line on the ground, inviting all who wanted wealth and glory to step over the line and join him.

Thirteen men crossed the line. Pizarro and "the famous thirteen" continued exploring the coast to a land they named Peru.

Pizarro then sailed to Spain to ask the king directly for authority to conquer Peru. This was granted. Pizarro left Spain with four of his half-brothers on Jan. 19, 1530. They sailed from Panama the following year. He had three vessels, fewer than 200 men, and about 40 horses.

The Spaniards took advantage of a civil war between two factions of Inca that was just ending. Pizarro spent a year conquering the coastal settlements. Then he marched inland to the city of Cajamarca. There he met with emissaries of Atahuallpa, the Inca emperor. Atahuallpa accepted an invitation to visit the Spanish commander, partly because the Spanish force was so small. He arrived attended by a few thousand Inca. Pizarro's followers, armed with muskets and cannons, were waiting. They seized the Inca emperor and slaughtered his attendants.

As ransom to obtain his freedom, Atahuallpa offered to fill with gold a room 17 by 22 feet (5 by 7 meters) to a point as high as he could reach. Pizarro accepted this immense fortune. He soon had Atahuallpa executed anyway, on Aug. 29, 1533. With news of Atahuallpa's death, the Inca armies surrounding Cajamarca retreated, and Pizarro progressed toward Cuzco, the royal capital. The Spaniards took possession of Cuzco without a struggle in November 1533. Spanish conquering expeditions soon set forth from Peru in all directions: to what are now Chile and Argentina to the south, Ecuador and Colombia to the north, and even the Amazon region to the east.

The Search for Fabled Riches

Much of the drive to explore and conquer northern South America came from tales of Eldorado—either a fantastically wealthy Indian ruler or a land filled with gold. In the 1530s three expeditions searching for this legendary source of riches arrived in New Granada (now Colombia) from different directions. The leaders of these expeditions were Gonzalo Jiménez de Quesada

Eldorado: The Legendary Land of Gold

The Spaniards found great riches, including gold, when they conquered the Aztec and Inca empires, and they hoped to find more. In the 1500s European explorers began hearing tales from local Indians about a wealthy Indian ruler. He supposedly ruled a town located somewhere near Bogotá (now in Colombia). This ruler was said to plaster his body with gold dust during festivals and then plunge into Lake Guatavita to wash off the dust. As part of the ceremonies, his subjects threw jewels and golden objects into the lake. This ruler became known as Eldorado, meaning "The Gilded One."

Europeans wanted to find this gold-strewn lake. A Spaniard reported that he had visited Eldorado in a city called Omagua. In 1538 Spanish and German explorers converged on the Bogotá highlands in search of the legendary ruler. No trace of him was found, but the area came under Spanish rule.

Eldorado soon came to mean an entire fabulous country of gold. It was said to have cities named Manoa and Omagua. In search of this country, the Spanish explorer Gonzalo Pizarro crossed the Andes Mountains from Quito (now in Ecuador) in 1541. One of his officers, Francisco de Orellana, sailed down the Napo and

The Granger Collection, New York

A gold figure made by Quimbaya Indians dates to about 1500. The Quimbaya lived in what is now Colombia.

Amazon rivers. The Spanish conqueror Gonzalo Jiménez de Quesada looked for Eldorado eastward from Bogotá in 1569–72. The English explorer Sir Walter Raleigh searched for Manoa in what is now Venezuela in 1595. Spaniards sought Omagua nearby. In 1603 Pêro Coelho de Sousa of Portugal explored northeastern Brazil. The golden city of Eldorado was shown on maps of Brazil and the Guianas for years thereafter.

Although there was no Eldorado, there was gold. Many of the Indian peoples of northern South America produced large quantities of gold jewelry and other ornaments of great artistry. Among them were the Chibcha, Tairona, Cenú, Quimbaya, Calima, and Manteño.

Eldorado was only one of the many mythical regions of great riches in the New World. Others included Quivira and the Seven Cities of Cíbola in North America and the City of the Caesars in South America. The search for these wealthy lands led to the rapid exploration and conquest of much of the Americas by Spaniards and others. Since then, Eldorado has come to mean any place where wealth can be quickly and easily gained. The name has been given to towns in Latin America and the United States and to a California county.

and Sebastián de Benalcázar of Spain and Nikolaus Federmann of Germany.

Jiménez de Quesada was trained as a lawyer and had no military experience. Nevertheless, he set off from the Caribbean coast of Colombia in 1536 to look for Eldorado and to try to find a land route to Peru. He led an expedition of 900 men up the Magdalena River into the interior of Colombia. After eight months of marching through tropical forests and struggling with hostile Indians, the expedition reached the great central plain of Colombia. This was the land of the Chibcha Indians, a group of tribes that had attained a relatively high state of culture. Although it was not the fabled land of Eldorado, the Chibcha did possess numerous ornaments of gold and jewels. The ruler of the Chibcha fled as Jiménez de Quesada's army approached, and the conquest of the area appeared to be accomplished. Jiménez de Quesada founded the city of Bogotá in 1538.

Two rival conquerors soon arrived in the area, however, and challenged Jiménez de Quesada's claim to Colombia. Federmann and his party had set off from the coast of what is now Venezuela and then explored to the south. Benalcázar, who had already conquered Nicaragua and Ecuador, arrived in Colombia from Peru. The three explorers agreed to submit their rival claims to the Spanish king. They sailed to Spain and plead their cases, but the governorship of Colombia was eventually awarded to another man.

Jiménez de Quesada led another expedition in search of Eldorado in 1569, when he was probably in his 70s. With a party of 500 men, he crossed the Andes and explored eastern Colombia. He returned after two years' wanderings with only 25 of his original company.

Gonzalo Jiménez de Quesada.

Museo Nacional Bogota—Gianni Dagli Orti/The Art Archive

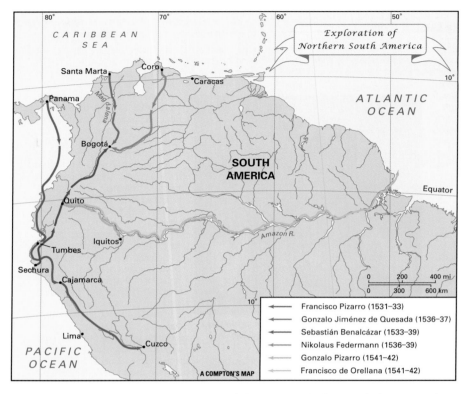

Exploration of
Northern South America

A COMPTON'S MAP

→ Francisco Pizarro (1531–33)
→ Gonzalo Jiménez de Quesada (1536–37)
→ Sebastián Benalcázar (1533–39)
→ Nikolaus Federmann (1536–39)
→ Gonzalo Pizarro (1541–42)
→ Francisco de Orellana (1541–42)

Francisco de Orellana, was sent off in search of provisions. He took a homemade ship and 50 men. Pizarro and his men waited in vain for Orellana's return. Forced to eat their dogs and horses, they finally staggered back to Quito in August 1542. Only about 80 of the men survived the disastrous expedition.

Orellana, however, made valuable explorations to the east. He reached the junction of the Napo and Marañón rivers. There, according to some accounts, his men persuaded him of the impossibility of sailing upstream to return to Pizarro. Instead, Orellana became the first European to explore the course of the Amazon River.

Orellana explores the Amazon. Meanwhile, another Spanish expedition had set out in February 1541 to search for a land rich in valuable cinnamon as well as gold. It was led by Gonzalo Pizarro, one of the half-brothers of Francisco Pizarro. With 200 Spaniards, some 4,000 Indians, and numerous horses and other animals, he set out into the unexplored region east of Quito. Food became scarce, however, and Pizarro's lieutenant,

Francisco de Orellana sails down the Amazon River in 1541.

The Granger Collection, New York

Drifting with the current, he reached the mouth of the Amazon in August 1542. The party continued to the West Indies and then to Spain. Orellana reported that the Amazon area had hoards of cinnamon and gold. He also told of encounters with tribes led by women warriors who resembled the Amazons of ancient Greek mythology. For this reason, he named the river the Amazon.

Raleigh explores the Orinoco. The English adventurer Sir Walter Raleigh sought the fabled Eldorado in Venezuela. In 1595 he sailed up the Orinoco River in the heart of Spain's colonial empire. He did locate some gold deposits, but the English did not support his project for colonizing the area. Back in England, he was accused of plotting to dethrone the king and was imprisoned for some 13 years.

Upon his release, Raleigh still hoped to exploit the wealth of Venezuela, arguing that the country had been ceded to England by its Indian rulers in 1595. With the king's permission, he financed and led a second expedition there in 1617. He promised to open a gold mine without offending Spain. However, a severe fever prevented him from leading his men upriver. His lieutenant burned a Spanish settlement but found no gold, and Raleigh's son died in the action. The expedition had not only failed but it had attacked the Spanish. The king of England had Raleigh executed in 1618.

Scientific Exploration

The first European expeditions explored South America mainly to conquer it and to amass wealth. Missionaries

The English adventurer Sir Walter Raleigh leads a raid on the island of Trinidad in 1599. Meanwhile, his men seize the Spanish governor of the island, Antonio de Berrio. Berrio had killed some English explorers and was one of Raleigh's rivals in the search for the gold of Eldorado.

The Granger Collection, New York

who wanted to convert the Indians to Christianity also traversed the continent. In the 18th and 19th centuries many scientific explorers arrived in South America to study its geography, peoples, plants, and animals.

La Condamine. One of the earliest of these scientific explorers was the French naturalist Charles-Marie de La Condamine. In 1735 he led an expedition of scientists to Ecuador to help determine the precise shape of the Earth (which is not a perfect sphere). The scientists accomplished this by measuring the length near the Equator of a degree of the meridian. Meanwhile, another French expedition took similar measurements in the Arctic. La Condamine and his group surveyed the Andes of Ecuador for several years. He noted the Indians' production and use of rubber and was the first person to scientifically describe this elastic but tough substance. He sent the first rubber samples to Europe, where the new material was a curiosity.

In 1743 La Condamine conducted the first scientific study of the Amazon River. He traveled from Quito and began a four-month raft journey down the entire length of the river, to its mouth. Along the way, he made scientific observations of the region's geography and the peoples he encountered. He later published a map of the Amazon and an account of his journey.

Humboldt. One of the most important scientists to explore South America was Alexander von Humboldt of Germany. His contributions are often called the "scientific discovery of America." Humboldt became one of the most famous men of Europe during the first half of the 19th century.

In the summer of 1799 Humboldt set sail from Marseille, France, accompanied by the French botanist Aimé Bonpland. The estate Humboldt had inherited from his mother enabled him to finance the expedition entirely out of his own pocket. Humboldt and Bonpland spent five years, from 1799 to 1804, in South America,

Central America, and Mexico. They covered more than 6,000 miles (9,650 kilometers) on foot, on horseback, and in canoes. It was a life of great physical exertion and serious deprivation.

Starting from Caracas, Venezuela, they traveled south through grasslands and scrublands until they reached the banks of the Apure River, a tributary of the Orinoco. They continued their journey on the river by canoe as far as the Orinoco. Following its course and that of the Casiquiare River, they proved that the vast river systems of the Amazon and the Orinoco are connected by the Casiquiare. For three months Humboldt and Bonpland moved through dense tropical forests, tormented by clouds of mosquitoes and stifled by the humid heat. Their provisions were soon destroyed by insects and rain. The lack of food finally drove them to subsist on ground-up wild cocoa beans and river water.

> *"What a fabulous and extravagant country we're in! … We've been running around like a couple of mad things; for the first three days we couldn't settle to anything: we'd find one thing, only to abandon it for the next. Bonpland keeps telling me he'll go out of his mind if the wonders don't cease."*
>
> —Alexander von Humboldt, describing Venezuela, 1799

Humboldt and Bonpland visited Cuba and then made an extensive exploration of the Andes. From Bogotá to Trujillo, Peru, they wandered over the Andean Highlands over a series of steep, rocky, and often very narrow paths. They climbed a number of peaks, including all the volcanoes around Quito. Humboldt climbed Chimborazo to a height of 19,286 feet (5,878 meters), but short of the summit. His ascent remained a world mountain-climbing record for nearly 30 years. All these achievements were carried out without the help of modern mountaineering

Alexander von Humboldt collects plant specimens near the Orinoco River of northern South America. Friedrich Georg Weitsch painted this portrait of Humboldt in 1806.

equipment. Humboldt and Bonpland suffered badly from mountain sickness, but Humboldt turned his discomfort to advantage, by describing it scientifically. He became the first person to ascribe mountain sickness to the lack of oxygen at great elevations.

Humboldt also studied the oceanic current off the west coast of South America that was later named after him. It is now known as the Peru Current. In the last year of the expedition, Humboldt and Bonpland explored Mexico, gathering information on geography and geology as well as political, social, and economic conditions.

Humboldt and Bonpland returned with an immense amount of information. They brought back a collection of several thousand new plants as well as data on longitudes and latitudes, measurements of Earth's geomagnetic field, and daily weather observations. Humboldt published 30 volumes containing the expedition's scientific results. His weather data and maps helped lay the foundation for the science of comparative climatology. Other important studies included pioneering work on the relationship between a region's geography and its plants and animals and on the role volcanoes play in the ongoing development of Earth's crust. Humboldt's volumes also contained an impassioned outcry against the enslavement of the Indians.

Darwin and other British naturalists. In the 18th century the British navy sent a series of expeditions to chart the coastlines of South America. Naturalists began to join these expeditions, which provided unique opportunities to study the natural histories of places

little known to Western science. Early in his career, the distinguished naturalist Sir Joseph Banks sailed around the world under Capt. James Cook in 1768–71. The expedition traveled along the east coast of South America, rounded Cape Horn at the continent's southern tip, and proceeded to Tahiti and Australia (*see* Australia and the Pacific Islands). Throughout the voyage, Banks and the Swedish botanist Daniel Solander collected, drew, and described a great number plants and animals. They obtained specimens of hundreds of previously unknown species. Banks later became the long-time president of the British Royal Society.

The most famous naturalist to join a British naval expedition was Charles Darwin. The observations he made on his journey aboard the *Beagle* in 1831–36 were to form the basis of his great theory of evolution. The expedition charted the southern coasts of South America and sailed around the world. Darwin was given time for many side trips on land. He examined geologic formations and collected numerous plants, animals, and fossils.

Darwin's main interest at the time was geology. However, his visit to the Galápagos Islands west of Ecuador aroused his interest in biology. He began to speculate about the curious animal life that varied from island to island. He wondered whether the development of these species was related to the isolation of the islands. He also considered the great diversity of the living things he saw on his travels around the world, even in the depths of the ocean where no humans could appreciate their beauty. He thought about how the fossils he collected suggested that some kinds of mammals had died out. And he returned home filled with questions. Back in England, Darwin quietly began work on what would become his theory of evolution by natural selection. He did not publish it until more than 20 years later, in 1859.

By that time, another British naturalist, Alfred Russel Wallace, had independently developed a similar theory

Alfred Russel Wallace, detail of a painting over a photograph.
Courtesy of the National Portrait Gallery, London

of evolution. Darwin developed his own theory in much greater detail, however. He also provided far more evidence for evolution and was mainly responsible for its acceptance.

Wallace and his naturalist friend Henry Walter Bates had traveled to Brazil in 1848 as self-employed specimen collectors. After several joint collecting ventures, the two young men amicably parted ways. Bates remained in the region for 11 years. He explored the entire valley of the Amazon River, where he collected about 14,712 species, including 8,000 previously unknown species. Most of these specimens were of insects.

Wallace spent four years traveling, collecting, mapping, drawing, and writing in unexplored regions of the Amazon River basin. He collected insects and birds and searched for clues to solve the mystery of the origin of plant and animal species. Disastrously, on his voyage home his ship went up in flames and sank. Nearly all his collections were lost, though he managed to save some of his notes.

Wallace made a second scientific voyage in 1854–62. This time he toured the Malay Archipelago of Southeast Asia. He traveled among the islands, collecting biological specimens for his own research and for sale. He also wrote scores of scientific articles. Among these were two extraordinary articles dealing with the origin of new species.

Naturalists continued to study Latin American flora and fauna throughout the 19th century. Biologists today still explore the region, particularly the Amazon Rainforest, which is the world's richest and most varied reserve of living things.

The search for lost worlds. The 19th and 20th centuries saw the arrival in Latin America of a new kind of scientist—the archaeologist. Archaeologists began searching for the ruins of Indian civilizations of the past. They were especially motivated by tales of "lost worlds"—ruins of cities that had not been seen by Europeans since the Spanish conquest of the 16th century.

The American traveler John Lloyd Stephens generated interest in the archaeology of the region with his discoveries of Maya ruins. In 1839 he set off for Central America, after having heard reports of the existence of ancient ruins there. He was accompanied by the English illustrator and archaeologist Frederick Catherwood. Their progress to Copán, Honduras, was imperiled, first by local strife and then by the hazards and extreme hardships of travel through dense, dark jungle. Their perseverance was eventually rewarded, when they uncovered a magnificently carved Maya stone slab.

Other discoveries—more carved slabs, terraces, stairways, and walls with strange and fantastic ornamentation—came in quick succession. Catherwood produced superb drawings of the Maya remains they found there and elsewhere, including Uxmal and Palenque in Mexico. The report of the expedition caused a storm of popular and scholarly interest in the Maya.

Interest in the Inca grew because of the work of the American archaeologist Hiram Bingham. In July 1911 Bingham directed an expedition to Peru to find the ruins of Vilcabamba, known as the "lost city of the Inca." From this city the last Inca rulers led a rebellion against Spanish rule. Prospects for locating Vilcabamba were poor. Clues from early chronicles of the Inca were scanty. The city was believed to be situated somewhere near the city of Cuzco, where the problems of crossing the Andes were great.

The expedition owed its success largely to Bingham's steadfastness and courage. He visited several Inca sites, sometimes risking his life to do so. His most significant find came on July 24, when a local resident, Melchor Arteaga, led him to the great ruins of Machu Picchu. The ancient Inca structures of white granite are nearly intact. Among them are temples, palaces, and small houses at various levels connected by stone staircases. Surrounding the residential area are hundreds of stone terraces for farming. Bingham thought that Machu Picchu was Vilcabamba. Most modern scholars believe

A carved stone altar is one of many Maya ruins at Copán, Honduras. The first Europeans to discover the site were John Lloyd Stephens and Frederick Catherwood.

© Sandra A. Dunlap/Shutterstock.com

that an Inca site found in 1964 by Gene Savoy is more likely to be the "lost city."

> *" ... suddenly we found ourselves in the midst of a jungle-covered maze of small and large walls, the ruins of buildings made of blocks of white granite, most carefully cut and beautifully fitted together without cement. Surprise followed surprise until there came the realization that we were in the midst of as wonderful ruins as any ever found in Peru. "*
>
> —Hiram Bingham, describing Machu Picchu, 1911

UNITED STATES AND CANADA

European exploration of what are now the United States and Canada was carried out mainly by the Spanish, French, English, and Dutch as they each tried to expand their empires and secure greater wealth. As in Latin America, European exploration of this vast area accompanied its colonization. The region was ultimately colonized primarily by the English and the French. At first, however, England lagged far behind in its colonization efforts. France was occupied with wars in Europe and was initially not able to devote as much time or effort to overseas expansion as did Spain and Portugal.

Portugal primarily focused on expanding its colonial empire in Africa and Brazil. Though initially lagging behind the Portuguese in the arts of navigation and exploration, the Spanish quickly closed that gap. First in the Caribbean and then in spectacular conquests of Mexico and Peru, they captured the imagination and envy of the European world. In the 16th century Spain hoped to find further riches in what is now the United States.

Spain in the South and Southwest

Spanish expeditions set out from or stopped off at Spanish colonies in Mexico and the Caribbean. Approaching from the south, the Spaniards began exploring the southern and later western regions of what is now the United States.

Ponce de León and the fountain of youth. The first European known to have visited what is now the U.S. mainland was the Spanish explorer Juan Ponce de León. While serving as governor of eastern Hispaniola, he had heard persistent reports that there was gold to be found on Puerto Rico. In 1508–09 he explored and settled that island. He founded the colony's oldest settlement, Caparra, near what is now San Juan.

The Spanish king encouraged Ponce de León to continue searching for new lands. The explorer learned from Indians of an island called Bimini (in The Bahamas). On this island there was said to be a miraculous spring or fountain that kept those who drank from it perpetually young. In search of this "fountain of youth," he led an expedition from Puerto Rico in March 1513. Although he never found the fabled fountain, he was the first European to encounter the ocean current known as the Gulf Stream. He was also the first to sight what is now Florida. In April he landed

The expedition of Juan Ponce de León searches for the "fountain of youth" in Florida in 1513.

on Florida's coast, near the site of what is today St. Augustine. He did not realize that he was on the mainland of North America but supposed that he had landed on an island.

Ponce de León claimed this land for Spain. He then coasted southward, sailing through the Florida Keys. He ended his search near Charlotte Harbor on Florida's west coast. He returned to Florida in 1521 to build a settlement, but he was slain by Indians.

Narváez meets disaster. Additional Spanish expeditions to colonize the region followed. The king gave Spanish conquistador Panfilo de Narváez authorization to subdue and colonize vast lands from Florida westward. (Narváez had earlier led one of the armies sent to arrest Hernán Cortés in Mexico.) He sailed from Spain on June 17, 1527, with five ships and about 600 soldiers, sailors, and colonists. He began to suffer losses early on. In Santo Domingo 140 men deserted the expedition. In Cuba a hurricane sank two of the ships, killing 50 men and several horses.

Narváez remained in Cuba until late February 1528. He then sailed with five ships and 400 followers to the region around Tampa Bay in Florida. He sent the ships to the north and began an overland expedition in May with about 300 men. The force made a difficult and distressing march northward, continually fighting Indians. Near the end of July, the survivors reached the area around what is now St. Marks, in Florida's panhandle region.

Narváez had expected to meet his ships on the coast, but they did not arrive. Instead, the expedition's suffering survivors had to build five new ships themselves. In late September the 245 surviving men sailed along the coast, hoping to reach Mexico. The ships drifted along the northern part of the Gulf of Mexico, passing Pensacola Bay and the mouth of the Mississippi River. As the journey progressed, the ships were gradually lost. In about early November 1528 Narváez disappeared when his own vessel was suddenly blown out to sea.

One of the vessels, commanded by Álvar Núñez Cabeza de Vaca, reached the shore near what is now Galveston, Texas. There, he and his men met survivors of two of the other ships. Of all these men, only 15 were still alive by the following spring. Eventually only Cabeza de Vaca and three others remained. Among these few survivors was a slave named Estéban, who was the first black man known to have entered Florida.

In the following years Cabeza de Vaca and his companions spent much time among nomadic Indians. They became slaves of various Indian tribes for a time in order to obtain food. Cabeza de Vaca later reported that he had pretended to be a healer in order to receive better treatment and more food from the Indians. The survivors eventually crossed the Rio Grande River and turned south. Though they found only the gravest hardship and poverty during their wanderings, the men made their way back to Mexico in 1536, some eight years after they had set out.

Although only four men returned from the disastrous expedition, they had been among the first Europeans to see the mouth of the Mississippi River. They had also been the first to see the American bison (buffalo). The men returned with stories of rich Indian civilizations that supposedly existed somewhere in the north. There were said to be seven "cities of gold," called the Seven Cities of Cíbola.

De Soto traverses the Mississippi. In April 1538 Hernando de Soto set off to search for gold in the region.

Álvar Núñez Cabeza de Vaca and his men were shipwrecked on the shores of what is now Texas in 1528. Cabeza de Vaca and three other survivors finally made it back to Mexico about eight years later.

He and his men did not find riches, but they became the first Europeans to travel on the Mississippi River. De Soto is often credited with being the European discoverer of the river, though other explorers had already seen its mouth.

De Soto had earlier participated in the Spanish conquests of Central America and Peru. He sailed on this expedition from Spain in command of 10 ships and 700 men. After a brief stop in Cuba, the expedition landed in May 1539 on the coast of Florida. After spending the winter at a small Indian village, de Soto and his men traveled to the north and west. They passed through Georgia, the Carolinas, and Tennessee. Along the way they met many Indian tribes. De Soto forced the Indians to furnish supplies and tortured their chiefs in a

Hernando de Soto, on horseback, finds the Mississippi River, in the painting Discovery of the Mississippi *by William H. Powell, 1853.*

A COMPTON'S MAP

Early Exploration of Southern North America

0 — 200 — 400 mi
0 — 300 — 600 km

Missouri River

St. Louis

Santa Fe

Arkansas River

Mississippi River

UNITED STATES

ATLANTIC OCEAN

MEXICO

Gulf of Mexico

Florida

← Juan Ponce de León (1513)
← Hernando de Soto (1539–42)
← Francisco Vázquez de Coronado (1540–42)

The expedition turned back to the Mississippi River early in 1542. Overcome by fever, de Soto died in Louisiana, and his comrades buried his body in the Mississippi. By this time, only about half of the original party remained. Luis de Moscoso led the expedition's survivors down the Mississippi on rafts. They reached Mexico in 1543.

Coronado explores the Southwest. Meanwhile, the Spanish leader of New Spain— which included Mexico, Central America and the Caribbean— had sent out an expedition in 1539. Its mission was to locate useless effort to make them tell where gold was hidden. They also abducted Indians to serve as their guides. This brutality led to many battles.

Although de Soto and his men did not find gold, they obtained an assortment of pearls. They turned southward into Alabama and headed toward Mobile Bay, where they expected to meet their ships. However, at a fortified Indian town, a confederation of Indians attacked the Spaniards. The Indians were decimated. The Spanish were also severely crippled, losing most of their equipment and all their pearls.

After a month's rest, de Soto decided to turn north again and head inland in search of treasure. This decision was to have disastrous results. Moving northwest through Alabama and then west through Mississippi, de Soto's party was attacked relentlessly by Indians. On May 21, 1541, the Spaniards saw for the first time the Mississippi River, south of Memphis, Tenn. The explorers built boats and crossed the river. They then made their way through Arkansas and Louisiana. Everywhere de Soto searched, the Indians reported gold "just ahead" in order to escape his torture. After three years, he still had found no gold.

the wealthy Seven Cities of Cíbola. The expedition was led by Marcos de Niza (or Fray Marcos), a Franciscan priest. The expedition's guide was Estéban, the black slave who had been shipwrecked with Cabeza de Vaca. The men journeyed northward from Mexico, across the desert to Arizona. Niza sent Estéban ahead to scout the area. He soon learned that Estéban had been killed by Indians. Niza continued on, until he reportedly saw the Seven Cities of Cíbola in the distance. He had perhaps actually seen towns of the Zuni Indians in New Mexico, which were small and poor. In any case, Niza did not visit the cities but returned to Mexico with tales of riches.

Niza's report of great wealth stirred interest in further exploration of the region. The leader of New Spain sent forth a large military expedition, led by Francisco Vázquez de Coronado, to conquer the fabled cities. Niza served as its guide. The expedition consisted of some 300 Spaniards, hundreds of Indian allies and Indian slaves, horses, and herds of sheep, pigs, and cattle. Two ships under the command of Hernando de Alarcón also sailed up the Gulf of California. This

Francisco Vázquez de Coronado, right, leads an expedition to find the legendary Seven Cities of Cíbola, in an illustration by Frederic Remington.

MPI—Hulton Archive/Getty Images

The slave Estéban explores what is now the American Southwest. He served as the guide for the Marcos de Niza expedition of 1539.

branch of the expedition discovered the mouth of the Colorado River.

The main force under Coronado departed in February 1540, traveling up the west coast of Mexico to Culiacán. A smaller unit rode north from there. The explorers encountered the Zuni towns but found no great wealth or treasure. Another scouting party, led by García López de Cárdenas, journeyed to the west. He and his men became the first Europeans to view the Grand Canyon of Arizona.

The expedition spent the winter in the valley of the Rio Grande in New Mexico. New hope came from a Plains Indian slave, whom the Spaniards called "the Turk." He told of a land to the northeast called Quivira that was very rich. With 30 men and the Turk as guide, Coronado set forth. After months they found Quivira in what is now central Kansas, but it held only Indian tepees, not gold. Coronado had the Turk executed.

The expedition returned to the Rio Grande. After wintering there, the men started homeward. The tattered army followed a route over deserts and mountains in blazing summer heat. In the fall of 1542 Coronado led only about 100 men into Mexico City. The remaining survivors trailed in during the next months. Coronado's expensive expedition had failed to find cities of gold. He had, however, established the basis for Spain's later claim to what is now the U.S. Southwest.

European discovery of California. In 1539 Francisco de Ulloa led a seaward expedition to find the fabled cities of gold. He sailed along the Pacific coast of Mexico and explored the Gulf of California. Sailing around Baja California (now part of Mexico), he proved that it is a peninsula, not an island as had been thought. According to some sources, Ulloa may have continued northward and sighted California.

The first European known to have reached California was Juan Rodríguez Cabrillo. It is not known for certain whether he was Spanish or Portuguese. In any event, he explored in the service of Spain. It is thought that Cabrillo embarked from the Mexican port of Navidad in June 1542. He explored most of the coast of California and entered San Diego and Monterey bays.

In 1579 the English navigator Sir Francis Drake sailed up the California coast beyond San Francisco Bay and claimed the land for England. He was leading the second expedition to sail around the world (*see* Australia and the Pacific Islands, "Sailing Around the World"). Spain's claim to California was strengthened in 1602 by the Spanish navigator Sebastián Vizcaíno, who charted the coast. He sailed from Mexico to the California coast, naming San Diego, Santa Catalina Island, Santa Barbara, and Monterey. He ultimately reached the Oregon coast.

The Spaniards did not launch many more expeditions to the region. Having found no cities of gold or other sources of great wealth, they did not care to explore further the disappointing lands north of Mexico. Spanish missionaries and settlers later established colonies in the areas already explored, in Florida, the Southwest, and California. However, most of Spain's colonial efforts were concentrated on exploiting the great riches already found in Mexico and South America.

France, England, and Holland in the Northeast

While Spain explored the south, the French, English, and Dutch approached North America from the east. Europeans still wanted to find a commercial sea route westward to Asia. Numerous expeditions searched for the Northwest Passage, a sea route to Asia through northern North America. It took centuries of effort, however, to find this route, which leads from the Atlantic Ocean to the Pacific Ocean through the Arctic islands of Canada. The first person to sail through the passage was the Norwegian explorer Roald Amundsen in 1906. All the earlier expeditions met with failure, and many with disaster. They nevertheless made valuable explorations in what are now the northeastern United States and Canada. (*See also* Polar Regions, "The Northwest Passage.")

Cabot reaches Canada. John Cabot's search for a westward passage to Asia made him the first European to arrive in what is now Canada after the Vikings, centuries earlier. Cabot was an Italian explorer who sailed for England. (His name in Italian is Giovanni Caboto.) Shortly after Columbus first reached the New World, King Henry VII of England authorized Cabot and his sons to undertake a voyage to the west in search of unknown lands. The same king had earlier rejected a similar proposal by Columbus.

In 1496 Cabot left from Bristol, England, with one ship. He was soon forced to turn back, however, because of poor weather, a shortage of food, and disputes with his crew. In May 1497 he tried again. He set sail from Bristol in the small ship *Matthew* with a crew of 18 men. He proceeded around Ireland and then to the north and west, making landfall on the morning of June 24. The site of his landfall is believed to have been in what is now southern Labrador, Cape Breton Island, or Newfoundland, in eastern Canada. On going ashore, Cabot noticed signs that the area was inhabited, but he saw no people. He nevertheless took possession of the land for the English king. He then explored the coastline from the ship before

John Cabot and his son Sebastian leave for North America in 1497. Their expedition would make the first successful English voyage to the New World.

returning with news of his discovery. Cabot arrived back in England on Aug. 6, 1497, believing that he had reached the northeast coast of Asia.

The following year Cabot set out on another voyage, probably with five ships and 200 men. This time he hoped to find Japan. Cabot was never seen again. Some evidence suggests that he may have reached North America, but he was probably lost at sea.

Cabot's successful voyage helped lay the groundwork for the later English claim to Canada. He also demonstrated that it was possible to sail a short route across the North Atlantic. This would later prove important in the establishment of English colonies in North America. Moreover, Cabot discovered that the northwest Atlantic waters were teeming with fish. Soon Portuguese, Spanish, French, and English fishing crews braved the Atlantic crossing to fish in the waters of the Grand Banks, southeast of Newfoundland. Some fishers began to land on the coast of Newfoundland to dry their catch before returning to Europe. This fishing ushered in the initial period of contact between the Europeans and the Indians of northern North America. Although each was deeply suspicious of the other, they traded now and then in scattered locations.

Cartier finds the St. Lawrence River. France soon began establishing its claim to northern North America. Francis I, king of France, sent the Italian navigator Giovanni da Verrazzano west to find the passage to Asia. In 1524 Verrazzano touched the American coast at what is now North Carolina and then sailed north to Newfoundland. He made several discoveries on the voyage, including the sites of what are now New York Harbor, Block Island, and Narragansett Bay. Verrazzano's report to the king contained the first description of the northeastern coast of North America. It also gave France its first claim to American lands by right of discovery.

King Francis I of France decided to send another expedition to explore the northern lands in the hope of discovering gold, spices, and a passage to Asia. The explorer Jacques Cartier set off from France on April 20, 1534, with two ships and 61 men. He reached North America a few weeks later. Cartier traveled along the

west coast of Newfoundland and discovered Prince Edward Island. He also explored the Gulf of St. Lawrence as far as Anticosti Island, claiming the shores of the gulf for the French king. He took two Indians with him on the journey back to France.

Francis I sent Cartier back the following year to explore further. Guided by the two Indians he had brought back, Cartier sailed up the St. Lawrence River as far as what is now Quebec city. He established a base near an Iroquois Indian village and proceeded with a small party as far as the island of Montreal. Cartier was welcomed by the local Iroquois. He learned from them

Jacques Cartier, in red, has a cross set up in Gaspé (now in Quebec) in 1534. By this act, he claimed the Canadian mainland for the king of France.

that two rivers led farther west to lands where gold, silver, copper, and spices abounded.

The severity of the winter came as a terrible shock. No Europeans since the Vikings had wintered that far north on the American continent. Scurvy claimed 25 of Cartier's men. To make matters worse, the explorers earned the ill will of the Iroquois. In May, as soon as the river was free of ice, the explorers seized some of the Iroquois chiefs and sailed for France. Cartier was able to report only that great riches lay farther in the interior and that a great river possibly led to Asia.

War in Europe prevented Francis I from sending another expedition until 1541. Concerned about Spanish claims to the Americas, he commissioned a nobleman, Jean-François de La Rocque de Roberval, to establish a colony in the lands discovered by Cartier. Roberval led the expedition, and Cartier served under him. Cartier sailed first, arriving at what is now Quebec city on August 23. Roberval was delayed until the following year.

The winter at Cartier's new base above Quebec proved as severe as the earlier one. He appears to have been unable to maintain discipline among his men, and their actions again aroused the hostility of the local Indians. But they found what appeared to be gold and diamonds in abundance. In the spring Cartier abandoned the base and sailed for France. On the way he stopped at Newfoundland. There he encountered Roberval, who ordered him back to Quebec. Cartier, however, stole away during the night and continued to France. There, his gold and diamonds were found to be worthless—they were really fool's gold (pyrite) and quartz. "False as a Canadian diamond" became a common French expression. Roberval enjoyed no better success. After one winter he abandoned the plan to found a colony and returned to France.

French disappointment at these meager results was very great. France lost interest in these new lands for more than half a century. Nevertheless, Cartier had made the European discovery of the St. Lawrence River, which was later to become France's great entranceway into North America. He also is credited with naming Canada, from the Huron-Iroquois word *kanata,* meaning a village or settlement. (Cartier used the name to refer only to the area around Quebec city.) Moreover, the French claim to the land remained; it had only to be made good by actual settlement.

England tries to set up colonies. After John Cabot's early voyages, English explorers did not return to the New World until the late 16th century. In 1576–78 the English mariner Martin Frobisher undertook three voyages in search of the Northwest Passage to Asia. He explored Canada's northeast coast and discovered the bay near Baffin Island that now bears his name. However, his single-minded pursuit of gold limited the exploratory value of his voyages.

Sir Humphrey Gilbert, an English soldier and navigator, wrote a paper about the Northwest Passage in 1566 that later inspired many explorers to search for the elusive route to Asia. He set sail on his own attempt on Nov. 19, 1578, with seven ships. He probably intended to cross to North America, but his ill-equipped, badly

At St. John's, Sir Humphrey Gilbert claims Newfoundland for the queen of England in 1583.

disciplined force quickly broke up. By the spring of 1579 some of the ships had drifted to England while others had turned to piracy.

Gilbert later undertook a more ambitious attempt to establish an English colony in North America. He sailed from Plymouth, England, on June 11, 1583. On August 3 he arrived at what is now St. John's, Newfoundland, which he claimed in the name of the queen. Sailing southward with three ships, he lost the largest of them on August 29. Two days later he turned homeward. Gilbert was last seen during a great storm in the Atlantic, shouting to his companion vessel, "We are as near heaven by sea as by land." Gilbert's ship was then swallowed by the sea.

With the failure of Gilbert's voyage, the English turned to a new man, Sir Walter Raleigh, to advance England's fortunes in the New World. They also tried a new strategy—taking a southern rather than a northern route to North America. Raleigh sponsored attempts in the 1580s to found a permanent colony off the coast of Virginia. Although his efforts finally failed with the mysterious destruction of the Roanoke Island colony in 1587, they awakened popular interest in a permanent colonizing venture. The English established their first permanent colony in the New World—Jamestown—in Virginia in 1607. The following year the French explorer Samuel de Champlain founded Quebec, France's first permanent colony in the Americas.

Champlain founds Quebec. French fishing fleets had continued to make almost yearly visits to the eastern shores of Canada. Chiefly as a sideline of the fishing industry, there continued an unorganized trade in furs. At home in Europe new methods of processing furs were developed, and beaver hats in particular grew very fashionable. Thus new encouragement was given to the fur trade in Canada.

In 1604 Pierre du Gua, sieur (lord) de Monts, received a French royal monopoly that gave him the exclusive right

Champlain's Explorations

←	1603
←	1604
←	1609
←	1615–16

Gaspé Pen.

St. Lawrence River

Quebec

Ottawa R.

Lake Champlain

L. Huron

L. Ontario

Hudson R.

Cape Cod

L. Erie

ATLANTIC OCEAN

0	100	200 mi
0	150	300 km

A COMPTON'S MAP

to this fur trade. That year he led his first colonizing expedition to Acadia, a region surrounding the Bay of Fundy on the eastern seaboard of Canada. Among the expedition's lieutenants was Samuel de Champlain, who was a geographer and navigator as well as a soldier.

Champlain spent three winters in Acadia. During the first winter the settlers stayed on an island in the St. Croix River. Scurvy killed nearly half the party. The second and third winters, at Annapolis Basin, claimed the lives of fewer men. During the summers Champlain searched for an ideal site for colonization. He carried out a major exploration of the northeastern coastline of what is now the United States, journeying down the Atlantic

Samuel de Champlain uses a navigational instrument called an astrolabe near the Ottawa River in 1613. He lost his astrolabe shortly thereafter, and it was not found again until the late 19th century.

The Granger Collection, New York

coast southward to Massachusetts Bay and beyond. He mapped in detail the harbors that his English rivals had only touched.

In 1608 Champlain was granted permission to undertake another expedition. He led a group of settlers to a site on the St. Lawrence River where they hoped to establish a center for controlling the fur trade. There he founded Quebec city and made friends of the Huron people of the region. In 1609 he went with the Huron to fight the Iroquois in New York. During this time he discovered Lake Champlain, which he named after himself. Not far from the lake he routed the Iroquois enemy with gunfire. Thereafter the Iroquois were bitter enemies of the French. Champlain later made several exploring trips in search of rivers that might lead to the Pacific Ocean. In 1615 he reached Georgian Bay and Lake Huron.

Hudson seeks a passage to Asia. The English explorer Henry Hudson tried to discover a short route from Europe to Asia by sailing both northwest and northeast through the Arctic Ocean. On his first two voyages, he searched for the Northeast Passage along northern Europe, but ice blocked his way. Both times he sailed for the English Muscovy Company.

Hudson undertook his third voyage in search of the Northeast Passage for the Dutch East India Company. He sailed from Holland in the *Half Moon* on April 6, 1609. When head winds and storms forced him to abandon his northeast voyage, he decided to instead seek the Northwest Passage. The ship reached eastern North America. While cruising along the Atlantic seaboard, Hudson entered a majestic river that Verrazzano had encountered in 1524. It was known from then on as the Hudson River. The expedition traveled up the river for about 150 miles (240 kilometers) to the vicinity of what is now Albany, N.Y. Hudson concluded that the river did not lead to the Pacific and began the return voyage. On his way to Holland, Hudson docked at Dartmouth, England. There the English government forbade him from undertaking any more explorations for other countries.

The British East India Company and other English merchants sponsored Hudson's fourth and final voyage, to search for the Northwest Passage. This time he wanted to follow up on a report by the English explorer Capt. George Weymouth regarding a possible channel to the Pacific. Weymouth had described an inlet—now named Hudson Strait—where a "furious overfall" of water rushed out with every ebb tide. This phenomenon suggested that a great body of water lay beyond the strait. Hudson was confident that it was the Pacific Ocean.

Hudson sailed from London on April 17, 1610, in the 55-ton vessel *Discovery*. He proceeded to the "furious overfall," between Baffin Island and what is now northern Quebec, Canada. Passing through the strait, he entered the large inland sea that is now named Hudson Bay. He followed the east coast southward, reaching James Bay. With no outlet to the Pacific Ocean to be found, Hudson cruised aimlessly until winter overtook him.

In the close confinement of an Arctic winter, quarrels arose. Some crew members suspected that Hudson was

After a mutiny in 1611, the crew of the Discovery cast Henry Hudson, his son, and seven others adrift in a small boat.
The Granger Collection, New York

secretly hoarding food for his favorites. On the homeward voyage, several of the crew rebelled. The mutineers seized Hudson, his son, and seven others, casting them adrift in Hudson Bay in a small open boat on June 22, 1611. The ringleaders and several other crew members never returned home, having been killed in a fight with Eskimos. Nothing more was ever heard of Hudson and his small party. His discoveries later formed the basis for the Dutch colonization of the Hudson River and for English claims to much of Canada.

Jolliet and Marquette travel the Mississippi. The French colonial possessions in what are now Canada and the United States were known as New France. Much of New France was explored by fur traders, colonists, and especially Jesuit and Franciscan missionaries. The missionaries wanted to convert the Indians to Roman Catholicism. Most of the explorations were thus private undertakings. In 1672, however, the governor of New France sponsored an expedition to the Mississippi River. The explorers were to determine the direction of the river's course and to find its mouth. The French hoped that the river emptied into the Pacific Ocean and would provide a passage to Asia. The expedition was led by Louis Jolliet, who had studied to be a Jesuit but worked as a fur trader. Jolliet's traveling companion was Jacques Marquette, a Jesuit priest. Marquette knew several Indian languages and served as an interpreter. The small party also included five other men.

On May 17, 1673, the expedition set out in two birchbark canoes from what is now St. Ignace, Mich., for Green Bay, on Lake Michigan. The men then paddled up the Fox River in central Wisconsin and down the Wisconsin River. About a month later they entered the Mississippi River. The explorers traveled the great river's upper course, pausing along the way to make notes, to hunt, and to glean scraps of information from local Indians. Marquette also preached to the Indians he met.

In July the explorers arrived at a Quapaw Indian village at the mouth of the Arkansas River, about 40 miles (65 kilometers) north of what is now Arkansas City, Ark. From personal observations and from the friendly Quapaw, they concluded that the Mississippi flowed south into the Gulf of Mexico and not the Pacific. The river's mouth thus lay in the region held by the Spanish. Indians also warned that they would face hostile Indian tribes if they continued on the river. The party decided to return home, and they traveled back via the Illinois River and Green Bay.

In less than five months the expedition had traveled more than 2,500 miles (4,000 kilometers). Although the explorers did not reach the mouth of the Mississippi, they reported the first accurate data on the river's upper course. Jolliet's maps and papers had been lost when his canoe tipped over. Fortunately, Marquette had described their journey in his journal, which has survived.

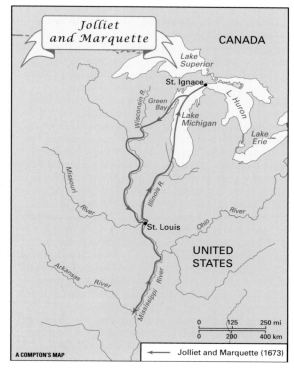

Jolliet and Marquette

CANADA

Lake Superior

St. Ignace

Wisconsin R.

Green Bay

Lake Michigan

L. Huron

Lake Erie

Missouri River

Illinois R.

Ohio River

St. Louis

UNITED STATES

Arkansas River

Mississippi River

0 125 250 mi
0 200 400 km

A COMPTON'S MAP

⟵ Jolliet and Marquette (1673)

While exploring the upper Mississippi River in 1673, Louis Jolliet and Father Jacques Marquette sometimes had to portage, or carry their canoe, over rapids.

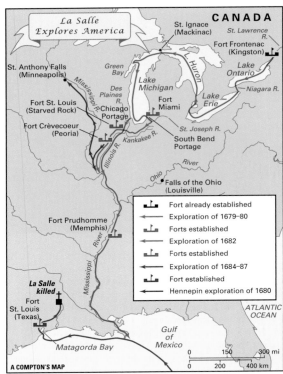

Jolliet later explored Hudson Bay, the coast of Labrador, and a number of Canadian rivers. In 1697 he was made the royal mapmaker of the waters of New France. Meanwhile, Marquette set out in 1674 to found a mission among the Illinois Indians. Caught by the winter, he and two companions camped near the site that later became Chicago. They thus became the first Europeans to live there. Marquette reached the Indians in the spring, but illness forced his return. While en route to St. Ignace, he died at the mouth of a river now known as Père Marquette.

La Salle reaches the river's mouth. Nine years after Jolliet and Marquette's voyage down the Mississippi, another French explorer reached the river's delta. René-Robert Cavelier, sieur (lord) de La Salle, was the first European to travel down the Mississippi River to the Gulf of Mexico. He claimed the entire region watered by the Mississippi and its tributaries for King Louis XIV of France, naming it "Louisiana."

La Salle was committed to expanding New France. In the winter of 1678–79 La Salle and his men built a fort at the Niagara River. There they built a 40-ton ship, the *Griffon.* La Salle's lieutenant was Henri de Tonty, an Italian adventurer and a trusted ally. The Indians called Tonty the "man with the iron hand" because he had a metal claw at the end of one arm to replace a hand blown off in battle.

On Aug. 7, 1679, the expedition sailed for Green Bay on the *Griffon.* It was the first voyage ever made by a ship on the Great Lakes. The explorers reached Green Bay in September and sent the ship back laden with furs. It was never heard from again. Early in 1680 the explorers built Fort Crèvecoeur near what is now Peoria, Ill. From this fort La Salle sent Louis Hennepin, a Franciscan friar, with two companions to explore the upper Mississippi.

Leaving Tonty in charge of the new fort, La Salle made a trip to another French fort for supplies. On his return, he learned that the Iroquois had destroyed Fort Crèvecoeur, and Tonty and his men had vanished. La

Salle traced them northward, meeting up with them in what is now Mackinaw City, Mich.

Early in 1682 La Salle and Tonty finally set out again for the Mississippi River. They canoed down the Illinois

An illustration from the late 1600s shows René-Robert Cavelier, sieur de La Salle, landing on the coast of the Gulf of Mexico in 1685.

River and the Mississippi, reaching the Gulf of Mexico on April 9. La Salle claimed the Mississippi valley for France. Within a generation, the Mississippi became a vital link between French settlements along the Gulf of Mexico and in Canada.

In 1684 La Salle made one more voyage to the Mississippi. He wanted to build fortified colonies at the river's mouth and to conquer part of the Spanish province of Mexico. This expedition was doomed from the start. Vessels were lost by piracy and shipwreck, and sickness took a heavy toll of the colonists. Finally, a gross miscalculation brought the ships to Matagorda Bay in Texas, 500 miles (800 kilometers) west of their intended landfall. After several fruitless journeys in search of his lost Mississippi, La Salle was murdered by a few of his men near the Brazos River.

The West

Expeditions began pushing farther and farther to the west. In 1690 the English explorer Henry Kelsey led a two-year expedition westward in Canada to promote trade with the Indians. He traveled through what are now Manitoba and Saskatchewan, reaching the Saskatchewan River and beyond. He is believed to have been the first European to visit the Canadian prairies. Kelsey's voyage was funded by the Hudson's Bay Company. This English corporation controlled trade in the Hudson Bay region. It sent out explorers to expand its trade, and they eventually established numerous fur-trading stations scattered over the vast northern regions of Canada.

Routes to the Pacific. Starting in the 1730s, a family of French-Canadian explorers built a string of trading posts and broke the monopoly of the Hudson's Bay Company. Pierre Gaultier de Varennes, sieur (lord) de La Vérendrye, and his sons made a series of overland explorations far to the west of Lake Superior. Their travels carried them into what is now the western United States, perhaps as far as the foothills of the Rockies. They visited Lake Winnipeg and the Red, Assiniboine, and Saskatchewan rivers. They searched for an overland route to the "western sea." The explorers did not reach the Pacific Ocean, but the posts they established strengthened, for a while, French claims in North America.

Although explorers were not yet able to reach the Pacific by land, several seaward expeditions charted the Pacific coast. Cabrillo and Drake had done so in the 16th century. The Spanish navigator Juan Pérez explored the west coast of Vancouver Island in 1774. The following year Bruno Hezeta reached the Washington coast and claimed the area for Spain. Capt. James Cook of England charted the coast from Oregon to the Arctic in 1778.

The first overland explorer to reach the Pacific Ocean was the Scottish-Canadian fur trader Alexander Mackenzie. In 1789 he followed the river that now bears his name from its source to the Arctic Ocean. Disappointed because he had not discovered a route to the Pacific, he set out on another expedition in 1792. After a strenuous journey over the most rugged terrain on the continent, Mackenzie and his companions at last crossed the Rocky Mountains to reach the Fraser River

© Sally Scott/Shutterstock.com

The Hudson's Bay Company set up the Fort Langley fur-trading post in 1827 near what is now Vancouver, B.C. Today, the post's buildings are preserved as a national historic site.

in 1793. From the Fraser they traveled on land to the Bella Coola River. The explorers canoed down the river until they sighted the long-sought "western sea," in what is now British Columbia. Only a few weeks earlier Capt. George Vancouver of England had explored the same part of the Pacific coast by sea.

The English explorer David Thompson crossed the Canadian Rockies in 1807–11. He crossed the mountains by the Howse Pass and built the first trading post on the Columbia River. Thompson then became the first European to explore the Columbia River from its source to its mouth. His maps of western North America served as a basis for all subsequent ones.

The first major explorers of the West were not members of expeditions, however, but pioneers known as mountain men. The mountain men went to the Rocky Mountain region first as fur trappers to obtain beaver pelts. The most experienced trappers were the French, who were joined by American and Spanish fur traders. Mingling extensively with the Indians, the mountain men adopted many of their manners of life and their beliefs. As permanent settlers arrived, many mountain men served as scouts and guides, but their way of life was gradually eliminated by advancing civilization.

Lewis and Clark expedition. In 1803 the newly founded United States bought the entire western half of the Mississippi River basin from France. La Salle had claimed this land for France under the name "Louisiana," so the transaction became known as the Louisiana Purchase. It doubled the size of the United States. For scientific, commercial, and political reasons, U.S. President Thomas Jefferson sent an expedition to explore the newly acquired land and to find a water route to the Pacific Ocean. He also wanted the explorers to make diplomatic contact with the Indians of the West and to expand the American fur trade.

Jefferson asked his personal secretary, Capt. Meriwether Lewis to lead the expedition. Lewis' considerable frontier skills, military service, physical

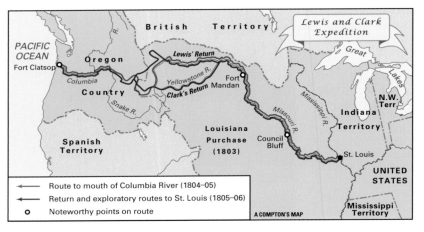

Lewis and Clark Expedition

- → Route to mouth of Columbia River (1804–05)
- → Return and exploratory routes to St. Louis (1805–06)
- o Noteworthy points on route

A COMPTON'S MAP

American frontiersman George Drouillard and Clark's African American slave, York. During the long journey, the expedition encountered large animal herds and ate well. They consumed about one buffalo, two elk, or four deer per day, supplemented by roots, berries, and fish. They named geographic locations after expedition members, peers, loved ones, and even their dog. The explorers suffered from dysentery, boils, tick bites, and injuries from prickly pear. However, only one man died during the expedition (apparently of appendicitis).

endurance, and intellectual prowess made him an excellent choice. Lewis invited his good friend William Clark to co-command the expedition. Like Lewis, Clark was familiar with the frontier and with some Indian groups through his service in the army. Lewis served as the expedition's field scientist, making observations on the plants, animals, Indians, climate, soil, and geography of the land they traversed. He also gathered plant, animal, and mineral specimens to send back for further study. Clark served as the expedition's principal waterman and mapmaker.

To prepare for the expedition, Lewis traveled to Philadelphia to study astronomy, botany, zoology, and medicine with some of the country's brightest scientists and doctors. He also began recruiting men and purchasing equipment and supplies. He purchased a dog, a Newfoundland named Seaman, to accompany the expedition. Lewis supervised the construction of a 55-foot (17-meter) covered keelboat and secured smaller vessels. Meanwhile, Clark recruited men and oversaw their training that winter.

The permanent exploring party—known as the Corps of Discovery—consisted of about 30 men, most of whom were soldiers. The party also included the part-Native

Along the way, the explorers held councils with the local Indians. The expedition staged military parades, handed out gifts, delivered speeches, promised trade, and requested intertribal peace. Most tribes welcomed trading opportunities and provided the expedition with food, knowledge, guides, and shelter.

The explorers set off on May 14, 1804. They started up the Missouri River. The explorers covered about 10 to 20 miles (16 to 32 kilometers) a day, poling, pushing, and pulling their keelboat and dugout boats up the river. On August 3 they held their first council with Indians, the Oto and Missouri, at a place the explorers named Council Bluff. The site is near what is today Council Bluffs, Iowa. In late October the party reached the earth-lodge villages of the Mandan and Hidatsa Indians, near what is now Bismarck, N.D.

Across the river from the Indian villages, the explorers built Fort Mandan and spent the winter. It was there that they hired Toussaint Charbonneau, a French interpreter, and his Shoshone Indian wife, Sacagawea, the sister of a Shoshone chief. While at Fort Mandan, Sacagawea gave birth to a baby boy. This did not stop her from participating in the group. She carried the child on her

A detail from The Lewis and Clark Expedition, *a painting by Thomas Burnham from about 1850, shows the explorers setting out into the unknown.*
Buffalo Bill Historical Center, Cody, Wyoming/The Art Archive

Sacagawea

A Shoshone Indian woman named Sacagawea served as interpreter to the Lewis and Clark expedition of 1804–06. She traveled thousands of miles through the wilderness with the explorers, from the Mandan-Hidatsa villages in the Dakotas to the Pacific Northwest and back again. Many memorials have been raised in her honor, in part for the fortitude with which she faced hardship on the difficult journey.

Separating fact from legend in Sacagawea's life is difficult. Historians disagree on the dates of her birth and death and even on her name. The most likely version of her name, Sacagawea, means "Bird Woman" in the Hidatsa language. Her name is sometimes spelled Sacajawea or Sakakawea. She is thought to have been born in about 1788, near the Continental Divide at what is now the Idaho-Montana border.

When Sacagawea was about 12 years old, a raiding party of Hidatsa Indians captured her near the headwaters of the Missouri River. The Hidatsa made her a slave and took her to their villages. In about 1804 she became one of the wives of the French Canadian fur trader Toussaint Charbonneau.

The explorers Meriwether Lewis and William Clark hired Charbonneau as an interpreter to accompany them to the Pacific Ocean. However, he did not speak Shoshone. The expedition would need to communicate with the Shoshone to acquire horses to help them cross the mountains. For this reason, the explorers agreed that the pregnant Sacagawea should also accompany them. On Feb. 11, 1805, she gave birth to a son, Jean Baptiste.

The expedition set off on April 7, ascending the Missouri River. On May 14, Charbonneau nearly capsized the dugout boat in which Sacagawea was riding. Remaining calm, she retrieved important papers, instruments, medicine, and other valuables that otherwise would have been lost. Sacagawea proved to be a significant asset in many other ways, such as in searching for edible plants and in making moccasins and clothing. She also helped allay the suspicions of approaching Indian tribes through her presence—a woman and child accompanying a party of men indicated peaceful intentions.

By mid-August the expedition encountered a band of Shoshone. Their leader was Sacagawea's brother Cameahwait. The reunion of sister and brother helped Lewis and Clark obtain the horses and guide that enabled them to cross the Rocky Mountains.

Sacagawea was not the guide for the expedition, as some have wrongly portrayed her. She did, however, recognize landmarks in southwestern Montana. She also informed Clark that Bozeman Pass was the best route between the Missouri and Yellowstone rivers on their return journey. Sacagawea and her family left the expedition when they arrived back at the Mandan-Hidatsa villages.

It is believed that Sacagawea died shortly after giving birth to a daughter, Lisette, on Dec. 20, 1812. She is thought to have died at Fort Manuel, near what is now Mobridge, S.D. Clark became the legal guardian of Sacagawea's two children.

The Granger Collection, New York

The Lewis and Clark expedition travels on the Columbia River, in a 1905 watercolor by Charles Russell.

" *This little fleet altho' not quite so rispectable [sic] as those of Columbus or Capt. Cook were still viewed by us with as much pleasure as those deservedly famed adventurers ever beheld theirs … we were now about to penetrate a country at least two thousand miles in width, on which the foot of civillized man had never trodden …* "

—Meriwether Lewis

back for the rest of the trip. As a Shoshone interpreter she proved invaluable.

In the spring of 1805 the explorers sent the keelboat back to St. Louis with natural history specimens, including live magpies and a prairie dog. Meanwhile, they had built canoes. On April 7 the party continued up the Missouri. On April 26 the explorers passed the mouth of the Yellowstone, and on June 13 they reached the Great Falls of the Missouri. Carrying the laden canoes 18 miles (29 kilometers) around the falls caused a month's delay. Their way was made even more difficult by broken terrain, prickly pear cactus, hailstorms, and numerous grizzly bears.

In mid-July the explorers launched the canoes above the falls. On the 25th the expedition reached Three Forks, where three rivers (the Madison, the Jefferson, and the Gallatin) join to form the Missouri. For some time the explorers had been within sight of the Rocky Mountains. Crossing them was to be the hardest part of the journey. The expedition decided to follow the Jefferson River, the fork that led westward toward the mountains.

On August 12 the group climbed to the top of the Continental Divide. They hoped to see the headwaters of the Columbia River close enough to let them carry their canoes and proceed downstream toward the Pacific. Instead they saw mountains stretching endlessly into the distance. The water route Jefferson had sent them to find did not exist.

They were now in the country of the Shoshone. Sacagawea eagerly watched for her people, but it was Lewis who found them. He met a Shoshone chief who turned out to be Sacagawea's brother. The chief provided the party with horses and a guide, Old Toby, for the difficult crossing of the lofty Bitterroot Range.

It took the Corps of Discovery most of September to cross the mountains. Hungry, sick, and exhausted, they

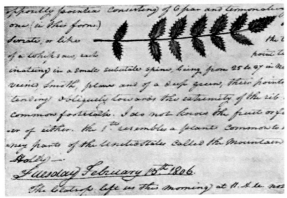

A page from William Clark's expedition journal includes a sketch of evergreen shrub leaves.

reached a point on the Clearwater River where Nez Percé Indians helped them make dugout canoes. From there they were able to proceed by water, via the Clearwater and Snake rivers. They reached the Columbia River on October 16. They finally arrived at the Pacific Ocean in mid-November.

Fierce storms delayed their progress for nearly a month. The members voted on where to spend the winter, and even York and Sacagawea were allowed to cast votes. Near what is now Astoria, Ore., the party built Fort Clatsop. There they endured a wet, miserable winter by journal writing, drying meat, making salt, and traveling to see a beached whale.

The explorers hoped to encounter ships on the Pacific that could transport them home. They found none, however, and the party started back. After stealing a Clatsop Indian canoe, they headed up the Columbia River on March 23, 1806. They arrived at the Nez Percé villages, gathered up their horses, and waited for the snows to melt. They crossed the mountains in June with Nez Percé horses and guides. Beside the Bitterroot River the party divided into groups to learn more about the country.

Several groups floated down to the Great Falls. Clark headed for the Yellowstone River and followed it to the Missouri. Lewis and several men struck off toward the northeast to explore a branch of the Missouri. On this trip he had a skirmish with Indians that left two Blackfeet dead, the only such incident of the entire journey. Later, while out hunting, Lewis was accidentally shot by one of his own men. He recovered after the party was reunited and had stopped at the Mandan-Hidatsa villages. There they left Sacagawea and her family.

The Corps of Discovery reached St. Louis on Sept. 23, 1806. Their arrival caused great rejoicing, for they had been believed dead. They had been gone two years, four months, and nine days and had traveled nearly 8,000 miles (13,000 kilometers).

Although Lewis and Clark were not the first non-Indians to explore the area, the expedition contributed important scientific and geographic knowledge of the West. Lewis, Clark, and several other members of the expedition had kept detailed journals. Lewis had identified 178 plants and 122 animals that were new to science. Clark's maps of the West were the best available until the 1840s. Their trail to the Pacific also paved the way for future explorers and traders who sought to colonize the West.

Pike explores the Southwest. While Lewis and Clark traveled to the Pacific Northwest, the U.S. Army officer Zebulon M. Pike tried to locate the source of the Mississippi River and explored new areas of the Southwest. In 1805 Pike led 20 men more than 2,000 miles (3,200 kilometers) in search of the Mississippi headwaters. They traveled both on foot and by boat from St. Louis, Mo., to Leech and Sandy lakes in northern Minnesota. Pike reported that Leech Lake was the river's source. This was later proved incorrect.

Pike's next major assignment was to explore the Southwest. His party departed in 1806 to explore the Red and Arkansas rivers and to obtain information about the adjacent Spanish territory in what is now New Mexico. Pike set up camp near what is now Pueblo, Colo. From there he led his party northwestward to the Rocky Mountains. At the Front Range of the Rockies, he discovered the peak now known as Pikes Peak. The explorers tried to climb the peak, but they were unsuccessful. Discouraged, they turned south and slowly made their way toward New Mexico. Spanish officials met and captured Pike and his party on the charge of illegal entry into New Mexico. They were taken across Texas to the Spanish-American border in Louisiana. On July 1, 1807, they were released. Pike wrote a report praising the Spanish Southwest that soon attracted American fur trappers, bison hunters, and traders into the area.

Climbing Mount McKinley

The highest mountain in North America, Mount McKinley is located in south-central Alaska, near the center of the Alaska Range. It rises 20,320 feet (6,194 meters) above sea level. Two peaks crown the mountain, with the south peak being the higher. The upper two thirds of the summits are covered with permanent snowfields that feed many glaciers.

The first European to see Mount McKinley was the English navigator George Vancouver. He sighted the mountain in 1794 from Cook Inlet, an arm of the Gulf of Alaska. In 1903 an American judge, James Wickersham, made the first attempt to climb Mount McKinley. He did not succeed. The American physician and explorer Frederick A. Cook said that he reached the top in 1906, but his claim proved to be false. Cook later claimed to have been the first person to reach the North Pole (*see* Polar Regions).

Local miners mounted the "Sourdough Expedition" to the mountain in 1910. Two of the miners reached the top of the lower North Peak in 1910. On June 7, 1913, the Americans Hudson Stuck and Harry Karstens led an expedition that reached the South Peak, the mountain's true summit.

A climbing party was first airlifted onto the mountain's flanks in 1932. Beginning in the 1950s, this became the standard way to attempt a summit climb, as it reduced the trip by several weeks. Most climbers are now flown to Kahiltna Glacier at an elevation of 7,200 feet (2,195 meters). On average, several hundred climbers reach the summit each year.

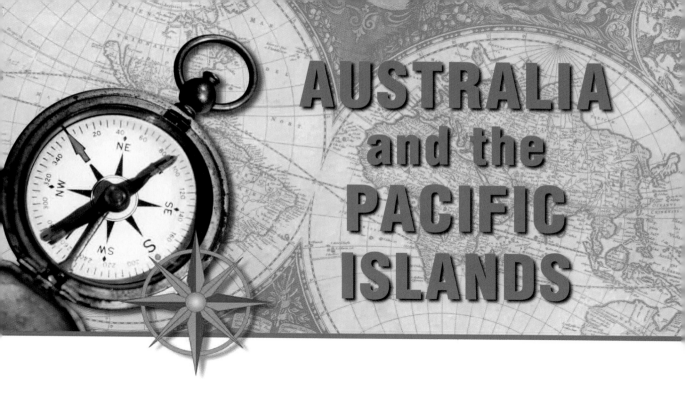

AUSTRALIA and the PACIFIC ISLANDS

The island-continent of Australia was explored and settled long before Europeans first sighted it. So, too, was Oceania, or the numerous islands scattered throughout the Pacific Ocean.

The first peoples to explore Australia were the ancestors of the Australian Aborigines. Scientists believe that they came to Australia from the islands of Southeast Asia some 40,000 to 60,000 years ago. Sea levels were lower then, and there were many land bridges between Asia and Australia. However, the ancestors of the Aborigines must have used watercraft for some passages. This is the earliest confirmed seafaring in the world. By about 35,000 years ago they had explored and occupied all parts of Australia. They had also settled the highlands of what is now the island of New Guinea.

POLYNESIAN EXPLORATION

The early Polynesians were intrepid explorers who settled far-flung islands in the Pacific. Their ancestors, the prehistoric Lapita people, were also seaborne explorers and colonists. The Lapita settled much of the region known as Polynesia, in the central Pacific. They also settled parts of Micronesia, in the western Pacific.

The Lapita are believed to have originally come from Taiwan and elsewhere in East Asia. They later settled in Southeast Asia. From there, Lapita people migrated to New Guinea and other nearby islands. These islands were already settled by other peoples. Generations of Lapita voyagers ranged northward into eastern Micronesia and eastward into Polynesia. By 2000 BC the Lapita had settled in the Bismarck Archipelago, northeast of New Guinea. Starting in about 1600 BC they spread to the Solomon Islands. They had reached Fiji, Tonga, and the rest of western Polynesia by 1000 BC. By 500 BC they had dispersed to Micronesia.

The Lapita are known mainly from the remains of their decorated cooking pots, bowls, and other fired pottery. Lapita pottery has been found from New Guinea eastward to Samoa. Fishhooks and shell jewelry are among the other main artifacts of the Lapita culture.

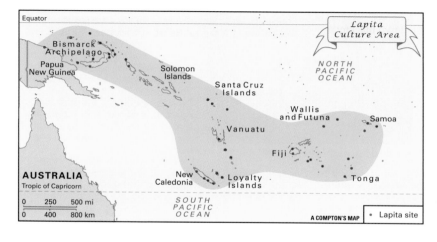

Equator
Bismarck Archipelago
Papua New Guinea
Solomon Islands
Santa Cruz Islands
NORTH PACIFIC OCEAN
Wallis and Futuna
Samoa
Vanuatu
Fiji
AUSTRALIA
Tropic of Capricorn
New Caledonia
Loyalty Islands
Tonga
0 250 500 mi
0 400 800 km
SOUTH PACIFIC OCEAN
A COMPTON'S MAP
Lapita Culture Area
• Lapita site

The early Polynesians carried out another major wave of exploration and colonization, starting perhaps about 1,200 years ago. From their homeland in Samoa and Tonga, they spread out to remote islands thousands of miles away. The Polynesians reached the Marquesas Islands, perhaps by about the 2nd century BC. From there, they began to settle the distant Hawaiian Islands in the central Pacific. They may have arrived at Hawaii by about AD 300. The Polynesians later colonized Tahiti and other Society Islands as well as Easter Island. Their voyages extended as far as Chile, about 2,200 miles (3,500 kilometers) east of Easter Island. A Polynesian people known as the Maori settled New Zealand starting in about AD 1250, or perhaps much earlier.

It is not known what drove the Lapita and later the Polynesians to "island hop" and then to settle increasingly distant islands. It is possible that growing populations set off in search of more living space and resources. Or perhaps people were exiled from their homeland and had to find a new place to live. Some of the journeys may have been accidental, with the sailors being blown far off course.

On most of their great voyages of exploration, the Lapita and the Polynesians sailed eastward. This course took them against the prevailing trade winds. Sailing directly into the wind made for a difficult outward journey. They were assured, however, that they could use the winds to return home if they did not find a new island or if they ran out of supplies.

Lee Foster/Alamy

The Hokule'a *is a reconstruction of the type of canoe the ancient Polynesians would have sailed on long sea voyages. The Polynesian Voyaging Society of Hawaii has successfully sailed the* Hokule'a *and other such canoes throughout the Pacific without using modern navigational instruments.*

The peopling of Polynesia was a remarkable feat of navigation. The Lapita and the early Polynesians must have been skilled sailors, navigators, and builders of

Heyerdahl and the *Kon-Tiki*

How did the Polynesians settle such distant, scattered islands in the Pacific? In the 20th century a Norwegian adventurer and anthropologist named Thor Heyerdahl developed unconventional theories about prehistoric exploration. He believed that it would have been too difficult for the Polynesians to have sailed eastward, against the trade winds. Instead, he concluded that peoples from South America may have settled the Pacific islands. They could have sailed westward, with the trade winds. American Indians would thus have been the ancestors of the Polynesians.

To test this theory, Heyerdahl re-created a possible voyage. He built a large raft similar to those used by the Inca of Peru at the time of European contact. The raft was made from balsa logs locally available in Peru. It had a square sail and a long steering oar. He named the raft *Kon-Tiki* after a legendary Inca god. In 1947 Heyerdahl and a five-person crew set off on the raft from Peru. Their journey ended 101 days later, at a reef in French Polynesia. The *Kon-Tiki* had successfully sailed across some 4,300 miles (6,900 kilometers) of ocean.

Heyerdahl had demonstrated that Indians could have made a journey to Polynesia. Of course, just because something is

Michel Lipchitz/AP

Thor Heyerdahl sails the Ra II *in 1970.*

possible does not mean that it happened. For the most part, scholars have not accepted this or other of Heyerdahl's theories. Scholars believe that the ancestors of the Polynesians came from Asia, on the basis of linguistic, archaeological, and now genetic evidence.

Heyerdahl later wanted to show that American Indians could have had contact with ancient Egyptians. In 1970 he sailed a replica of an ancient Egyptian reed boat, the *Ra II*. He and a small crew crossed the Atlantic Ocean from Morocco to Barbados, in the West Indies. The trip took 57 days.

On the *Tigris* expedition of 1977–78, Heyerdahl and his crew sailed 4,000 miles (6,440 kilometers) on a craft made from reeds. They traveled from Iraq, across the Arabian Sea to Pakistan, ending in the Red Sea. Heyerdahl undertook this journey to prove possible contact by the ancient Sumerians with Southwest Asia and the Arabian Peninsula.

Starting in 1976, the Polynesian Voyaging Society has conducted several expeditions using replicas of ancient Polynesian craft. The society has shown that the early Polynesians could have sailed eastward into the wind.

A 16th-century world map shows an enormous southern continent that many people mistakenly thought must exist. The map was created in 1570 by Abraham Ortelius.
National Library of Australia

watercraft. They had no magnetic compasses or other such navigational instruments. Instead, they used a keen knowledge of the sky and sea. They "read" the stars, Sun, sea swells, and winds to guide them across thousands of miles of open ocean.

The Lapita may have used bamboo rafts or other simple watercraft for their earliest voyages of discovery. They later must have developed more advanced craft, probably including paddle-driven rafts and dugout canoes. A dugout canoe is formed by hollowing out and shaping a log. For long-range voyages the early Polynesians probably used large dugouts that were stabilized with outriggers—floats attached by long poles to one side. Some of these canoes were quite long and had two hulls. The canoes were built of wide planks of wood bound together with coconut fibers. They were powered by one or two triangular sails and steered by paddle.

THE SEARCH FOR THE FABLED SOUTHLAND

Europeans did not sight the Pacific islands until the 16th century and Australia until the early 17th century. During the Age of Discovery explorers sailed around the world for the first time. Europeans expected to find a large continent south of Eurasia. For several centuries they had theorized that Europe and Asia might be balanced by land in the Southern Hemisphere. They believed that this balance of land kept Earth spinning at an even rate. The great southern continent appeared on many maps. Eventually, European navigators set out to find the continent that they imagined. They called it Terra Australis Incognita, meaning the "Unknown Southern Continent."

No such enormous continent exists. Nevertheless, the search for the fabled southland brought European explorers to many Pacific islands. It also led them to "discover" a smaller southern continent—Australia.

Sailing Around the World

In 1519–21 the expedition of Ferdinand Magellan became the first to circumnavigate, or sail completely around, the globe (*see* The Americas). Magellan was a Portuguese navigator who sailed for Spain. He died along the way, but other crew members completed the journey. Magellan and his crew missed the main island groups of the Pacific. However, they probably reached Guam and Pukapuka Atoll (now in French Polynesia). After Magellan's death, the expedition encountered some of the Caroline Islands.

The second expedition to sail around the globe was led by the English mariner Francis Drake in 1577–80. One of Drake's aims was to find the fabled southern continent. Although he was not able to locate this theoretical land, he did accomplish another of his goals: piracy. Drake was actually considered a "privateer" and

Francis Drake.
Archivio I.G.D.A./© DeA Picture Library

not a pirate. Privateers sailed privately owned vessels that were licensed by their government to attack another country's ships.

Drake sailed from England in five small ships and fewer than 200 men. He commanded a ship he later named the *Golden Hind*. The fleet sailed to the southern tip of South America. Drake intended to continue westward in search of the great southland. Once the *Golden Hind* passed through the Strait of Magellan, however, strong winds made him turn north. Drake's ship then sailed alone along the coast of Peru. There he surprised and plundered Spanish ships laden with gold, silver, and jewels. His fortune made, he explored the west coast of North America. He later traveled westward to the Philippines, sailed around the southern tip of Africa, and returned to England.

The Spanish and the Portuguese

The Portuguese took the lead in the Age of Discovery. They were probably the first Europeans to encounter New Guinea. They sighted the island in 1511 but made no landing until 1527.

The leaders of Spain's American empire regularly sought new lands. They had found great wealth in Peru and Mexico and hoped to find more in the Pacific. After Magellan, the next major Spanish exploration of the Pacific was made by Álvaro de Mendaña de Neira. He set out in 1567 from Peru in search of the great southern continent. Instead, he "discovered" the Solomon Islands. However, navigators of the time had no way to measure longitude (east-west position) precisely. Mendaña failed to find the islands again on another journey, in 1595. On that voyage, he became the first European to reach the Marquesas and Santa Cruz islands.

Mendaña's chief pilot, the Portuguese explorer Pedro Fernández de Quirós, continued the search for the fabled southland. He wanted to establish Christianity there. Quirós set off from Peru with two ships in late 1605. He located part of the Tuamotu Archipelago and reached the northern Cook Islands. He also discovered an island in what is now Vanuatu. He believed that he had indeed found the unknown southern continent. However, troubles soon forced his ship to return to Latin America.

The other ship of the expedition was commanded by the Spanish mariner Luis Vaez de Torres. It went on to sail through a channel—now known as the Torres Strait—between New Guinea and Australia. The explorers thus showed that New Guinea was an island, not part of a southern continent. However, they almost certainly failed to sight Australia. The Spanish kept their discovery of the Torres Strait a secret for more than 150 years.

The Dutch

The Dutch were already established in the Dutch East Indies (now Indonesia). The powerful trading company known as the Dutch East India Company dominated the spice trade. It also helped expand the overseas commercial empire of the Netherlands, or Holland. The company's navigators explored Southeast Asia and the Pacific. Like the Spanish, they too looked for an enormous southern continent. What they found was Australia. For many years, it was known as New Holland.

Jansz sights Australia. Late in 1605 the Dutch mariner Willem Jansz (or Janszoon) sailed from Java in the Dutch East Indies. He hoped to find New Guinea and a route to the Pacific. He commanded the *Duyfken* (Little Dove), a small ship of the Dutch East Indies Company.

Jansz reached the Torres Strait a few weeks before Torres. Not realizing that it was a channel, Jansz sailed right past it. He and his men then made the first European sighting of Australia, in the Gulf of Carpentaria, in 1606. They did not know, however, that they had found a new continent. The expedition explored the shores of Cape York Peninsula. Charting a

The ships of Abel Tasman's expedition, right-center, and Polynesian outrigger canoes, front, meet off the coast of one of the Fiji Islands in 1643. This engraving is based on a drawing by Tasman.

The Granger Collection, New York

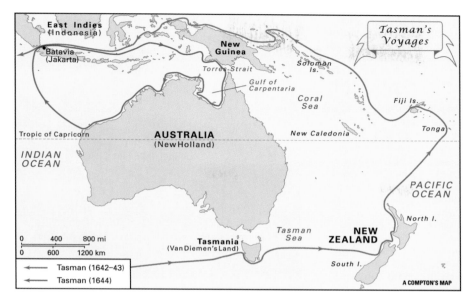

East Indies
(Indonesia)

New
Guinea

Batavia
(Jakarta)

Torres Strait

Gulf of
Carpentaria

Solomon
Is.

Coral
Sea

Fiji Is.

Tropic of Capricorn

AUSTRALIA
(New Holland)

New Caledonia

Tonga

INDIAN
OCEAN

PACIFIC
OCEAN

North I.

0   400   800 mi
0   600   1200 km

Tasman (1642–43)
Tasman (1644)

Tasmania
(Van Diemen's Land)

Tasman
Sea

NEW
ZEALAND

South I.

A COMPTON'S MAP

Tasman's
Voyages

to Batavia at the last possible moment. But not all turned north in time. Several Dutch navigators thus discovered the west coast of Australia between 1616 and 1628.

The first of these navigators was Dirck (or Dirk) Hartog. In January 1616 he sailed as skipper of the *Eendracht*, a Dutch East India Company ship. He set off from the Netherlands for the Dutch East Indies. He reached the Cape of Good Hope in August.

After rounding the cape, Hartog used the newly adopted faster route. He sailed eastward before the strong trade winds. With the navigational aids available at the time, however, he could not accurately determine the ship's longitude, and thus when to turn north. Hartog sailed too far east and sighted Australia's west coast. On October 25 the ship arrived at an offshore island near the mouth of what is now Shark Bay. Today the island is named Dirk Hartog Island. Hartog and some of his crew explored the island for a couple of days. As he sailed the *Eendracht* north to continue his trading mission, he charted a section of the west coast.

Europeans first sighted the south coast of Australia in 1626–27. The Dutch East India Company ship *Guilden Zeepaard* (Golden Seahorse) arrived at Cape Leeuwin, in the southwest. It too might have inadvertently carried too far east. Francois Thyssen commanded the ship, which carried aboard a company official named Pieter Nuyts. The men explored almost 1,000 miles (1,600 kilometers) of the south coast.

Tasman finds Tasmania and New Zealand. Other Dutch expeditions added to knowledge of the north and west coasts of Australia. Most important of all was the work of Abel Janszoon Tasman. Anthony van Diemen, the governor-general of the Dutch East Indies, chose Tasman to lead an important expedition to the southern Pacific and Indian oceans. Although the Dutch had charted several portions of the Australian coast, it was not known if these coasts were connected to the great southern continent. Tasman was assigned to solve this problem. Another part of his mission was to try to discover a passage to Chile. He was also supposed to explore New Guinea and to find the Solomon Islands, which had been discovered earlier by the Spanish.

Tasman set out from Batavia on Aug. 14, 1642, with two ships, the *Heemskerk* and the *Zeehaen*. He sailed first to Mauritius, in the western Indian Ocean, then east and south to 49° latitude. After turning north to avoid bad weather, on November 24 he discovered a large island—

Rob Griffith/AP
The Duyfken *is a modern replica of the ship Willem Jansz sailed when he made the European discovery of Australia in 1606.*

portion of the north coast of Australia, the explorers created the first European map of the continent.

The *Duyfken* also landed briefly on western Cape York Peninsula. Its men became the first Europeans to encounter Australian Aborigines. This first encounter proved fatal, as one of the Europeans was killed.

Hartog reaches the west coast. The next Dutch landings in Australia were accidental. The capital of the Dutch East Indies was Batavia (now Jakarta, Indonesia). Sailing ships bound for Batavia began to follow a faster route. The brisk westerly winds of the Indian Ocean could propel ships eastward from the Cape of Good Hope, at Africa's southern tip. The ships then cut north

now known as Tasmania. He named the island Van Diemen's Land, after the governor-general. Continuing eastward, he sighted the coast of New Zealand's South Island on December 13. Tasman explored the coast northward. He entered the strait between North Island and South Island, supposing it to be a bay. He left New Zealand on Jan. 4, 1643.

Convinced that a sea passage to Chile existed, Tasman again sailed northward. He discovered Tonga on January 21 and the Fiji Islands on February 6. Turning northwest, the ships reached New Guinea waters on April 1. After exploring New Guinea, he returned to Batavia, arriving on June 14, 1643. Tasman had sailed completely around Australia without seeing it. He had thus established that Australia was separated from the hypothetical southern continent.

The Dutch East India Company was nevertheless dissatisfied. It sent Tasman on another expedition in 1644. His mission was to determine the relationship between New Guinea, Tasmania, and the southern continent. He sailed from Batavia, steering southeast along the south coast of New Guinea. He then sailed southeast into the Torres Strait, which he mistook for a bay. He followed the north coast of Australia and then the west coast to 22° S. Tasman thus mapped a substantial portion of the coast. This second expedition was also a disappointment to the company, however, because Tasman had found no lands of great wealth.

The Dutch spent little more effort in exploration. On a later notable voyage the Dutch admiral Jacob Roggeveen crossed the Pacific from west to east in 1722. He became the first European to land on Easter Island. Roggeveen

Louis-Antoine de Bougainville and his men meet a group of islanders on Tahiti in 1768.

also discovered Samoa and some of the Society Islands, including Bora-Bora.

The British and the French

Starting in the late 17th century, the British and the French were the most active explorers of the Pacific. The British mariner William Dampier explored parts of the coasts of Australia, New Guinea, and New Britain for the British Admiralty. He had earlier been a type of pirate known as a buccaneer, chiefly along the west coast of South America and in the Pacific. In 1688 he reached Australia, probably the north coast near Melville Island. He found nothing to plunder, however, and took a dislike to the people and their customs.

Dampier published an account of his travels in 1697. His book became famous and further popularized the idea of there being a great southern continent. The following year the British Admiralty appointed him captain of the *Roebuck* to explore the South Seas.

Dampier set off from England in January 1699. He reached an inlet off western Australia on July 26. He named this inlet Shark Bay. Dampier explored the coast northward to a group of islands that were from then on called the Dampier Archipelago. He continued to New Guinea and then sighted and named New Britain. With a deteriorating ship and a discontented crew, he was unable to visit Australia's east coast, as he had intended. Instead, he continued to Java for repairs and provisions.

On Oct. 17, 1700, Dampier sailed for England. However, the *Roebuck* sank off Ascension Island, in the South Atlantic, on Feb. 22, 1701. The crew remained on the island until April 3, when they were picked up by a convoy of British ships.

Dampier had traversed the west coast of Australia for some 1,000 miles (1,600 kilometers). His reports were so critical of the land and its people, however, that a British

Jeanne Baret

The first French expedition to sail around the world harbored a secret. One member of the supposedly all-male crew was actually a woman: Jeanne Baret. The expedition was led by Louis-Antoine de Bougainville in 1766–69. Baret would not have been able to join it if her gender were known; women were forbidden on French naval vessels. Seeking adventure, she disguised herself as a boy named Jean. In this identity, she was hired as a servant to the ship's naturalist, Joseph-Philibert Commerson. Baret was about 25 years old.

Baret successfully passed herself off as male. She helped Commerson with his botanical work, following him into the jungles in search of new plants. She carried his gear and also assisted him in storing and documenting the plant samples they collected. She helped him so ably that he called her his "beast of burden."

When the expedition landed in Tahiti, the Tahitians immediately recognized that Baret was a woman. With her secret revealed, she confessed the truth to the shocked Bougainville. He allowed her to sail back with the expedition.

According to some accounts, Baret was Commerson's lover all along and he had smuggled her aboard the ship. Other sources tell that Commerson had not known or even remotely suspected that she was a woman. In any event, Baret traveled all the way around the world. She left the expedition with Commerson in Mauritius, in the western Indian Ocean. Baret is believed to have later returned to France, thereby completing her circumnavigation.

expedition did not visit Australia again for several decades.

Further exploration of the Pacific was also delayed for many years by wars in Europe. In 1765 the British admiral John Byron set off in search of the supposed southern continent. He was the grandfather of the famous poet Lord Byron. The admiral explored the northern Marianas and discovered islands in the Tuamotu, Cook, and Tokelau groups.

In 1767 the British Admiralty sent Samuel Wallis and Philip Carteret to follow up on Byron's expedition. As Wallis and Carteret entered the Pacific, however, their ships were separated. Wallis became the first European to discover Tahiti. He also found more of the Tuamotus and the Society Islands. Meanwhile, Carteret reached Pitcairn Island and the Solomons.

The French sponsored a major expedition to the Pacific in 1766–69, led by Louis-Antoine de Bougainville. It was the first French expedition to sail completely around the world. Bougainville sailed to Tahiti, Samoa, Vanuatu, New Guinea, and the Solomons. Along the way, the expedition gathered scientific data. The ship's astronomer calculated accurately the location of islands they visited. The ship's naturalist collected numerous species of plants and animals that had been unknown to science. After he returned, Bougainville published an account of his journey that described the "noble savages" of Tahiti. His book helped popularize a belief in the moral worth of human beings in their natural state, without their having been "civilized."

The Voyages of James Cook

Meanwhile, the British explorer James Cook had set out on a highly significant expedition. A British naval captain and navigator, Cook had already explored the seaways and coasts of Canada. He now led three wide-ranging expeditions to the Pacific. Cook surveyed a greater length of coastline than any other man and remade the map of the Pacific. He also claimed New Zealand and eastern Australia for Britain.

First voyage. In 1768 the Royal Society and the British Admiralty chose Cook to lead the first British scientific expedition to the Pacific. Cook's orders were to convey Royal Society scientists to Tahiti. There they would observe the planet Venus passing in front of the Sun, a type of eclipse that occurs only rarely. Other scientists would observe this "transit" of Venus from different spots around the world. The scientists' observations would enable them to more accurately calculate the distance from Earth to the Sun. Once at sea, Cook was also supposed to open a set of secret instructions. These told him to search for the great southern continent. If he could not find it, he was to explore New Zealand.

The leader of the scientists was Joseph Banks, an enthusiastic and able naturalist. At the places the ship visited, he collected numerous specimens of plant species unknown in the West. Banks was assisted by the Swedish botanist Daniel Solander. The expedition also carried astronomers, including Cook himself, as well as artists to document the scientists' discoveries.

The expedition sailed in the HMS *Endeavour*, a former coal-hauling bark. The ship weighed just 368 tons and was less than 98 feet (30 meters) long. It carried a crew of 94 men, including the scientists and their assistants.

The explorers set off from Plymouth, England, on Aug. 26, 1768. They sailed southward in the Atlantic to the east coast of South America. After rounding the southern tip of that continent, they sailed northwestward into the Pacific. The *Endeavour* reached Tahiti in April 1769. The Tahitians were quite friendly to the Europeans, and the scientists observed the transit of Venus in June.

From Tahiti, Cook sailed as far as latitude 40° S. in search of the fabled southern continent, as instructed. He did not, however, think that such a continent existed. Finding no land, he turned west to New Zealand. Cook located the two main islands of New Zealand and charted their coasts with great accuracy. This difficult job took six months to complete.

James Cook claims New South Wales, Australia, for Britain in 1770.

The Print Collector/Heritage-Images

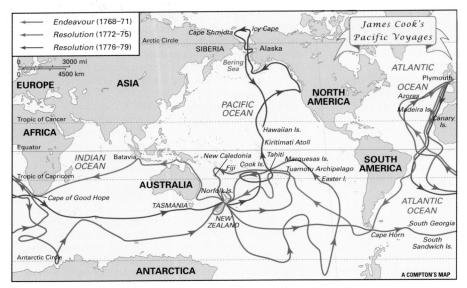

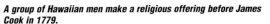

expedition had made significant explorations of little-known lands. It had also collected an unprecedented amount of scientific data.

The expedition was also notable for the health of its crew. Although some of the crew died of diseases contracted on land in Batavia, Cook kept the men remarkably healthy at sea. None of the crew died of scurvy, a dietary disease now known to be caused by a lack of vitamin C. At the time, scurvy regularly decimated the crews of ships on long voyages. Cook insisted that the crew's diet include all probable remedies for the disease. They thus ate cress, sauerkraut, and a kind of orange extract, all of which effectively prevented scurvy. He also made sure that the crew's quarters were clean and well ventilated.

Second voyage. Cook soon began to organize another expedition to the South Pacific. This one was even more ambitious. He intended to sail around the world from the far southern latitudes. On this voyage Cook commanded the small ship *Resolution*. It was accompanied by the *Adventure*.

The ships left England on June 21, 1772. The explorers were the first to circumnavigate the globe from west to east. They were also the first people to sail completely around Antarctica, though they did not sail close enough

At numerous points along the way, the explorers made contact with the Maori people. Their first contact with the Maori was violent, but more peaceful relations were established later. Cook was impressed by the Maori's social organization, intelligence, and artistic abilities. In his journal, which was later published, he stressed that the land would be suitable for British colonies. Soon colonists as well as other explorers followed Cook to New Zealand.

From New Zealand, Cook sailed westward across the Tasman Sea. He arrived at southeastern Australia on April 19, 1770. He and his men were the first Europeans to reach the east coast. Cook sailed north along Australia's entire east coast, surveying as he went. The expedition landed first at a natural harbor near what is now Sydney. The harbor soon became known as Botany Bay because the naturalists found a great richness and variety of vegetation growing there.

Continuing northward, Cook successfully navigated the Great Barrier Reef, an enormous complex of coral reefs off the coast of what is now Queensland. The Great Barrier Reef is now known to be one of the greatest navigational hazards in the world. One night the ship touched on a coral spur. The ship withstood the impact, however, and the explorers were at last able to free it. They did what they could to repair the badly leaking vessel on the nearby coast.

At Cape York on August 23, Cook took possession of the whole eastern coast of Australia for Britain. He named this land New South Wales because he thought it resembled the south coast of Wales in Britain. Cook then sailed through the Torres Strait. As he made this passage, he realized that New Guinea was an island and not part of a great southern continent.

Cook then sailed for England. Along the way, he stopped at Batavia for supplies and ship repairs. The men fell ill there, and about 30 of them died of fever and dysentery. The *Endeavour* returned to England in July 1771, having sailed completely around the globe. The

A group of Hawaiian men make a religious offering before James Cook in 1779.

The Granger Collection, New York

to see it (*see* The Polar Regions). The explorers journeyed beyond latitude 70° S. They traveled through freezing fog in waters filled with icebergs, farther south than any known person before them. However, they found no trace of the great southern continent. Cook thus showed once and for all that there was no new southern continent except Australia and whatever frozen land might exist around the South Pole—Antarctica. There was no great southland after all.

On his second voyage, Cook also charted Pacific islands that had been found by earlier explorers but then lost. Cook determined the islands' exact locations. On this trip, he tested one of the earliest chronometers, a type of precision watch used as a navigational instrument. This newly invented instrument allowed explorers to determine longitudes accurately for the first time. In 1774 Cook charted islands in the Tuamotus, the Cooks, the Marquesas, Fiji, Tonga, and Vanuatu, as well as Easter Island. He also discovered Norfolk Island and New Caledonia. The explorers arrived back in England on July 30, 1775. Remarkably, once again not one person on Cook's ship had died of scurvy.

> *"I have now done with the Southern Pacific Ocean, and flatter my self that no one will think I have left it unexplor'd ..."*
>
> —Capt. James Cook, 1774

Third voyage. There was one more secret of the Pacific to be discovered: whether the Northwest Passage existed. The passage is a sea route around North America between the Pacific and the Atlantic. European explorers had long sought this passage, mainly from the North Atlantic. Although their efforts had been in vain, it was thought that a search from the North Pacific might be successful. The person to undertake the search obviously was Cook.

On July 12, 1776, Cook set off again in the *Resolution*. This time, it was accompanied by the *Discovery*. The two ships sailed southward through the Atlantic and then eastward to the South Pacific. Cook charted Kiritimati Atoll and some of the Tongan islands. He landed in the Hawaiian Islands at Waimea, Kauai Island, on Jan. 30, 1778. He and his crew were the first Europeans known to have visited the Hawaiian Islands. Cook named them the Sandwich Islands, in honor of the earl of Sandwich, first lord of the Admiralty. He then turned north, sailing along the coast of North America to the Bering Strait between Alaska and Siberia. The ship encountered an ice barrier, and Cook found no way through it.

Unable to locate a passage, Cook turned southward. The expedition arrived back in the Hawaiian Islands to spend the winter, a visit that led to Cook's death. He and his men explored the islands further. Trouble arose when one of the ship's boats was stolen. On Feb. 14, 1779, Cook took some men ashore at Kealakekua Bay, on the island of Hawaii, to recover the boat. Violence broke out, and Cook was killed by Hawaiians.

Cook's voyages left little land to be discovered in the Pacific. His maps and charts were so accurate that many have never needed to be substantially revised. Cook was arguably the greatest European explorer of his time, because of his navigator's skill and his ability to keep his crew healthy. He also seems to have had honorable, largely peaceful interactions with indigenous peoples.

EXPLORING AUSTRALIA

Not long after James Cook claimed eastern Australia for Britain, the first British settlers began arriving. British navigators charted more of the continent's coastline. Some colonists also began to explore the vast interior, as they searched for more agricultural land.

A New British Penal Colony

The British government decided to colonize New South Wales by setting up an overseas penal (prison) settlement. Convicts would be "transported" to eastern Australia to serve their sentences—so far from home they could never hope to return. The British planned to put the convicts to work on government farms. Former convicts and other free settlers would farm their own small plots.

Arthur Phillip was chosen to command the first colonizing expedition and then to serve as the first

Contact Between Europeans and Aborigines

Europeans began to settle Australia in 1788. By that time, the Aborigines had explored and spread out through the entire continent. They had adapted successfully to a wide range of terrain and climates, from tropical rainforests to deserts. Estimates of the Aboriginal population in 1788 vary from 300,000 to more than 1,000,000. The various groups of Aborigines spoke more than 200 different languages.

European contact with the Aborigines was a painful and tragic tale of incomprehension and greed. Many European explorers reported contact with hostile natives. However, blame for the violent welcomes could often be placed on Europeans. Many of the Europeans believed that it was their right to take prisoners, slaves, and treasure whenever they desired. The earliest British settlers did not recognize Aboriginal rights to the land. Instead they reported that the continent was *terra nullius*—a land unoccupied and unclaimed by prior inhabitants. The Aborigines lacked agriculture, permanent homes, written languages, and the use of metal. For these reasons, the Europeans viewed the Aborigines as being uncivilized.

Many Aboriginal groups were physically or culturally exterminated. They were uprooted from land which held for them sacred, ceremonial, or hunting significance. The Europeans employed massacres, food poisoning, rape, and punitive expeditions. European diseases also took a heavy toll because the Aborigines had no immunity to them.

Some Aborigines initially welcomed the new arrivals. Some even believed that the light-skinned invaders were the returned ghosts of their ancestors. But in most areas Aborigines responded to the invaders by fighting vicious guerrilla wars. White farmers and police responded with unmatched savagery and cruelty. They sometimes, for example, slaughtered Aboriginal women and children in response to Aboriginal raids on sheep and cattle. The Europeans often believed that they were only "defending" innocent people—and civilization itself—in a strange land.

governor of New South Wales. He and the First Fleet set out from Portsmouth, England, on May 13, 1787. The fleet consisted of 11 ships carrying 443 seamen, 778 convicts, 211 marines, and officials, wives, and children. They arrived at Botany Bay, the site of Cook's first landing, on Jan. 18–20, 1788, minus those who had died en route.

Finding Botany Bay too exposed and lacking drinking water, Phillip investigated the next inlet north. There he found a superb natural harbor, Port Jackson, or Sydney Harbour. He selected a deepwater cove with a freshwater stream and named it Sydney Cove. He officially started the settlement on Jan. 26, 1788, which is now celebrated as Australia Day.

The first years of the colony were ones of hardship. Disease and pests abounded. The soil was poor, and the land was rough and had to be cleared by hand. Few of the convicts proved able laborers. In addition, conflicts often arose between the newcomers and the original settlers of the land, the Aborigines.

Flinders and Bass Chart the Coasts

Cook's voyages led to settlement and provided the first European knowledge of the east coast. However, exploration of the coasts was not complete. Marion Dufresne of France skirted Tasmania in 1772, seeing more than had Tasman. In 1791 the British navigator George Vancouver surveyed the southern shores discovered by Dutch explorers years before.

Two British sailors—the navigator Matthew Flinders and the naval surgeon George Bass—completed extensive surveys of Australia's coasts. Together they entered some harbors on the southeast coast near Botany

Bay in 1795 and 1796. Bass also studied the animals and plants of the region.

Bass ventured farther south in 1797–98, pushing around Cape Everard to Western Port, southeast of what is now Melbourne. He discovered a channel—now named Bass Strait—between Australia and Tasmania. Flinders also explored that region early in 1798. He charted the Furneaux Islands, off the coast of northeastern Tasmania. Late in 1798 Flinders and Bass sailed completely around Tasmania in the *Norfolk*. They thus established that Tasmania is an island.

In 1801 Flinders was appointed to command an expedition that would circumnavigate Australia and virtually complete the charting of the continent's coasts. Over the next three years Flinders proved equal to this task. Above all, he left no doubt that the Australia was a single landmass and not a group of islands. The continent was still known as New Holland. Flinders urged that the name Australia be used instead, and this change received official British backing from 1817.

The charting of the coasts was almost complete. More exploration was needed only in the north, from Arnhem Land to Cape York Peninsula. Two British expeditions—under Phillip Parker King (1817–22) and John Clements Wickham (1838–39)—filled this gap in knowledge.

Into the Interior

The penal colony at Sydney was initially barely able to feed itself. The settlers needed more grazing land for their animals. Some settlers, along with escaped convicts and their pursuers, had explored coastal land to the north and south. From early days, the settlers sought a way over the Blue Mountains of the Great Dividing Range. These mountains lay some 50–100 miles (80–160 kilometers) west of the colony. The task was finally accomplished in 1813 by the Australian explorers Gregory Blaxland, William Charles Wentworth, and William Lawson. Across the mountains, the settlers discovered the fertile inland plains. Ranchers drove their sheep and cattle inland, leaving the penal colony behind.

The map of inland Australia was gradually and arduously compiled by the explorers who traversed its length and breadth between 1815 and 1939. Settlers who followed them pushed

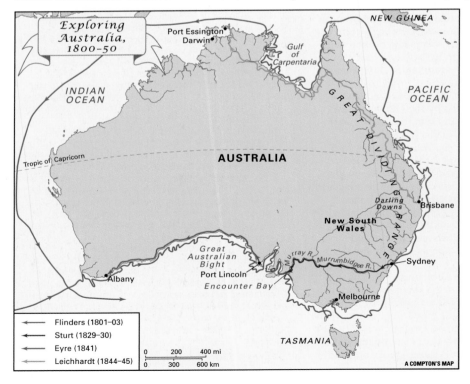

Exploring Australia, 1800–50

- Flinders (1801–03)
- Sturt (1829–30)
- Eyre (1841)
- Leichhardt (1844–45)

NEW GUINEA

Port Essington
Darwin

Gulf of Carpentaria

INDIAN OCEAN

PACIFIC OCEAN

GREAT DIVIDING RANGE

Tropic of Capricorn

AUSTRALIA

Darling Downs
Brisbane

New South Wales

Murray R.
Murrumbidgee R.
Sydney

Great Australian Bight
Port Lincoln
Encounter Bay
Albany

Melbourne

TASMANIA

0   200   400 mi
0   300   600 km

A COMPTON'S MAP

the pioneering frontier as far as they could. They moved into the arid center and the tropical north, first from the southeast and then from the southwest.

The search for an inland sea. Many explorers hoped to find great rivers and lakes in the interior of Australia, as there were on the other inhabited continents. In 1815 George William Evans discovered the Lachlan River, which he followed as far as Mandagery Creek. John Oxley and Evans further mapped the inland plains and rivers, especially the Lachlan and Macquarie rivers in 1817–18. They traversed both these rivers until they met with impassable marshes. Oxley also explored the southern coasts of what is now Queensland in 1823. At Moreton Bay, near what is now Brisbane, he met three castaway sailors who showed him a river. He named the river the Brisbane. In 1827 Allan Cunningham explored inland, discovering the region west of Brisbane now known as the Darling Downs.

Although explorers had found rivers beyond the mountains, they did not behave as expected. Oxley observed: "On every hill a spring, in every valley a rivulet, but the river itself disappears." He guessed that the great fan of rivers that drained the western slopes of the mountains fell into a vast inland sea.

This vision of a well-watered interior inspired several other explorers, notably Charles Sturt. He traced the Murray River to its outlet but later went half-blind in the blazing heat of the Simpson Desert. He explored major rivers and revealed extensive areas of land for development in what is now South Australia.

Sturt led the first of his major expeditions in 1828–29. He traced the Macquarie, Bogan, and Castlereagh rivers and discovered the Darling River. In November 1829 he led an expedition to the Murrumbidgee River southwest of Sydney. The explorers traveled down the river by boat to its junction with the Murray River, the principal river of Australia. They followed the Murray to its mouth near what is now Adelaide, dealing peaceably with many Aborigines along the way. The explorers returned to Sydney in May 1830. Exhausted and nearly blinded because of poor diet and overexertion, Sturt went to England for a couple of years to recuperate.

In 1844–46 Sturt led an expedition north from Adelaide to the edge of Simpson Desert. It discovered no fertile land and was eventually driven back by heat and scurvy. However, his party was the first to penetrate the center of the continent.

It later became clear that Sturt and others had searched for an inland sea in vain. The interior consists largely of vast deserts and dry grasslands. Australia is in fact the driest continent except for Antarctica.

Linking the ports. Meanwhile, other explorers forged overland routes between the coastal ports. In 1824–25 Hamilton Hume and William Hovell were the first to traverse the 540 miles (870 kilometers) between what are now the cities of Sydney and Melbourne.

Edward John Eyre was commissioned in 1841 to find a land route between South Australia and Western Australia. Eyre had already explored to the north of Adelaide. In 1841 he made the hazardous journey westward across southern Australia to Albany. He

Edward John Eyre in about 1870.
The Granger Collection, New York

traveled along the coast of the Great Australian Bight of the Indian Ocean. In crossing the Nullarbor Plain on foot, he found no running water for 1,240 miles (2,000 kilometers).

> "The incessant walking … the low and unwholesome diet we had lived upon, the severe and weakening attacks of illness … having daily, and sometimes twice a day, to dig for water, to carry all our firewood from a distance upon our backs…usually so completely exhausted us that we had neither spirit nor energy left."
>
> —Edward John Eyre, 1841

Ludwig Leichhardt and his party were the first explorers to cross northeastern Australia. Their epic overland journey took them across nearly 3,000 miles (4,830 kilometers) of the continent. Leichhardt discovered a route across reliable rivers from Brisbane to the north coast. In August 1844 he sailed from Sydney to Moreton Bay. He and 10 companions, including two Aboriginal guides, set off in October from Jimbour, in the Darling Downs region. Two members of the party turned back, and one was killed by Aborigines. The rest of the explorers reached Port Essington, on the north coast, in December 1845. From there they sailed back to Sydney.

The party had been given up for dead, and their return was greeted with astonishment and joy. Leichhardt became one of Australia's earliest heroes. The expedition had discovered extensive areas suitable for settlement and many important streams. It also provided an early map.

Leichhardt set out on a second expedition in December 1846. He intended to cross from Darling Downs to the west coast and then south to a settlement

Ludwig Leichhardt
© Photos.com/Jupiterimages

on the Swan River. The explorers fell ill, however, and most of the animals they had brought to eat ran away. Within a few months, they were forced to turn back.

In March 1848 Leichhardt organized a party of six others and set out on what would be his final expedition. He was last seen in early April, leaving a point near what is now the town of Roma. After that he and his party were never heard from again. Their mysterious disappearance captured the imaginations of many people. Several search parties set out to try to find the explorers or clues to their disappearance. The searches began in 1852 and continued into the 1930s, spurred on at times by rumors of white men living among the Aborigines. The mystery was never solved. However, many of the search parties brought back valuable information for later settlement.

Crossing the continent. Starting in 1860 two rival expeditions backed by two different colonies raced to be the first to cross the continent from south to north. The expedition led by Robert O'Hara Burke and William Wills trekked from Victoria to the Gulf of Carpentaria. It

reached the north coast first, but both Burke and Wills died on the return journey. The Scottish-born explorer John McDouall Stuart left from South Australia. Unlike Burke, Stuart was an experienced explorer with some bush skills. In a series of expeditions, Stuart crossed the very center of the continent to reach Darwin.

The Burke and Wills expedition was sponsored by the Royal Society of Victoria. It was the largest and most expensive expedition in Australian history. The party that left Melbourne on Aug. 20, 1860, consisted of 18 men. Burke led the expedition, and Wills was second in command. The explorers took 25 camels to carry the

The Burke and Wills expedition departs from Melbourne, Australia, on Aug. 20, 1860. The exploring party brought along many camels as well as horses.

The Granger Collection, New York

Explorers of the South Australian Burke Relief expedition are beset by crocodiles while crossing a river. Led by John McKinlay, the men explored the Australian interior while searching for the missing Burke and Wills expedition in 1861–62.

The Art Archive/Picture Desk

supplies needed for the long and arduous trek. They intended to establish a series of bases across the desert. At these bases they would leave supplies for their use on the return trip.

Burke was impatient about the delays caused by setting up the bases and by traveling with the entire expedition. At Menindee, in New South Wales, the bulk of the party was left behind. Seven men and 15 camels continued to the Barcoo River (now Cooper's Creek). There, about halfway to their destination, they set up camp. Again impatient, Burke decided to continue northward with only three companions—Wills, Charles Gray, and John King. The rest of the party agreed to wait at the camp for at least three months for their return.

The four men left the camp on Dec. 16, 1860, and reached the far north on Feb. 9, 1861. They were only a few miles away from their destination, the Gulf of Carpentaria. However, impenetrable swamps and jungle scrub prevented them from reaching the coast. The expedition started back. Gray was overcome by exhaustion and died on the return trip. The others reached the Barcoo camp on April 21 but found it deserted. The rest of the party, after having waited for more than four months, had left for Melbourne that same morning. They had buried some food for the men at a marked spot. Burke and King decided to head for Adelaide on the south coast. In late June, however, Wills became too weak to travel. Burke and King left him behind, intending to find food and return. Wills died soon thereafter. Burke also died of starvation, and King returned to look for Wills.

Four rescue missions were sent to find the explorers. In September a search party located King living among some Aborigines and brought him back to a joyous welcome in Melbourne. They also brought back Wills's journal of the expedition, a rough map, and a few letters. The rescue parties added greatly to the knowledge of the interior.

Meanwhile, Stuart had set out from Adelaide in March 1860. He and his companions trekked northward through the central deserts. They reached the MacDonnell Ranges and then what they determined to be the very center of the continent. Provisions began to run low, and the men became ill with scurvy. In late June an attack by Aborigines at what is now called Attack Creek forced the explorers to turn back. They had come within only about 200 miles (320 kilometers) of the ocean.

> " We then gave three hearty cheers for the flag . . . and may it be a sign to the natives that the dawn of liberty, civilization, and Christianity is about to break upon them. "
>
> —John McDouall Stuart, describing why he planted a British flag in central Australia, April 23, 1860

Stuart's next two expeditions were sponsored by the South Australian government. It was hoped that he would find an appropriate route for the first telegraph line across the continent. In 1860–61 Stuart pressed farther north than on the last attempt. Short on food and water, however, he prudently chose to turn back.

The explorers set out from Adelaide again on Oct. 26, 1861. They reached Attack Creek in March. In the far north the explorers had to pass through thick scrub. On July 24, 1862, they finally reached the Indian Ocean near the mouth of the Adelaide River, east of Darwin. The return trip proved difficult. Suffering from scurvy and nearly blind, Stuart had to be carried on a sling between two horses. Although he returned to Adelaide in triumph, his health was destroyed. He died about four years later, at the age of 50.

A decade after Stuart's successful expedition, a telegraph line stretched from Adelaide to Darwin along the route he had taken. Australia was at last connected to the outside world. The Burke and Wills and Stuart expeditions had traveled through the center of the continent but had found only·desert there. Additional explorers set out over the next several years to search for the great inland sea but would not find one. White settlement of the continent, however, continued apace.

AFRICA

It is now widely recognized that Africa was the birthplace of humankind. Archaeological evidence indicates that the continent has been inhabited by humans and their ancestors for some 4,000,000 years or more. Anatomically modern humans are believed to have appeared about 100,000 years ago in eastern Africa. Somewhat later, groups of these early humans became the first explorers. They spread into northern Africa and the Middle East and, ultimately, to the rest of the world.

The coasts of northern Africa were known to peoples of Europe and Asia since ancient times. Non-Africans later gained knowledge of the west, south, and east coasts. However, the interior of Africa remained largely a mystery to foreigners until the mid-19th century. It was the last of the inhabited continents to be thoroughly explored by outsiders, along with Australia. Africa lies very close to southern Europe and even closer to the Middle East region of Asia. Nevertheless, Europeans explored the distant Americas first.

Africa posed several challenges to foreign explorers. The interior of the continent is vast, and much of the land lies far from any coast. Europeans had easy access to the north coast along the Mediterranean Sea. Just to the south their way was hindered, however, by a formidable barrier—the Sahara, which is the largest desert in the world.

Unfavorable winds and ocean currents make it difficult to sail to most of the rest of Africa's shores. Off the west coast just north of the Equator lie the doldrums, an area of very light winds. The crews of sailing ships dreaded the doldrums because their ships were often stuck there for long periods without winds to propel them. By contrast, fierce storms are common on the south. On parts of the coast, explorers also had to sail along dangerous, uncharted "lee shores," where the wind blows toward the coast. In a storm, a ship could be dashed upon these shores. Moreover, Africa's coasts largely lack good natural harbors that provide safe landing places.

Travel in the interior was also difficult. Boats cannot journey far on most of the continent's great rivers. The way is often blocked by waterfalls and rapids. Large parts of the interior consist of deserts or jungles. The extremely hot, humid, and wet climate in the tropics presented serious problems to Europeans. Diseases such as malaria and yellow fever killed many explorers. Sleeping sickness and other diseases also affected the explorers' horses and pack animals. In many places expeditions had to travel on foot and hire human porters. Wild animals such as lions and crocodiles also posed a threat in some areas. Finally, the continent was already occupied by millions of Africans, who often did not welcome the European newcomers. Explorers had to contend with the possibility of hostile encounters with local peoples.

EARLY CONTACTS AND COLONIES

The northern coast of Africa was considered part of the ancient Mediterranean world. The great civilization of ancient Egypt arose in northern Africa. The Egyptians explored parts of the Nile River and developed trading contacts throughout the region. The Phoenicians and the Greeks explored northern Africa as they established colonies along the coast. The region subsequently came under Roman and later Arab rule.

Phoenicians and Greeks

Great traders and seafarers, the Phoenicians of Lebanon colonized the north coast of Africa in the 1st millennium

A Phoenician ship stands on the beach at the Mediterranean port of Sidon (now in Lebanon) in ancient times.

North Wind Picture Archives/Alamy

BC (*see* Eurasia, "Early European Exploration.") The Phoenicians mainly wanted to establish places where their trading ships could stop on their way across the Mediterranean Sea to Spain. Their largest colony was Carthage (now in Tunisia), which itself became an important commercial power. The Greeks also built colonies in the region, notably at Cyrene, in what is now Libya.

The Phoenicians were skilled sailors, and they began to explore Africa's coasts. According to the ancient Greek historian Herodotus, some Phoenicians sailed completely around Africa in about 600 BC. They were sent to circle Africa by the Egyptian pharaoh Necho II. The Phoenicians sailed from east to west, setting off from the Red Sea. When they returned two to three years later, they reported "unbelievable" things about what they had seen. For example, they told that, after a certain point in their voyage, the Sun lay to their right (northward). The Sun would have been in this position as they sailed around southern Africa. It is not known whether the Phoenicians actually succeeded in sailing around the entire continent, which would have been a remarkable feat indeed.

Carthage was the starting point for many explorers and colonists. The Carthaginian named Hanno was one of the greatest of the ancient explorers. In about 500 BC he led an expedition to the west coast of Africa. Its aim was to set up new settlements, as well as to explore. It is said that Hanno had 60 vessels, each driven by 50 oars, and that he started with 30,000 men and women. He left some people at each place he stopped to begin new settlements.

Some scholars believe that Hanno reached only as far as Morocco. However, he reported having seen a "deep river infested with crocodiles and hippopotamuses." Some scholars think the river he saw was the Sénégal River of western Africa. Hanno also described an island where men "scampered up steep rocks" and threw

stones at the explorers. This may have been an island off the coast of what is now Sierra Leone. It is possible that Hanno ventured as far as Cameroon. In any case, there is no record that anyone followed up Hanno's voyage until the 15th century AD, more than 1,900 years later.

Herodotus also tells of explorations of the African interior. He wrote about five young adventurers of the tribe of the Nasamones. They journeyed from Libya to the southwest for many months across the desert. Eventually, they reached a great river flowing from west

Ptolemy's World Map

The astronomer, mathematician, and geographer Ptolemy flourished in the 2nd century AD. He lived in Egypt, which was then part of the Roman Empire, but he was of Greek descent. In several fields his writings represent the crowning achievement of ancient Greek and Roman science. He is particularly well known for his model of the universe in which the Sun and all the planets revolve around Earth.

Ptolemy's geographic writings and world map were also very influential. His eight-volume *Guide to Geography* was one of the first geography texts. It provided all the information and techniques required to draw maps of the world. His world map shows only Europe, Asia, and northern Africa. The rest of Africa, the Americas, and Australia were unknown to people in the Roman Empire.

Ptolemy recorded longitudes and latitudes in degrees for roughly 8,000 locations on his world map. This great innovation made it possible for others to make exact duplicates of his map. Ptolemy's map is seriously distorted in size and orientation compared to modern maps. These errors are a reflection of the incomplete and inaccurate descriptions of road systems and trade routes that were available to him.

Arab scholars translated Ptolemy's works into Arabic. Ptolemy's world map was rediscovered in Europe in about 1300. In the later Middle Ages, Arab and European world maps were often based on Ptolemy's. For a copy of Ptolemy's map from the 1400s, *see* p. 22.

Ptolemy
© Photos.com/Thinkstock

to east. This river was presumably the Niger, though Herodotus thought it to be the Upper Nile.

Herodotus, who lived in the 5th century BC, traveled widely himself. He visited what are now southern Egypt, Libya, and Syria, as well as many places in the Middle East and southern Europe.

Although Africa's north coast was well explored, nonnatives mostly did not venture into the Sahara. Since prehistoric times, however, African caravans had crossed the desert along trade routes linking the north coast to the interior. The Carthaginians apparently continued these commercial relationships with the interior.

The Romans later took control of much of northern Africa. They led a series of expeditions in the Sahara between 19 BC and AD 86. The descriptions of the Sahara in the works of ancient geographers also reflect growing interest in the desert. The Greek geographer Strabo, the Roman writer Pliny the Elder, and the Egyptian geographer and astronomer Ptolemy all wrote about the Sahara. Exploration of the region by Arabs was widespread during what were the Middle Ages in Europe.

Arabs and Muslims

In the 7th and 8th centuries the Arabs conquered first Egypt, then the rest of northern Africa. They converted the peoples who lived there to Islam. The Arabs in the north continued the trade with African kingdoms in the western interior. From the interior came African slaves, ivory, and above all gold. Salt, copper, and other goods were sent from northern to western Africa.

Since Arabs controlled the northern ends of the trade routes, they gained access to more and more information about the land south of the Sahara. The study of geography and history flourished throughout the Muslim world from about the 9th to the 14th century. Muslim travelers also brought back much geographic information. From all over the Muslim world, the faithful traveled on pilgrimages to Mecca (now in Saudi Arabia). Muslims also journeyed to visit notable Islamic scholars.

Among the Muslim travelers who visited Africa was the geographer al-Ya'qubi. In the 9th century he traveled in northern Africa and wrote about the Sahara and the cities of the north coast. The 12th-century geographer ash-Sharif al-Idrisi was born in Morocco. As a young man he traveled throughout northern Africa and Spain and published detailed and accurate information on both regions. He later became famous for the world maps and geographic texts he produced for the king of Sicily.

The best-known medieval Arab traveler, Ibn Battutah, also visited Africa on his long and many journeys. He too was born in Morocco. On his pilgrimage to Mecca in 1325–27, he traveled across northern Africa to Egypt. On his second voyage, Ibn Battutah sailed along the east coast of Africa as far as Kilwa, in what is now Tanzania. He visited several cities along the way. After traveling extensively in Asia, his final voyage took him across the Sahara to western Africa. He spent a year in the Mali empire, then at the height of its power. His account of his trip is one of the most important sources for the history of that part of Africa at the time. (*See also* Eurasia, "Muslim Travelers.")

> "They are more thickset than horses and they have manes and tails, their heads are like the heads of horses and their legs like the legs of elephants. ... The boatmen feared them and came in close to the shore so as not to be drowned by them."
>
> —Ibn Battutah, describing hippopotamuses in Mali, 1353

THE PORTUGUESE

The Portuguese wanted to end Muslim control over northern Africa. This desire was one of several reasons why Portugal explored the continent in the 15th century. Spreading Christianity in Africa was another motive for Portuguese exploration, along with scientific curiosity. They also sought great wealth.

Portugal's exploring aims were largely commercial. The Portuguese wanted to find a sea route around Africa to the riches of Asia. Like other European powers, they wanted to trade directly in valuable Asian spices. The older trade routes to Asia were becoming increasingly blocked to them.

The Portuguese also wanted to establish trade with western Africa. Gold, ivory, and African slaves had long been traded across the Sahara to Muslims in the north. The Portuguese sought to establish new trade routes to channel these profitable items instead to the west coast. From there, they would be carried by ship across the sea to Portugal. They would make much greater profits,

The Granger Collection, New York

The Portuguese built a fortress at what is now Elmina, Ghana, on Africa's west coast, in 1481–82. It served as a gold-trading post as well as a supply base for the country's navigators.

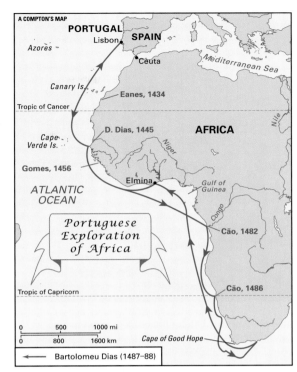

since they would not have to pay Muslim middlemen. The Portuguese ultimately succeeded in setting up this trade. Part of the west coast of Africa became known as the "Gold Coast." The Atlantic slave trade also began. Africans were eventually shipped across the ocean in great numbers to provide slave labor in European colonies in the Americas.

Henry the Navigator

In the 1400s Prince Henry of Portugal sent ship after ship to explore the west coast of Africa. These voyages initiated the Age of Discovery, a great period of maritime exploration in which Europeans sailed completely around the world. They also "discovered" the Americas during this period (*see* The Americas, "The Age of Discovery"). Henry is often called "Prince Henry the Navigator" because he sponsored so many voyages of exploration. He did not himself join the expeditions.

In 1415 Henry took part in the Portuguese capture of Ceuta, a port at the northern tip of what is now Morocco. While he was in Ceuta he became interested in Africa and decided to send out exploring expeditions. He first sent ships to the islands west of northwestern Africa. Portuguese ships reached Madeira in about 1419, followed by the Canary Islands and the Azores. These islands would later become important staging points for ships traveling to the Americas. After about 1445 the Portuguese set up colonies on the Azores and Madeira and grew sugar on plantations there.

Meanwhile, Henry's ships were pushing southward, charting Africa's west coast. An important achievement came in 1434, when the navigator Gil Eanes rounded Cape Bojador (now in Western Sahara). This cape is a dangerous reef-lined stretch of the coast. Modern scholars think that Eanes may have actually rounded another cape to the north.

During the next years, Henry's captains pushed southward beyond the Río de Oro. From 1440 Portuguese expeditions were equipped with a new and lighter type of ship, the caravel. In 1445 the Portuguese

navigator Dinís Dias sailed a caravel past the mouth of the Sénégal River. He mistakenly thought this river was a branch of the Nile. Dias continued southward, reaching the westernmost point of Africa. He named it Cape Verde, meaning "Green Cape," because the headland had tall trees and fragrant vegetation.

In 1456 Henry sent the navigator Diogo Gomes to continue the coastal exploration. Gomes sailed south beyond the Gêba River, which is now in Guinea-Bissau. On the return trip he traveled up the Gambia River to the town of Cantor (now Kuntaur, The Gambia). There he met men from the important trading city of Timbuktu, in the Mali empire. He could not explore any farther inland, because his crew had fallen ill. On a second voyage, in about 1460, Gomes landed at São Tiago in the Cape Verde Islands. The Portuguese soon began colonizing these islands.

Seaway to India

By the time Henry died in 1460, his navigators had explored the coast as far south as Sierra Leone. For a time the Portuguese were busy fighting the Moroccans, and few exploring expeditions were sent out. John II became king of Portugal in 1481. Under John, the Portuguese once again began exploring Africa regularly. In 1481–82 they established a fortress and trading post at Elmina (now in Ghana), on the Gulf of Guinea.

In 1482 John sent the navigator Diogo Cão to search for a seaway around southern Africa to India. Cão instead discovered the mouth of the Congo River. There he set up a stone pillar to mark his discovery and to claim Portuguese authority over the area. Cão then

traveled southward along the coast of what is now Angola. He put up a second stone pillar at Cape Santa Maria. Other Portuguese explorers later stood pillars at other points on the African coast. On a second voyage, in 1485–86, Cão reached Cape Cross (now in Namibia).

In 1487 John sent Pêro da Covilhã and Afonso Paiva to visit India and Ethiopia by an overland route. That same year the king had Bartolomeu Dias take over the task of finding the southern end of Africa. In an impressive feat of navigation, Dias rounded the stormy Cape of Good Hope at Africa's southern tip in 1488. He reached the continent's east coast and then returned home. The seaway from western Europe to India at last lay open. In 1497–99 the Portuguese navigator Vasco da Gama made the first trip around the Cape of Good Hope to India. Along the way, he explored the coasts of eastern Africa. The Portuguese soon captured trading cities all along the east coast. (*See also* Eurasia, "The Sea Route to India.")

The Portuguese had thus completed many of their main objectives in exploring Africa. They had established profitable trade with western Africa and had found a route to India. They had also charted the coasts of Africa that had long been unknown to foreigners, discovering the continent's true outline.

The interior of Africa is quite difficult to explore, and Portugal's great talents lay in sea travel. Instead of venturing farther inland, the Portuguese focused on maintaining and exploiting their colonies on the coasts. They continued to trade in gold and slaves in Africa and in spices in Asia. However, Jesuit missionaries from Portugal began to travel through the interior in order to convert Africans to Christianity. These Jesuits became the first Europeans to reach many areas of inland Africa. The Portuguese kept much of the work of their explorers secret. The achievements of the early Jesuit explorers thus remain less well known than those of later explorers.

THE MYSTERIES OF THE GREAT RIVERS

After the Portuguese expeditions, European exploration of Africa largely ceased for some two hundred years. European countries were more interested in exploiting the trade in slaves and gold at the west coast. In the 19th century the growing movement to abolish slavery began to draw attention to the continent. Scientific curiosity also sparked new interest in the interior. Europeans wanted to solve the "mysteries" of this vast land. Indeed, it was seen as a rebuke to modern science that one of the continents remained largely unknown.

Explorers also trekked into the interior in search of new avenues for profitable trade. Europeans wanted to bring new commerce and "progress" to a land they thought was "uncivilized." Africa was long known to Europeans as the "Dark Continent" because they thought it was a land of ignorance and backwardness. Europeans believed that it was their moral duty to bring Christianity and Western civilization to the "primitive" peoples of Africa. They viewed native African religions and cultures as markedly inferior. Christian missionaries from Great Britain, France, Germany, and the Netherlands became active in Africa.

Travel in the interior remained challenging. Explorers had to contend with the extreme climates of the deserts and the rainforests. Diseases such as malaria, yellow fever, dysentery, and sleeping sickness abounded. Because of these dangers, Europeans began to view the continent's explorers as dashing and romantic figures. It became fashionable to seek adventure in what Europeans viewed as an exotic and "savage" land. By the end of the 19th century, the renewed European interest in Africa had led to the colonization of nearly the entire continent.

The focus of European explorers was to understand at last the geography of Africa's great river systems. It was hoped that the rivers could provide transportation into the interior. Better transportation would help to advance trade and development. The "golden age" of African exploration began with Scottish explorer James Bruce. He searched for the source of the Nile River during daring and difficult travels in Ethiopia in 1768–71. The "riddle" of where the Nile arose was not solved, however, for about a hundred more years. Meanwhile, Europeans explored the Niger River in the west, the Zambezi and Congo rivers in the central regions, and the East African lakes.

James Bruce
© Photos.com/Jupiterimages

The Europeans were, of course, exploring a land that was already populated. They were usually assisted in their explorations by local Africans. Africans served as guides, envoys, servants, laborers, and porters for the explorers. African interpreters were essential. They helped the explorers communicate with various local peoples along the way.

The Niger and Western Africa

Many expeditions to the interior were sponsored by the African Association. This British organization was founded in 1788 to promote the scientific exploration of Africa. One of the association's founders and leaders was Joseph Banks. He was president of Britain's scientific Royal Society. Banks was also an explorer, having served as a naturalist on James Cook's first voyage around the world. In 1830 Britain's Royal Geographical Society was founded. It soon absorbed the African Association and continued its mission of funding African exploration.

The African Association initially emphasized western Africa. Since ancient times, Europeans had known that a great river—the Niger—existed in the western interior. However, the river's source, direction of flow, and outlet were still unknown. Some people believed that the Niger River emptied into the Sénégal River. Others thought that its outlet was in the Gambia, the Congo, or even the Nile.

The African Association sent several explorers to the Niger River. The first few expeditions were not successful. For example, the explorer Daniel Houghton did not reach the river on his quest in 1790–91. However, he heard from local people that the river flowed eastward. He sent news of this discovery back to England, but he never returned himself. Houghton was robbed by some traders and abandoned in the desert of western Mali, where he died.

Park reaches the Niger. The African Association next asked a young Scottish surgeon named Mungo Park to investigate the Niger. Park began his exploration at the mouth of the Gambia River on June 21, 1795. He traveled up that river for 200 miles (320 kilometers) to a British trading station called Pisania (now Karantaba, Gambia). He continued inland on the river and then set off on foot. Hampered by fever and other hardships, he crossed the basin of the upper Sénégal River. Park was robbed, and most of his servants deserted him. An Arab chief then captured and imprisoned him for four months. Park escaped on July 1, 1796. However, he had to continue his journey with little more than a horse and a compass.

Mungo Park, right, rests in a hut at Ségou (now in Mali) during his first expedition to the Niger River.
Classic Image/Alamy

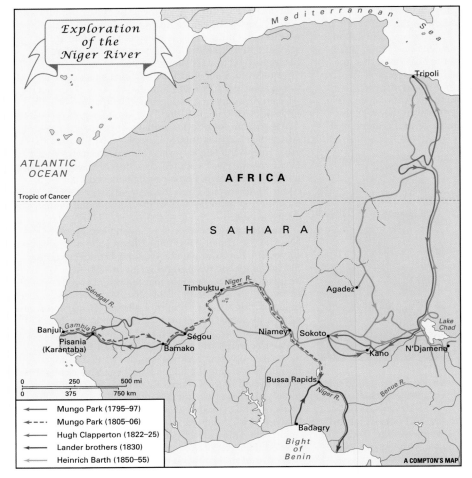

Exploration of the Niger River

Mediterranean Sea

Tripoli

ATLANTIC OCEAN

Tropic of Cancer

AFRICA

SAHARA

Timbuktu Niger R. Agadez

Lake Chad

Banjul Gambia R. Niamey Sokoto

Pisania (Karantaba) Ségou Kano N'Djamena

Sénégal R. Bamako

Bussa Rapids Niger R. Benue R.

| 0 | 250 | 500 mi |
| 0 | 375 | 750 km |

Badagry

Bight of Benin

A COMPTON'S MAP

→ Mungo Park (1795–97)
←--- Mungo Park (1805–06)
← Hugh Clapperton (1822–25)
← Lander brothers (1830)
← Heinrich Barth (1850–55)

On July 20 Park reached the Niger River near Ségou (now in Mali). He determined once and for all that the river flows from west to east. He traveled on the Niger downstream for 80 miles (130 kilometers) to the village of Silla. He was finally forced to turn back for lack of supplies.

Traveling on foot, he took a more southerly route on his return. After crossing mountainous country, he became dangerously ill with fever for seven months. With the assistance of a slave trader, he reached Pisania on June 10, 1797. He returned to Britain and wrote an account of his adventures. The book became a popular success and made him famous.

A few years later the British government asked Park to head a second expedition to the Niger. Commissioned a captain, he led a party of 40 Europeans, mostly soldiers. Park first traveled to Pisania. On Aug. 19, 1805, he reached Bamako (now in Mali) on the Niger River. By then all but 11 of his party had died of disease. Resuming the journey by canoe, he and his surviving companions reached Ségou. The local ruler gave him permission to continue his voyage down the unexplored river. Hoping to reach the river's mouth at the coast, he

set sail with eight companions on Nov. 19, 1805. The explorers left from Sansanding, a little below Ségou. They were never heard from again. In 1812 it was learned that the explorers had sailed more than 1,500 miles (2,400 kilometers) down the river. They reached the rapids at Bussa, where they were attacked by local inhabitants and Park was drowned.

Clapperton explores Nigeria. Hugh Clapperton was the first European to return with a firsthand account of what is now northern Nigeria. In 1821 he joined an expedition to the Niger River basin that was sponsored by the British government. The party also included Walter Oudney and Dixon Denham. The men left Tripoli (now in Libya) and journeyed southward across the Sahara. They successfully crossed the great desert. In early 1823 they became the first Europeans to view Lake Chad. They were also the first to enter the province of Bornu (now in Nigeria).

In December 1823 Denham explored the region around Lake Chad. Meanwhile, Clapperton and Oudney

Hugh Clapperton
The Granger Collection, New York

Mary Kingsley

In the late 19th century Mary Kingsley became famous for her travels to Africa. It was then considered inappropriate for Englishwomen to explore foreign lands, especially "uncivilized" places such as tropical Africa. Disregarding the conventions of her time, she journeyed through western and equatorial Africa. She became the first European to enter parts of Gabon.

Mary Henrietta Kingsley was born on Nov. 13, 1862, in London. She was a niece of the clergyman and author Charles Kingsley. She led a secluded life until age 30, when she decided to visit western Africa. She wanted to study African religion and law. She hoped this research would help her complete a book left unfinished by her deceased father.

In 1893–94 Mary Kingsley visited coastal Angola and southeastern Nigeria. She also traveled to the island of Fernando Po (Bioko), off the coast of Cameroon. Around the

Courtesy of the Royal Geographical Society, London

lower Congo River, she collected specimens of beetles and freshwater fishes for the British Museum.

Kingsley began her second African trip in December 1894. She visited the Congo region and then journeyed to Gabon. In this area she had many adventures and narrow escapes traveling up the Ogooué River. She passed through the country of the Fang, a tribe with a reputation for cannibalism. She then visited Corisco Island, off Gabon, and also climbed Mount Cameroon.

Kingsley returned to England with valuable national history collections. Between 1896 and 1899 she lectured widely throughout the country about her travels. Her writings, which express her strong sympathies for black Africans, include *Travels in West Africa* (1897) and *West African Studies* (1899). Kingsley died on June 3, 1900, in what is now South Africa while nursing sick prisoners during the Boer War.

"*For crocodiles can, and often do … grab at people in small canoes. On one occasion, one chose to get his front paws over the stern of my canoe, and endeavoured to improve our acquaintance. I had to retire to the bows, to keep the balance right, and fetch him a clip on the snout with a paddle, when he withdrew. … I should think that crocodile was eight feet long. … This was only a pushing young creature who had not learnt his manners.*"

—Mary Kingsley, *Travels in West Africa* (1897)

set out westward. Oudney died within about a month. Clapperton continued on, traveling to the cities of Kano, Katsina, Sokoto, and Zaria (all now in Nigeria). He and Denham returned to England in June 1825.

Almost immediately afterward, Clapperton sailed to western Africa to begin a second expedition. In December 1825 he journeyed inland from the Bight of Benin, a bay of the Atlantic Ocean off of Africa's west coast. The expedition also included Richard Lander, Clapperton's servant. The explorers crossed the Niger River and traveled via Kano to Sokoto. Clapperton became ill and died near Sokoto in April 1827. Lander returned to Kano and then traveled back to the coast.

The fabled Timbuktu. The ancient city of Timbuktu (now in Mali) had long captured the imagination of explorers. Rumors of its great wealth in gold and of its many scholars had reached Europe centuries earlier. Several explorers, including Mungo Park, had tried in vain to reach the fabled city. Timbuktu has often been used as a symbol for remoteness. Some routes to the city took explorers through disease-ridden jungles. The other routes passed through deserts where explorers were attacked by bandits.

The Scottish explorer Alexander Gordon Laing was the first European known to have visited Timbuktu. He took the desert route. In July 1825 he left the north coast at Tripoli on his journey across the Sahara. He reached

Ghadamis (now in Libya) by September. He then entered the vast country of the nomadic people known as the Tuareg. One night in early 1826 some Tuareg attacked the explorers in their tents. Laing had to fight for his life and was severely wounded. He recovered and continued onward with the other survivors. Eventually, however, all his remaining companions died of disease.

After trekking alone through the desert, he finally reached Timbuktu on Aug. 18, 1826. The local ruler urged him to depart because he was concerned that a

An illustration of Timbuktu was drawn in 1830 by René-Auguste Caillié, the first European to visit the fabled city and survive to describe it.

The Granger Collection, New York

non-Muslim would not be safe in the area. Laing left Timbuktu on September 24 and was murdered by Tuareg people two days later.

The French explorer René-Auguste Caillié was the first European to reach Timbuktu and survive. Caillié had studied Islam and learned Arabic. He reached Timbuktu disguised as an Arab. He left the coast of western Africa in April 1827, but his journey was interrupted by five months of illness. Caillié at last reached Timbuktu on April 20, 1828. He remained there for about two weeks, finding the city significantly less impressive than was suggested in legend. Timbuktu had declined; it had no fabulous wealth, and it was no longer a great center of scholarship. Caillié returned across the Sahara to France, via Morocco, with firsthand knowledge of the city.

" I looked around and found that the sight before me … did not answer my expectations. I had formed a totally different idea of the grandeur and wealth of Timbuktu. The city presented, at first view, nothing but a mass of ill-looking houses, built of earth. "

— René-Auguste Caillié, 1828

The Lander brothers. At the request of the British government, the English explorer Richard Lander (who had earlier traveled with Hugh Clapperton) returned to western Africa. This time he traveled with his brother John. The Lander brothers sailed to the Bight of Benin. They landed at Badagry (now in Nigeria), on March 22, 1830. From there they traveled inland to Bussa and explored the Niger River upstream for about 100 miles (160 kilometers). The brothers then began a hazardous canoe trip downstream to the river's delta. They became the first Europeans to reach the mouth of the Niger River. They thus confirmed that the river empties into the Atlantic Ocean. While exploring the delta, the Lander brothers were seized by local tribesman. They were held captive until a large ransom was paid.

The Benue River. The greatest tributary of the Niger River is the Benue. In the second half of the 19th century two German explorers—Heinrich Barth and Eduard R. Flegel—charted the course of the Benue River.

Barth was a scholar who was fluent in French, Spanish, Italian, English, and Arabic. He participated in an expedition sponsored by the British government that aimed to suppress the slave trade. Early in 1850, he set out from Tripoli. The expedition was led by the English explorer and antislavery activist James Richardson. The party also included the German geologist and astronomer Adolf Overweg.

From Tripoli, the men crossed the Sahara. When Richardson died in March 1851 in northern Nigeria, Barth assumed command of the expedition. He explored the area south and southeast of Lake Chad. He also mapped the upper reaches of the Benue River. Overweg died in September 1852. Barth continued on to the city of Timbuktu, remaining there for six months. He returned to London, via Tripoli in 1855. Despite ill health and the loss of his colleagues, he had traveled

Heinrich Barth
© Photos.com/Thinkstock

some 10,000 miles (16,000 kilometers). He had returned to Europe with the first account of the middle section of the Niger River.

Flegel was the first European to reach the source of the Benue River. In 1879 he traveled about 525 miles (845 kilometers) up the Benue. In 1880 he sailed on the Niger River to Sokoto. With a local ruler's permission, he explored the Benue River basin in 1882–84. In the course of his travels, he reached the Benue's source, near Ngaoundéré (now in Cameroon).

Livingstone in the Heart of Africa

For more than 30 years the Scottish missionary Dr. David Livingstone explored Africa. He traveled the continent from near the Equator to the Cape and from the Atlantic to the Indian Ocean. On long voyages in southern and central Africa, he explored the Kalahari basin and the Zambezi River. He later investigated the East African lakes.

Livingstone gained worldwide fame as an explorer. His exploits helped awaken the interest of the outside world in the then largely unknown continent. In so doing, he helped pave the way for its European colonization later in the 19th century. Livingstone believed deeply, however, that Africans could advance into the modern world. In this sense, he later served as an inspiration for African nationalism and independence.

Of working-class origins, Livingstone studied theology and medicine in Glasgow while working part-time in a cotton mill. He had originally intended to work in China as a medical missionary—introducing Western medicine and Christianity. He was prevented from going to China, however, when war broke out between China and Britain. He later met Robert Moffat, the noted missionary to southern Africa. This meeting convinced Livingstone that he should instead take up his work in Africa. On Nov. 20, 1840, Livingstone was ordained as a missionary. He set sail for South Africa at the end of the year and arrived at Cape Town on March 14, 1841.

The "White Man's Grave"

There were several obstacles to European exploration of tropical and subtropical Africa, not least of them disease. Numerous explorers died of malaria, yellow fever, and infections of the gastrointestinal tract. Much of the continent was considered "unhealthy" for Europeans, who seemed to die in greater numbers than the local Africans. Today, it is known that the Europeans had no immunity to many of the diseases and so were more susceptible to them. Disease killed so many Europeans in western Africa that Europeans began calling the region the "white man's grave." From 1819 to 1836, for example, nearly half of all British soldiers in Sierra Leone died of disease.

Malaria was the greatest killer. Even those who did not die of the disease could be severely weakened by it. Malaria causes periodic attacks of chills and fever, nausea and vomiting, muscle aches, anemia, and enlargement of the spleen. People realized that malaria was associated with swamps and marshes. But no one knew what caused it. Nevertheless, an effective remedy was discovered in the bark of the cinchona tree, which contains the active ingredient quinine. The tree is native to the Andes Mountains of South America. Its bark was introduced into Spain from Peru in the 1630s. However, this life-saving medicine was not widely available until the mid-19th century. It became much more common after Europeans smuggled cinchona seeds from South America to plantations in Asia in the 1850s and 1860s. Scientists also learned how to extract quinine from the bark and to produce new high-yield strains.

Bibliotheque des Arts Decoratifs Paris—Gianni Dagli Orti/The Art Archive

Cinchona tree

In his journeys across Africa in the mid-19th century, the explorer Dr. David Livingstone used quinine to treat malaria. At the time, the amount of quinine typically given to patients was too low to be very effective. Livingstone initially used low doses, but later tried much higher doses—which he found very effective. Fewer of his explorers died than was common on other African expeditions. He was unable, however, to prevent his wife, Mary, from dying of malaria. The use of quinine subsequently helped Europeans explore more of the African interior, and then to colonize it.

Several other drugs to treat malaria have since been developed. In addition, the cause of malaria is now known. Several one-celled parasites can cause the disease. They are transmitted to humans by the bite of certain types of mosquitoes. Measures to reduce mosquito populations are thus an important part of malaria prevention. Nets treated with insecticide, for instance, are placed over beds to protect people from getting bitten in their sleep. Still, the disease remains a major killer. About 900,000 people die of malaria each year; most of them are young children in Africa.

From the moment he arrived, Livingstone determined to become an explorer. He wanted to open up the continent for Christianity and European commerce and civilization. He believed that accomplishing this would help to end the slave trade, which he strongly opposed. In addition, the delights of geographic discovery soon became apparent to him. A major aim of his great journeys was to gather new information about the continent.

Crossing the Kalahari. For the next 15 years, Livingstone was constantly on the move into the African interior. First, he ventured north of Cape Town into the Kalahari, a vast dry plain. By 1842 he had already traveled farther north in the Kalahari than any other European. In 1844 he traveled to Mabotsa to establish a mission station. Along the way, he was mauled by a lion, and his left arm was injured. The following year, Livingstone married Moffat's daughter Mary. She accompanied him on many of his travels.

With assistance from local peoples, Livingstone crossed the Kalahari in 1849. He was accompanied by William Oswell, an English big-game hunter. It is very difficult to travel in the Kalahari, large parts of which are desert. Although other parts receive slightly more rainfall, they completely lack surface water. Much of the basin is also covered by deep sands. The expedition traversed the Kalahari from south to north with great effort. The men used local water holes, found by local guides.

On Aug. 1, 1849, Livingstone and his companion became the first Europeans to see Lake Ngami. For this discovery, Livingstone was awarded a prize from the

David Livingstone
© Photos.com/Thinkstock

David Livingstone, holding his child's hand, leads an expedition to Lake Ngami (now in Botswana), in 1849. His wife and children accompanied him on many of his early journeys in southern Africa.
© Photos.com/Thinkstock

Royal Geographical Society. This was the beginning of his lifelong association with the society, which encouraged him to continue his explorations.

Livingstone crossed the Kalahari again in 1851. This time his pregnant wife and their three children joined him. Livingstone eventually reached the Zambezi River.

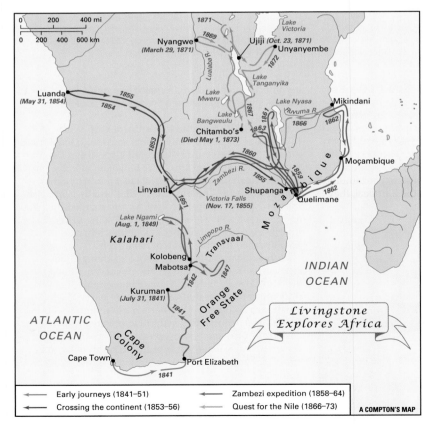

Livingstone Explores Africa

Early journeys (1841–51)
Crossing the continent (1853–56)
Zambezi expedition (1858–64)
Quest for the Nile (1866–73)

A COMPTON'S MAP

On the journey back, Mary gave birth to another child. In 1852 she and the children returned to Britain, because of her health and the children's need for security and education.

Crossing the continent. With his family safely in Scotland, Livingstone was able to set out on his next major journey. His first goal was to reach the Atlantic coast to open up a new avenue of commerce that would undercut the slave trade. In a famous statement in 1853 he made his purpose clear: "I shall open up a path into the interior, or perish." On Nov. 11, 1853, he set out northwestward from Linyanti at the approaches to the Zambezi River. He carried little equipment and traveled with only a small party of Africans.

Livingstone completed a long, arduous journey that would have wrecked the health of many people. He first canoed upstream on the Zambezi. He then continued on land, crossing the watershed of central Africa. Although Livingstone was ill with malaria, he reached Luanda, Angola, on the west coast, on May 31, 1854. He began the return trek in September, reaching Linyanti about a year later. He fell ill again along the way.

Continuing eastward, Livingstone explored the

Zambezi River regions downstream. He reached the east coast at Quelimane, Mozambique, on May 20, 1856. His most spectacular visit on this leg of his journey was to the thundering, smokelike waters about midway along the Zambezi. On Nov. 17, 1855, he became the first European to see this mighty waterfall. The local Africans called the waterfall "The Smoke That Thunders" in their language. Livingstone named it Victoria Falls after the British queen.

Livingstone returned to England on Dec. 9, 1856, a national hero. During the previous three years, news about his travels had stirred the imagination of English-speaking peoples everywhere. He recorded his achievements in a book, *Missionary Travels and Researches in South Africa* (1857). The book quickly sold more than 70,000 copies. He spent six months on a speaking tour in the British Isles. Honors flowed in upon him. His increased income meant that he was now able to provide adequately for his family, which had lived in near poverty since returning to Britain.

Zambezi expedition. Back in Africa in 1858, Livingstone began an expedition to navigate the Zambezi River. He believed that the river was "God's highway," through which the British would bring Christianity, British commerce, and European civilization to the peoples of the African interior.

The British government sponsored this expedition. It was much better equipped and organized than Livingstone's previous journeys. This time the expedition included 10 Africans and six Europeans, including his brother Charles. Livingstone's wife later returned from Britain to join him. The expedition took a paddle-wheeled steamboat and other vessels and was well stocked with provisions. The explorers set off from Quelimane on March 12, 1858. They traveled upstream (westward) on the Zambezi River.

The Zambezi expedition was beset by troubles. Quarrels broke out among the Europeans, and some of them were dismissed. Several members of the expedition were dissatisfied with Livingstone's leadership. Moreover, the explorers discovered that is impossible to travel to the middle course of the Zambezi River by ship. Their way was barred by rapids in western Mozambique. After traveling back downstream on the Zambezi, they explored the Shire River of eastern Africa instead.

In September 1859 Livingstone and his party were the first British people to reach the districts around Lake Nyasa (Lake Malawi). These districts looked like promising places to set up British colonies. Livingstone made two attempts to find a route to these districts that would bypass Portuguese territory. He explored the Ruvuma River but could not find a good route. To add to Livingstone's troubles, Mary fell ill with malaria. She died at Shupanga, on the Zambezi River, on April 27, 1862.

The expedition was not successful from a commercial point of view. The British government ended it in 1863. On the journey back, Livingstone took a small vessel on a hazardous voyage of 2,500 miles (4,000 kilometers) across the Indian Ocean to India. From there, he returned to Britain. Although the Zambezi expedition had not met its goals, it had gathered valuable scientific information. On his voyages along the Zambezi, Livingstone had charted the river's course. His map of the river remained the most accurate until the 20th century. His exploration of the Lake Nyasa region led to later British missionary activity and colonization there, in what later became Malawi.

In 1864 Livingstone and his brother Charles wrote a book about their Zambezi voyage. Livingstone soon returned to Africa on what would be his last expedition—a quest to find the source of the Nile River.

The Nile and Eastern Africa

The whereabouts of the source of the Nile River had intrigued people since ancient times. The river, which is the world's longest, rises in eastern Africa and flows generally northward to the Mediterranean Sea. The great civilization of ancient Egypt was centered on the Nile. The ancient Egyptians were probably familiar with the river as far as what is now Khartoum, Sudan. They also knew of the Blue Nile, the Nile's largest tributary, as far as Lake Tana, Ethiopia. However, they showed little or no interest in exploring the section of the Nile known as the White Nile, in central Sudan. The source of the Nile was unknown to them.

In 457 BC the Greek historian Herodotus traveled up the Nile. He journeyed as far as the first cataract, or waterfall, at Aswan. In about the second century BC the Greek writer Eratosthenes sketched a nearly correct route of the Nile to Khartoum. He correctly suggested that lakes are the source of the river.

A Roman expedition searched for the source of the Nile in AD 66. The explorers were impeded in south-central Sudan by the swamps of Al-Sudd and had to turn back. Ptolemy, a Greek astronomer and geographer

A papyrus painting from ancient Egypt shows a boat traveling on the Nile River.

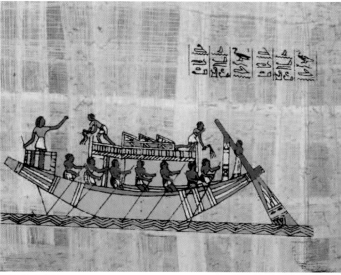

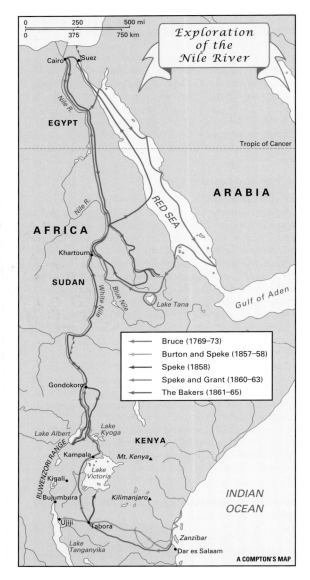

Exploration of the Nile River

←	Bruce (1769–73)
←	Burton and Speke (1857–58)
←	Speke (1858)
←	Speke and Grant (1860–63)
←	The Bakers (1861–65)

A COMPTON'S MAP

discoveries to the French court first. Reports by later travelers, however, confirmed the accuracy of Bruce's information. However, the spring he visited was not the source of the Nile.

Modern exploration of the Nile basin began when Egypt conquered northern and central Sudan starting in 1821. As a result, the Egyptians learned more about the courses of the Blue Nile and the White Nile. A Turkish officer, Selim Bimbashi, led three expeditions between 1839 and 1842. Two of them reached the point in southern Sudan where rapids make navigation of the Nile very difficult.

After these expeditions, traders and missionaries began to establish stations in southern Sudan. From an Austrian missionary, Ignaz Knoblecher, came reports in 1850 of lakes farther south. In the 1840s the German missionaries Johannes Rebmann and Johann Ludwig Krapf established a mission station in eastern Africa. In 1848 Rebmann became the first European to see the snow-topped Mount Kilimanjaro. The following year Krapf ventured still farther inland and discovered Mount Kenya. He and Rebmann also heard from traders of a great inland sea that might be a lake or lakes. On the basis of Arab information, another missionary, Jakob Erhardt, created a map that showed an enormous inland lake.

Back in Europe, people did not believe the news that there were snowcapped mountains so close to the Equator until more than a decade later. However, Rebmann, Krapf, and others thought these peaks might be the "Mountains of the Moon" that Ptolemy had described some 1,700 years earlier.

Burton and Speke. The reports of these mountains and large inland lakes stimulated fresh interest in finding the source of the Nile. The English explorers Richard Burton and John Speke tried to solve the mystery of the river in 1857–58. They set off from the island of Zanzibar, off the coast of east-central Africa,

Richard Burton, in about 1880

© Photos.com/Jupiterimages

who lived in Egypt, wrote about the Nile. In AD 150 he identified the source of the White Nile as being in the high snow-covered "Mountains of the Moon." Today, it is thought that he was referring to the Ruwenzori Range, in central Africa.

From the 17th century onward several attempts were made to explore the Nile. In 1618 Pedro Páez, a Spanish Jesuit priest, correctly traced the source of the Blue Nile to a spring near Lake Tana. He was the first European to visit the lake, but at the time few people learned of his achievement. In 1770 the Scottish explorer James Bruce also visited the spring. He thought that he had found the source of the main Nile River as well as the Blue Nile. Bruce published a vivid account of his journeys, but many people in Britain doubted whether it was true. They were suspicious partly because he had reported his

John Speke rests and reads while African porters carry him during his 1862 expedition to the source of the Nile River.

and followed an Arab trade route inland. They suffered almost every kind of hardship Africa could inflict. On Feb. 13, 1858, they became the first Europeans to discover Lake Tanganyika. When they finally arrived on its shores, however, Burton was so ill from malaria he could not walk. Speke was virtually blind. Moreover, the explorers realized that the lake they had found was not the source of the Nile.

Ailing and disappointed, Burton wished to return and prepare a new expedition. Speke, who had recovered more quickly, pushed on alone to the northeast. On July 30, 1858, he discovered a large lake. He named it Lake Victoria, after the queen of Great Britain. Without exploring farther, Speke returned to England, sure that he had found the true source of the

Nile. He was correct; Lake Victoria is the river's chief source. Speke had not, however, seen the outlet. Burton was unwilling to accept that Lake Victoria was the source without further exploration. This disagreement led to a long and bitter public feud between the two former partners.

Speke was the first to return to London. There, the Royal Geographical Society honored him and gave him funds to return to Africa. Burton, largely ignored and denied financing for a new exploration of his own, felt betrayed.

Speke, Grant, and Baker. Speke returned to Africa in 1860. On this journey he was accompanied by his friend James A. Grant, a Scottish soldier and explorer. The explorers trekked from Zanzibar to the land west of Lake Victoria. They became the first Europeans to see the Virunga Mountains and the Kagera River. On July 28, 1862, Speke found the Nile's exit from Lake Victoria and named it Ripon Falls. (Grant was not with him at the time.) The party then tried to follow the river's course, but an outbreak of tribal warfare required them to change their route. The explorers continued northward to Gondokoro (in Sudan).

At Gondokoro, Speke and Grant met two other explorers—Samuel White Baker of England and Florence von Sass of Hungary. Baker had earlier purchased von Sass from a slave market. She helped him explore eastern Africa and later became his wife. In 1861 Baker and von Sass had explored the tributaries of the Nile around southern Ethiopia. They reached Gondokoro by February 1863. There, Speke and Grant told them of another lake that was rumored to lie west of Lake Victoria. This information helped the Baker party to locate Lake Albert in March 1864.

Meanwhile, Speke and Grant had returned home. Speke's claim to have found the Nile source was again challenged in England. A public debate was set up in which he and Burton would present their arguments. On

Two teams of explorers—John Speke and James A. Grant, and Samuel White Baker and Florence von Sass—meet at Gondokoro (now in Sudan).

the day of the debate, however, Speke was killed in a hunting accident. Burton and some others thought that he committed suicide.

Livingstone's quest for the Nile. In 1866 David Livingstone, then world famous, embarked on another expedition. He wanted to explore the central African watershed and find the ultimate sources of the Nile. As on previous journeys, he also sought to spread Christianity and expose the horrors of the slave trade.

The party struck out from Mikindani on the east coast. Raids by the Ngoni people soon compelled them to change routes. In September some of Livingstone's followers deserted him. To avoid punishment when they returned to Zanzibar, they said that Livingstone had been killed by the Ngoni. Although it was proved the following year that Livingstone was still alive, a touch of drama was added to the reports about his expedition.

Drama mounted as Livingstone traveled northward from the south end of Lake Nyasa. Early in 1867 a deserter carried off Livingstone's medical chest, but he pressed on into central Africa. He was the first European to reach Lake Mweru (Nov. 8, 1867) and Lake Bangweulu (July 18, 1868). Assisted by Arab traders, Livingstone reached Lake Tanganyika in February 1869. Despite illness, he continued onward. On March 29, 1871, he reached Nyangwe, on the Lualaba River, in what is now the Democratic Republic of the Congo. This point was farther inland than any European had ever reached from the east coast.

Livingstone returned to Ujiji on the eastern shore of Lake Tanganyika on Oct. 23, 1871. He was by then very ill. Search parties had been sent to look for him because he had not been heard from in several years. The Welsh American journalist Henry M. Stanley, a correspondent of the *New York Herald*, was finally successful. Leading a well-funded expedition, Stanley and his caravan forced their way through land disturbed by fighting. He headed for Ujiji, Livingstone's last known port of call.

There, in October or November, he found the old hero, ill and short of supplies. Stanley greeted him with the famous words, "Dr. Livingstone, I presume?" (The exact date of the encounter is unclear, as the two men wrote different dates in their journals.)

> "*As I advanced slowly towards him I noticed he was pale, looked wearied, had a grey beard. … I would have run to him, only I was a coward in the presence of such a mob—would have embraced him, only, he being an Englishman, I did not know how he would receive me; so I did what cowardice and false pride suggested was the best thing—walked, deliberately to him, took off my hat, and said: 'Dr Livingstone, I presume?'*"
>
> —Henry Morton Stanley, describing his famous meeting with David Livingstone, 1871

Stanley brought much-needed food and medicine, and Livingstone soon recovered. A cordial friendship sprang up between the two men. Together, they explored the northern reaches of Lake Tanganyika and began trekking eastward. However, Livingstone refused all of Stanley's pleas to leave Africa with him. On March 14, 1872, Stanley departed alone for England. There he published *How I Found Livingstone*, which immediately became a best seller.

Livingstone moved south again, obsessed by his quest for the Nile sources and his desire to destroy the slave trade. His illness finally overcame him. On May 1, 1873, at Chitambo (now in Zambia), Livingstone's servants found him dead.

Soon thereafter, the question of the source of the Nile was finally settled by the British general Charles George Gordon. Between 1874 and 1877, he and his officers followed the river and mapped part of it.

Cameron crosses the continent. Meanwhile, in 1873 the Royal Geographical Society had sent out an expedition to offer aid to Livingstone. It was led by

Henry Morton Stanley, raising his hat at left, meets David Livingstone in 1871 at Ujiji (now in Tanzania).
The Granger Collection, New York

Verney Lovett Cameron. He departed from Bangamoyo, on the coast opposite Zanzibar, in late March 1873. In October the expedition met Livingstone's servants bearing his dead body. They were carrying his embalmed body to the coast, where it could be sent to England for burial. The difficult journey ultimately took them nine months.

Cameron continued to Ujiji, where he recovered some of Livingstone's papers. He then set out to explore the southern half of Lake Tanganyika. He discovered that its outlet is the Lukuga River, a tributary of the Congo River. Cameron then traced the Congo-Zambezi watershed for hundreds of miles. He reached the west coast of Africa near Benguela, Angola, on Nov. 7, 1875. He was the first European to cross equatorial Africa from sea to sea.

Stanley explores central Africa. When Livingstone died, Stanley resolved to take up the exploration of Africa where he had left off. He secured financial backing from the *New York Herald* and the *Daily Telegraph* of London. On Nov. 12, 1874, he led a caravan out of Zanzibar to Lake Victoria. His visit to a local ruler led to the eventual establishment of a British protectorate in Uganda. On the shores of Lake Victoria, a number of the expedition's men died in skirmishes with suspicious tribespeople. These casualties gave rise in England to criticism of this new kind of traveler with his journalist's outlook and forceful methods.

Lordprice Collection/Alamy
Henry Morton Stanley

Stanley and his men next explored Lake Tanganyika. From there, they journeyed westward to the Lualaba River, in what is now the Democratic Republic of the Congo. This river proved to be the headstream of the Congo River. He proceeded to follow the Congo to its mouth. When he embarked on his long journey, however, he had no way of knowing what river it was or where it would lead him. Livingstone had also

The Scramble for Africa

One of the goals of 19th-century European explorers was to open up Africa to the outside world. Over the course of many long and perilous journeys, they revealed the geography of much of the interior. They also found routes to the continent's economic resources. The work of the explorers paved the way for European colonization. In the late 19th century the "golden age" of African exploration came to an end, as European powers began to take control of nearly the entire continent. The countries of Europe rushed to claim territory. This race to obtain colonies became known as the "scramble for Africa."

In the mid-19th century the European colonial presence was confined to the southern and northern ends of Africa. There were Dutch and British settlers in South Africa and British and French soldiers in northern Africa. Later in the century, advances in technology—along with the explorers' new maps—suddenly made it possible for Europeans to take over the enormous continent. New weapons such as machine guns gave European armies a great military advantage. The use of quinine to treat malaria was a key discovery. It allowed Europeans to travel through the tropics more safely. The development of the railroad and the steamship also aided European colonization.

Two events in 1869 focused European attention on the continent's economic and strategic importance. Diamonds were discovered in South Africa, and the Suez Canal was opened in Egypt. The canal was the gateway to India and East Asia. It was thus a vital strategic interest for the British Empire. Britain soon established control over Egypt and Sudan, along with much of southern Africa. Parts of eastern and western Africa also became part of the vast British Empire. France began to rule a large territory in western and northern Africa. Germany claimed land in the southwest and east. Belgium, Italy, Portugal, and Spain also rushed to gain territory. The increasing number of participants led to heightened rivalry and sped up the race for conquest. By 1900 the map of Africa looked like a huge jigsaw puzzle. The continent was almost completely divided into separate territories controlled by European countries.

discovered the Lualaba River. Noting that the river flowed northward, he had hoped that it might be the headwaters of the Nile. But as Stanley journeyed downstream, the river turned westward. He decided, as Livingstone himself had suspected, that it might be the Congo River. The Congo's mouth on the west coast was already known. After a difficult journey of some 2,000 miles (3,200 kilometers), Stanley and his men reached the Atlantic Ocean on Aug. 12, 1877. He described his epic journey in *Through the Dark Continent* (1878).

Stanley wanted to open up the Congo region for colonization. Failing to enlist British support, he entered the service of the king of Belgium, Leopold II. From 1879 to 1884 Stanley explored the Congo basin for the king. His work led to the creation of the Congo Free State, which was ruled with great brutality by King Leopold.

Within a few years several European countries were competing with each other to found African colonies. They were wildly successful; nearly the entire map of Africa was carved up into European territories.

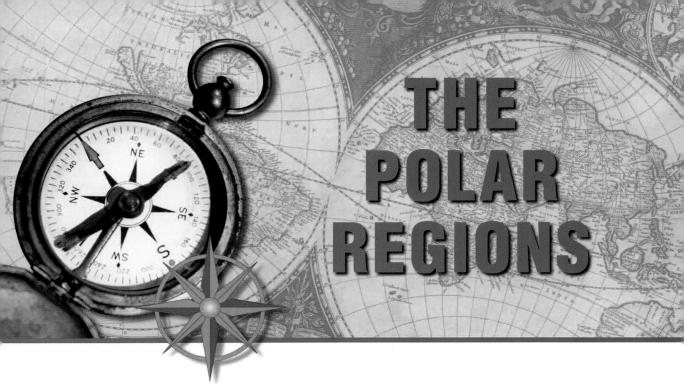

THE POLAR REGIONS

For hundreds of years the icy areas at each end of the globe have challenged explorers. Many brave people have risked their lives and some have lost them investigating the frigid regions of the Arctic and the Antarctic. Some of the early explorers were seeking short sailing routes from Europe. Others were searching for good sealing and whaling grounds. Still others wanted to reveal the geography of the polar regions and to study them scientifically. Many were driven by the explorer's longing to make the first footprints in an unknown land. For many years reaching the North Pole, and then the South Pole, was the supreme challenge to daring explorers.

Modern investigators are more likely to be scientists than sailors. They are seeking for the answers, which lie at the ends of the Earth, to questions about the world's climate, geology, and plant and animal life.

The Arctic regions are the northernmost parts of the world. They encompass the Arctic Ocean as well as Greenland and many other northern islands. Also included is the far northern rim of mainland Canada; Alaska, U.S.; Siberia, Russia; and part of Europe. In much of the Arctic the ground is frozen solid permanently. An imaginary line known as the Arctic Circle is drawn on maps at latitude 66°30′ N. North of this line there is at least one day each year when the Sun does not set and at least one day when it does not rise. These periods of continuous day or night are longer in the regions farther north. In winter the North Pole receives no direct sunlight for six months. The Arctic regions are only sparsely populated.

Antarctica, on the other hand, has no permanent population. A vast ice sheet covers nearly the entire continent. Surrounding Antarctica are ice-choked, stormy seas—the Southern Ocean, or the southernmost parts of the Atlantic, Pacific, and Indian oceans. The South Pole is located in Antarctica's interior, near the center of the continent. Most of the continent lies south of the Antarctic Circle and so experiences a period each year when the Sun never rises and one when the Sun never sets. Like the North Pole, the South Pole is plunged into darkness for six months of each year.

HARDSHIPS OF POLAR EXPLORATION

The remoteness and harsh climate of the polar regions has made them very difficult and expensive to explore. More than half of the Arctic Ocean is covered with a layer of ice all the time. Much of it stays in place as a jumbled mass called pack ice. The waters around Antarctica are likewise frozen. Sea ice up to 10 feet (3 meters) thick forms outward from Antarctica every winter, making a belt 300 to 1,000 miles (500 to 1,600 kilometers) wide. Even in summer the belt of sea ice is 100 to 500 miles (160 to 800 kilometers) wide in most places. Aircraft and icebreakers (ships that are specially equipped to break the sea ice) now make access to the polar regions relatively easy, though still not without hazard in stormy conditions.

Before the 1920s, explorers could approach these frozen regions only by ship. Metal articles may become brittle and break if placed under strain in extreme cold. For this reason early polar explorers usually used wooden ships, especially if the ship might be locked in ice. Large sheets of floating ice, called floes, constantly threatened to crush ships. After landing, the explorers continued, if possible, on foot, often wearing snowshoes or sometimes skis. Their provisions were carried on sledges hauled by dogs, ponies, or often the explorers themselves. They took great risks. Huge crevasses open in the ice, and these cracks can swallow sledges, animals, and people.

Extreme Cold and Hunger

In winter the polar regions can be extremely cold, though temperatures vary greatly from place to place. The coldest part of the Arctic lies in Siberia, where the temperature can reach −90° F (−68° C) in January. Antarctica is still colder. The world's record low temperature of −128.6° F (−89.2° C) was recorded there. The mean annual temperature of the Antarctic interior is only −70° F (−57° C).

The cold is severe enough to kill a person quickly who becomes stranded away from shelter. Hypothermia, or an abnormally low body temperature, is the greatest killer. Exposed skin can also freeze in minutes. The freezing of living tissue is known as frostbite. The affected parts, often the toes, fingers, ears, or tips of the nose, may need to be amputated.

Proper clothes and food can help defeat cold. Some early explorers adopted the fur clothing of the Inuit (Eskimos), who live in Arctic lands. As well as being warm, leather and fur made the best windbreaks. Other early explorers wore layers of clothing of cotton, wool, and other natural fabrics. Today, polar researchers rely on synthetic fabrics that are waterproof and windproof. The Antarctic coasts are among the windiest places on Earth, and parts of the Arctic also have very strong, persistent winds. People have to find shelter or perish.

Early polar explorers also risked starvation and scurvy, a serious disease that is now known to be caused by a lack of vitamin C in one's diet. Before about the 1930s, expeditions did not allow sufficient food rations for the explorers. At the time, it was not known that humans need greater than normal amounts of calories to withstand the extreme cold and to work harder (such as by hauling a sledge).

Food sources are quite scarce in most polar areas, especially during the long winters. Fresh fruits and vegetables can prevent scurvy, but in most polar lands there is little or no vegetation. Explorers had to bring and transport large amounts of preserved food. Biscuits and pemmican—dried meat pounded with fat—became staples. The explorers also hunted animals. However, Antarctica lacks land animals besides insects. When they could, explorers in the southern polar regions killed and ate marine animals such as seals and penguins. Explorers who ate fresh meat that was raw or lightly cooked were much less likely to get scurvy. (It is now known that seal and other fresh meat contains vitamin C, though cooking can destroy the vitamin.)

The Use of Airplanes

Modern polar explorations make extensive use of satellite data and airplanes, as well as snowmobiles and other motorized vehicles. Airplanes are used to carry supplies and personnel into and out of hard-to-reach areas. They also allow explorers to survey and photograph vast areas of land and sea quickly from

Kyodo/Landov

A Japanese icebreaker plows through the frozen waters surrounding Antarctica.

above. Instruments on board the plane can determine what kind of rocks lie beneath the snow and ice and can measure the depth of glaciers. Unmanned aircraft, controlled remotely and equipped with scientific instruments, are often used as a safer alternative to manned craft.

Nevertheless, many problems still arise in providing equipment for polar exploration. Fuel and lubricants for motors must be usable at extremely low temperatures. When airplanes are grounded, the motors are covered with tenting and kept heated so that they can be started easily. Ice crystals form in gas lines. Moisture freezes on insulators so that the base cannot contact the plane in flight. Oil freezes. Tires turn "square" from being parked on ice. Grease freezes, and landing gear wheels skid instead of roll. Storms are severe.

The worst condition of polar flying is the "white out," when winds blow snow through the air, making visibility extremely poor. With only white to be seen in every direction, it can be difficult to tell which direction is up. Pilots have said that it is like "flying in a bowl of milk."

THE ARCTIC

Probably the first explorer to approach the Arctic regions was Pytheas, a Greek from what is now France (*see* Eurasia, "Shores of the Mediterranean and the Atlantic"). In about 300 BC he sailed through the Mediterranean Sea and around Great Britain. He continued northward, reaching a place that he called Thule. This place may have been Iceland or islands off the coast of Norway. For centuries, the idea of Thule— shrouded in fog and believed to be the end of the Earth—caught the imagination of many.

Irish monks visited Iceland in the 8th and 9th centuries. Vikings from Norway settled the island late in the 9th century. Over the course of the next four

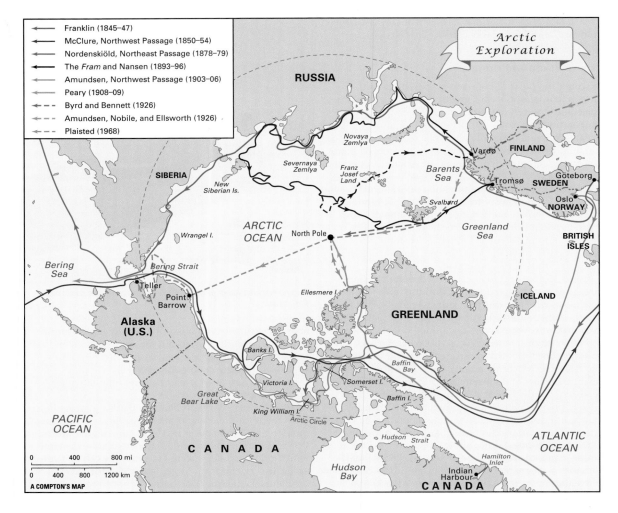

Arctic Exploration

Franklin (1845–47)
McClure, Northwest Passage (1850–54)
Nordenskiöld, Northeast Passage (1878–79)
The *Fram* and Nansen (1893–96)
Amundsen, Northwest Passage (1903–06)
Peary (1908–09)
Byrd and Bennett (1926)
Amundsen, Nobile, and Ellsworth (1926)
Plaisted (1968)

A COMPTON'S MAP

centuries, these hardy sailors explored several northern places. They visited Greenland and founded two settlements on the southwest coast. They also reached the coast of North America (*see* The Americas, "Early European Explorers"). The Vikings established trade routes to the White Sea, an extension of the Arctic Ocean along the shores of northwestern Russia. They probably also reached the Arctic islands of Svalbard and Novaya Zemlya. However, the Vikings left scant records of their voyages, and many of the places they visited had to be rediscovered by others.

The Northeast Passage

The English and the Dutch. After the decline of the Vikings, there was a lull in Arctic exploration. In the early 16th century the English and the Dutch began actively exploring the northern waters. Their motive was to establish direct trade with East Asia, which would be very profitable. Portugal and Spain claimed exclusive control of the known sea routes from western Europe to Asia. These long, arduous sea routes involved first sailing far to the south, and the overland routes to Asia

were even more difficult. The English and the Dutch wanted to find a shorter, northern sea route to Asia. Their merchants tried to find both a Northeast Passage, around northern Russia in Asia, and a Northwest Passage, around northern North America. Their attempts led to much Arctic exploration.

In 1553 the English sent three ships to the northeast under the command of Hugh Willoughby. The chief pilot was Richard Chancellor, whose ship became separated from the others in a gale. The other two ships wintered in a harbor on the Kola Peninsula, in Russia's far north. Willoughby and all his men died there. Meanwhile, Chancellor continued on, reaching what is now Arkhangelsk, Russia. From there, he made an overland journey to Moscow before returning home to England. It is interesting to note that the waters that Willoughby and Chancellor explored were already well known to Russians. Russian sailors were using the route around North Cape, Norway, to western Europe as early as 1496.

In Moscow, Chancellor had met with the Russian tsar and negotiated favorable conditions for English trade with Russia. Soon after, English merchants formed the

Willem Barents and his men contend with polar bears and rugged ice floes in the Arctic.
The Granger Collection, New York

Muscovy Company. The lucrative trade that developed with Russia distracted the English from the Northeast Passage. Nevertheless, they sent out two more expeditions in the 1500s. Both were stopped by ice and fog, but one succeeded in entering the Kara Sea, off the western part of Siberia.

In the meantime, the Dutch had taken up the search. The Dutch navigator Willem Barents became one of the most important early Arctic explorers. In 1594 he discovered Novaya Zemlya and sailed to its northern tip. As Barents coasted northward, he saw wrecked ships and grave markers at many points along the shore, indicating that Russians had been there before him. He led another expedition the following year but did not reach much farther.

Barents was more successful in 1596. Heading north from Norway, he discovered Bear Island and Svalbard, which he mistook for Greenland. He then headed east and rounded the north end of Novaya Zemlya. He and his men were forced to winter on the island's northeast coast. They built a house of driftwood and passed the season with remarkable success; only two men died of scurvy. They thus became the first Europeans known to have wintered successfully in the Arctic. However, their ship was hopelessly damaged. In the spring they escaped across the open Barents Sea in two small boats. Barents died on the journey.

In 1605–07 the Englishman Henry Hudson sailed in the service of the Dutch East India Company. He found that ice blocked the way both east and west of Svalbard. He then sailed to North America in search of the Northwest Passage.

The Russians. In the 17th century the Russians tried to establish a commercial sea route around the Taymyr Peninsula, in Siberia. Farther east, they explored the entire Siberian coast from the mouth of the Olenek River to the mouth of the Kolyma River. In 1648 Semyon Dezhnyov sailed east from the mouth of the Kolyma. He became the first European to sail through the Bering Strait between Russia and Alaska. He thus proved that Asia and North America are separated. His report lay buried in a Russian archive for about a century, however, so his discovery went unnoticed.

Not knowing of Dezhnyov's discovery, Tsar Peter the Great sent out an expedition in the 1720s to determine the geography of the Bering Strait area. He chose Vitus Bering, a Danish officer in the Russian navy, to lead the expedition. Bering put to sea from the east coast of Kamchatka, in far-eastern Russia, in 1728. He pushed well north through the Bering Strait and into the Chukchi Sea, part of the Arctic Ocean. He had not seen the Alaskan coast, however, so he could not know for sure whether he had actually entered the Arctic Ocean. Four years later, Ivan Fyodorov and Mikhail Gvozdev became the first Europeans to see any part of Alaska.

Vitus Bering's ships are wrecked upon the Aleutian Islands in 1741.

North Wind Picture Archives/Alamy

The Russian Admiralty next mounted an operation that has had no equal in the history of polar exploration: the Great Northern Expedition of 1733–43. Bering led the undertaking, which consisted of seven detachments totaling 977 men. Each was responsible for exploring different sections of the Arctic or Pacific coast. The expedition's vessels were repeatedly blocked by ice and were forced to winter in the Arctic or to return to base and try again the following year. Almost all the exploring parties endured extreme hardships. There were numerous deaths from scurvy, including Bering's. However, the explorers charted the entire Arctic coast from Arkhangelsk to Cape Bolshoy Baranov, off the East Siberian Sea.

Conquest. Finally, in 1878–79 the Northeast Passage was conquered by a Swedish expedition. It was led by Adolf Erik, Baron Nordenskiöld, aboard the steam vessel *Vega*. He left from Tromsø, Norway, on July 21, 1878. From the end of September until July 18, 1879, the *Vega* was frozen in the ice near the Bering Strait. Resuming its course, the *Vega* reached Port Clarence, Alaska, on July 22. It returned to Europe by way of China, Sri Lanka, and the Suez Canal.

The first accident-free, one-season passage of the Northeast Passage was made from west to east by the Russian icebreaker *Fedor Litke* in 1934. In the following season it escorted the first freighters through the passage, in the opposite direction. Since then, hundreds of vessels have completed the passage in both directions. Since the late 1960s icebreakers have kept the passage open in the summer months.

The Northwest Passage

As with the Northeast Passage, knowledge of the Northwest Passage came slowly, over hundreds of years. The search for the Northwest Passage began with the European discovery of America (*see* The Americas, "France, England, and Holland in the Northeast"). The voyages of Jacques Cartier and his successors to the St. Lawrence River of North America were undertaken with the aim of finding the passage. So too were the expeditions of John Cabot and the brothers Gaspar and Miguel Corte-Real to Newfoundland and Labrador (now in Canada).

Early expeditions. The first such voyage to enter the Arctic, however, was that of the English navigator Martin Frobisher in 1576. He made his North American landfall on the southeast coast of Baffin Island (now part of Nunavut, Canada). He then sailed about 60 miles (100 kilometers) up what is now named Frobisher Bay. He returned home mistakenly believing that he had found gold. He made two more voyages to establish a gold mine, but neither was successful.

Many explorers died while searching for the Northwest Passage. Humphrey Gilbert, whose writing about the passage inspired many others to take up the search, drowned on his own attempt in 1583 (*see* The Americas, "England Tries to Set up Colonies").

Next to seek the passage was another Englishman, John Davis, in three voyages in 1585–87. Davis was one of the finest of the early seamen and something of a

scientist as well. He rediscovered Greenland, which had been lost to Europeans since the decline of its Viking settlements. He also traced the coasts of Baffin Island and Labrador from Cape Dyer south and explored Cumberland Sound.

In 1602 George Weymouth sailed a short way into Hudson Strait, between Baffin Island and mainland Canada. In 1610 Henry Hudson sailed the *Discovery* into what is now named Hudson Bay. After a mutiny, Hudson and some of his men were set adrift in a small boat to die. They were never heard from again. (*See also* The Americas, "Hudson Seeks a Passage to Asia.")

In 1616 William Baffin, the outstanding navigator of his day, explored what is now named Baffin Bay, between Baffin Island and Greenland. He discovered the three sounds that lead out of Baffin Bay—Smith, Jones, and Lancaster. However, he mistakenly thought that they were bays and that there was no passage out of Baffin Bay. Further, his map was never published. In time the very existence of Baffin Bay came to be doubted. The significance of Baffin's exploration was not recognized for 200 years; in fact, the Northwest Passage runs through Lancaster Sound.

19th century. The British government sent a series of large naval expeditions to search for the Northwest Passage in the 19th century. The first, under Captain John Ross in 1818, retraced almost exactly Baffin's journey of two centuries earlier. It repeated his error of mistaking the sounds for bays. Second in command to Ross was William Parry. He was not convinced that Baffin Bay had no outlet. In 1819–20 he sailed through Lancaster Sound to Melville Island, where he wintered. He tried two routes to the Arctic, but his way was barred by ice.

On a privately financed venture in 1829–33, John Ross sailed down Prince Regent Inlet, between Baffin and Somerset islands, into the Gulf of Boothia. The expedition added greatly to the extent of mapped territory. Ross's nephew, James Clark Ross, also located the north magnetic pole. After three winters trapped in the ice, however, the explorers had to abandon their ship. They retreated by sledge and boat, spending a

John Ross
© Photos.com/Thinkstock

On an ill-fated Arctic expedition in search of the Northwest Passage, John Franklin and many of his men die by their boat.
The Granger Collection, New York

fourth winter on the way before being picked up by a whaler.

The British were also attacking the problem from the west by both sea and land. Admiral John Franklin led expeditions in 1819–22 and 1825–27. He surveyed the coast from about 200 miles (320 kilometers) east of Canada's Coppermine River, to Cape Beechey, Alaska. He explored overland and by boat from wintering bases in the Mackenzie River basin. Frederick W. Beechey reached Point Barrow, the northernmost point of Alaska, from the west in 1825–26.

By the mid-19th century, most of the continental coastline and a considerable amount of the Canadian Arctic Archipelago had been charted. Still the Northwest Passage remained elusive. The British government sent out one last expedition. This was the famous and tragic last voyage of John Franklin. He sailed from England on May 19, 1845, with two ships, the *Erebus* and the *Terror*, which carried 128 men. They were last seen by British whalers north of Baffin Island at the entrance to Lancaster Sound in late July. Franklin and his men were never heard from again.

The loss of this admiral and famous Arctic explorer produced a reaction of profound shock. Over the course of 12 years, numerous expeditions searched for Franklin and his men. In 1850 as many as 14 ships and a land expedition were in the area searching for Franklin at the same time. The fate of the expedition was finally determined by a search mission sent by Franklin's wife, Lady Jane Franklin. This mission was led by Capt. Francis McClintock. In 1859 he reached King William Island, southwest of Lancaster Sound. The search mission found skeletons of the vessels' crews and a written account of the expedition through April 25, 1848.

Franklin and his men had wintered at Beechey Island at the west end of Lancaster Sound. They later found a passage from Peel Sound to Victoria Strait. In September 1846 the ships became trapped in the ice near King William Island. Franklin and 23 others died there. In April 1848 the 105 survivors finally abandoned the ships and set out on foot on the Canadian mainland. They apparently resorted to cannibalism along the way, but all of them died anyway. An old Inuit woman told McClintock of how the starving men fell down and died as they walked. Autopsies were conducted on the preserved bodies of several crew members. They suggested that the men may have gotten lead poisoning from eating faultily canned food. This may have contributed to the mental and physical decline of the expedition.

The many missions that searched for Franklin contributed tremendously to geographic knowledge. One of them found the elusive Northwest Passage. A search party led by Capt. Richard Collinson departed in 1850 with two ships. Collinson commanded one ship, and Robert McClure the other. After the ships became separated in the Pacific, Collinson and his men spent three years on Victoria Island. Meanwhile, McClure, in the *Investigator*, entered the Bering Strait. Heading eastward north of Alaska, he found two entrances to the Northwest Passage around Banks Island (now part of

Robert McClure's ship the Investigator *becomes trapped in the ice north of Banks Island.*

North Wind Picture Archives/Alamy

Canada's Northwest Territories). The *Investigator* became trapped in the ice just north of Banks Island. Two years later the explorers abandoned the ship. McClure and his men were rescued by another expedition and returned home in 1854 by the eastern route. McClure had thus discovered the Northwest Passage, though he had traveled through it in more than one ship and partly on foot.

20th century. The Northwest Passage was at last found to be a reality. The great Norwegian explorer Roald Amundsen became the first person to sail through the entire passage. In 1903 he sailed down Peel Sound in his tiny yacht *Gjöa* and passed around the east side of King William Island. He spent two winters there, making scientific observations. He spent another winter west of the Mackenzie River. In 1906 he passed through the Bering Strait, becoming the first person to navigate the Northwest Passage.

The first single-season transit of the passage was achieved by Henry A. Larsen of the Royal Canadian Mounted Police. He made it through in 1944 in a schooner. In 1969 the *Manhattan*, a large American ship, was sent to assess the commercial feasibility of the passage. It smashed through some 650 miles (1,050 kilometers) of ice between Baffin Bay and Point Barrow, Alaska. Navigating the Northwest Passage ultimately proved to be impractical. It has not been used as a regular commercial route.

Whalers and Fur Traders

Many advances in geographic knowledge came about because of the whale fisheries that flourished in the Arctic for three centuries. By far the most famous of the whalers were the William Scoresbys, father and son. Scoresby Sr. was a first-rate navigator. He invented the crow's nest and other aids to ice navigation and was the first to suggest the use of sledges to reach the pole. The

scientific age of polar exploration began with his son, who wrote two important books on the Arctic. In 1806 the Scoresbys reached latitude 81°12′ N., north of Spitsbergen, in the Svalbard archipelago. At the time, this was a record for the northernmost point reached.

Just as whaling led to improved knowledge of the coastlines, the fur trade helped to open the interiors of Arctic lands. The Hudson's Bay Company was formed in 1670. It established a fur-trading post at the foot of James Bay. Soon other company posts were set up on the west side of the bay, and these served as bases for further exploration. Samuel Hearne was sent out in 1770 with a band of Indians to look for a source of copper. They made a remarkable journey to the mouth of the Coppermine River, returning by way of Great Slave Lake. They walked some 5,000 miles (8,000 kilometers). In 1789 Alexander Mackenzie of the rival North West Company of Montreal traveled by canoe from Lake Athabasca down the Mackenzie River to the Arctic Ocean.

By the time the two companies merged in 1821, there were trading posts on Great Slave Lake and down the Mackenzie River to Fort Good Hope. These posts made possible the overland expeditions of Franklin and his successors, among whom were many Hudson's Bay Company men.

Pushing westward into Alaska, the Hudson's Bay Company met Russian traders working from the west coast. The Russians had established settlements in Alaska toward the end of the 18th century and carried out a vigorous trade there.

Quest for the North Pole

The North Pole did not become in itself a goal of exploration until fairly late. The few early expeditions that tried to reach the pole were looking for a polar route to Asia rather than for the pole itself. In 1607

Alexander Mackenzie, second from left, views the Arctic Ocean for the first time, in 1789.

The Granger Collection, New York

Henry Hudson tried to discover a passage "by the North Pole to Japan and China." Like many others, he wrongly believed that he would find an ice-free sea around the North Pole. This belief would persist for more than two hundred years.

After Hudson's attempt, more than 150 years elapsed before the next one. In 1764 the Russian Admiralty sent an expedition to establish an advance base in Svalbard. It was led by Vasily Yakovlevich Chichagov. With three ships, he pushed north to 80°26′ N. before being forced by ice to retreat. Seven years later Capt. John Constantine Phipps of Britain's Royal Navy, tried to reach the pole from the same starting point but fared no better. In 1818 David Buchan and John Franklin were no more successful.

All these attempts had been made in the area between Greenland and Svalbard. This area was not the accessible route to the Arctic Ocean that it appeared to be, owing to the strong southerly drift of the ice. The search for Franklin opened a new route, up the west coast of Greenland. In 1860 the American physician Isaac Israel Hayes attempted to reach the pole by this route in the schooner *United States*. Hayes was a firm believer that the polar sea was ice-free. Ironically, he met with unusually heavy ice conditions and got only as far as the coast of Smith Sound.

In 1871 Charles Francis Hall, another American, with more luck and a better ship, reached 82°11′ N. He charted both sides of the Robeson Channel to its entrance to the Lincoln Sea. Hall himself died during the winter. His ship, the *Polaris*, was caught in the ice on the voyage south and drifted to Smith Sound, where it was almost wrecked.

In 1875–76 a British expedition under Capt. George Strong Nares reached the Lincoln Sea by ship. The expedition's sledge parties traced part of the coasts of Greenland and Ellesmere Island, off Greenland's northwest coast. One sledge party, under Albert Hastings Markham, reached 83°20′ N., setting a new record.

Nansen and the *Fram*. An entirely new approach was tried in 1879 by a U.S. expedition led by George Washington De Long. In the belief that Wrangel Island was a large landmass, he hoped to sail north along its coast and then sledge to the pole. However, his ship, the *Jeannette*, was caught in the pack ice. The ship drifted for 22 months, passing north of Wrangel Island and revealing its limited extent. In June 1881 the *Jeannette* was crushed by ice and sank near the New Siberian Islands. Enduring extreme hardships, the crew traveled by boat and sledge to the Lena River delta. De Long and many of the others died of starvation and exposure to the severe weather.

Wreckage from the *Jeannette* was later found on the southwest coast of Greenland. It had apparently drifted in the ice right across the Arctic Ocean. The Norwegian explorer Fridtjof Nansen conceived the daring idea that a ship might be made to do the same. Such a trip would provide a base for scientific investigation of the Arctic Ocean and also be a means of reaching the pole. Nansen had a ship, the *Fram* (Forward), built according to his

Fridtjof Nansen, 1896

design. It was shaped so that it would be lifted but not crushed when caught by the ice.

" Faster and faster I go flying on, while the ice gets more and more difficult. "

—Fridtjof Nansen, describing his 1888 trip across Greenland on skies

Nansen left Norway in the *Fram* on June 24, 1893, with 12 other men. Near the place where the *Jeannette* sank, they intentionally drove the *Fram* into the pack ice and allowed it to freeze in. The ship then began a slow drift that lasted almost three years. It ended with the safe release of the vessel north of Svalbard in 1896.

The expedition collected a large amount of scientific data, including measurements of the depths of the sea. In accord with popular opinion, Nansen expected to find only shallow water in the north polar region. However, his measurements gave depths ranging from about 11,000 to 13,000 feet (3,300 to 4,000 meters), which showed that there was a deep basin under at least part of the north polar sea. These deep soundings mark the true discovery of the Arctic Ocean.

Nansen himself left the *Fram* in 1895 with one companion, Hjalmar Johansen, in an attempt to ski to the pole. (Nansen had earlier skied across Greenland, becoming the first person to cross its ice fields.)

Dogsleds carried their supplies and kayaks. The explorers started from 84° N. and set a new record of reaching 86°13′ N. However, the ice conditions compelled them to turn back. The two men wintered on one of the islands of Franz Josef Land (now in Russia). There they built a hut of stone and covered it with a roof of walrus hides. They lived mainly on polar bear and walrus meat, using the blubber as fuel.

By a strange and lucky coincidence, the pair met the British explorer Frederick Jackson in the spring. Jackson had been investigating Franz Josef Land as a possible stepping-stone to the pole. Nansen and Johansen returned home with Jackson in his ship. Nansen went on to become a statesman and humanitarian; he won the Nobel peace prize in 1922.

The rival claims of Peary and Cook. Up to that time, the desire to reach the North Pole had been coupled with that of mapping unexplored territory and collecting scientific data. After the *Fram* expedition there was no longer any doubt that the central part of the polar basin was an ice-covered sea. There were no major land discoveries left to be made.

The quest for the pole then degenerated into something like an international sporting event. Many teams raced to be the first to arrive. Several expeditions tried to reach the pole from Franz Josef Land. An Italian expedition led by the duke d′Abruzzi set a new record in 1900, when Capt. Umberto Cagni reached 86°34′ N.

The American explorer Robert E. Peary started working toward his polar expeditions in two long journeys across northern Greenland in 1891–92 and

Matthew Henson

The African American explorer Matthew Henson accompanied Robert E. Peary on most of his Arctic expeditions. In 1909 Henson, Peary, and a few others reached what they believed was the North Pole. Whether the spot was actually the pole or some miles short is a matter of controversy. If they did reach the North Pole, they were the first people to do so.

Henson was born on Aug. 8, 1866, in Charles county, Md. Orphaned as a youth, he went to sea at the age of 12 as a cabin boy on the sailing ship *Katie Hines*. Later, while working in a store in Washington, D.C., he met Peary. Peary hired him as a valet for his 1888 expedition to Nicaragua.

Impressed with Henson′s abilities and resourcefulness, Peary employed him as an attendant on his seven expeditions to the Arctic, from 1891 to 1909. On these voyages, Henson learned the language of the Inuit. The kinship that Henson established with the Inuit and his skill at handling dog sledges made him indispensable to Peary. On April 6, 1909, Peary, Henson, and four Inuit traveled to what Peary thought was the North Pole. Henson planted the American flag that marked the spot.

Henson′s account of the journey, *A Negro Explorer at the North Pole*, appeared in 1912. The following year, by order of U.S. President William Howard Taft, Henson was appointed a clerk in the U.S. Customs House in New York City. He held this post until his retirement in 1936.

When the 1909 Peary expedition first returned home, Henson′s accomplishments were mostly overlooked. This was largely due to racial prejudice. Henson later gained more recognition for his achievements. In 1944 he received the Congressional medal awarded to all members of the Peary expedition. Henson died on March 9, 1955, in New York City. In 1988 the U.S. government honored him by reburying him next to Peary at Arlington National Cemetery, in Virginia.

1893–95. In these early Arctic travels, Peary found evidence that Greenland is an island. He also studied an isolated Inuit tribe who helped him greatly on later expeditions.

"Remember, Mother, I must have fame, and I cannot reconcile myself to years of commonplace drudgery and a name late in life ... I want my fame now."

—Robert E. Peary, in a letter to his mother

Peary then made three attempts to reach the North Pole. In 1898–1902 he sledged around the north coast of Greenland and pushed north onto the pack ice from Ellesmere Island, reaching 84°17′ N. On this journey, he lost most of his toes to frostbite.

On a second attempt to reach the pole, Peary sailed the *Roosevelt* to Ellesmere Island in 1905. The sledging season was unsuccessful, however, owing to adverse weather and ice conditions. Although his party failed to reach the pole, they sledged to 87°06′ N., setting a new record.

Peary sailed to Ellesmere Island on July 6, 1908, for his third attempt. Early the following March he set off from Cape Columbia, at the northern edge of Ellesmere, onto the polar pack ice. As in his other expeditions, the

Robert E. Peary wears polar expedition gear aboard his ship the Roosevelt. *For his Arctic explorations, he adopted the warm fur clothing of the Inuit.*

Library of Congress, Washington, D.C.

Matthew Henson, right, poses on a sledge that he, Robert Peary, and four Inuit took on the last leg on their quest for the North Pole. With Henson are other members of the Peary expedition—from left to right, Donald Baxter MacMillan, George Borup, and Thomas Gushue.

Libary of Congress, Washington, D.C. (neg. no. LC-USZ62-68223)

explorers progressed in relays, with advance support parties preparing the trail, constructing shelters, and depositing supplies. These support parties consisted of 24 men, 19 sledges, and 133 dogs. The expedition included many Inuit, and Peary and the other explorers adopted Inuit customs to help them survive. They dressed in warm furs, slept in igloos, and killed and ate walrus and seals.

For the last stage of the trek, Peary sent everyone back except his longtime associate Matthew Henson and four Inuit: Egingwah, Seeglo, Ootah, and Ooqueah. The six men made a dash for the pole. They purportedly reached the North Pole on April 6, 1909.

Peary returned to civilization only to discover that Dr. Frederick A. Cook was claiming to have reached the North Pole first. A former colleague, Cook had accompanied Peary on his first expedition to Greenland. Cook had spent 1907–09 in the Arctic. He claimed that on April 21, 1908, he had reached the North Pole with two Inuit. The rival claims of Peary and Cook generated considerable controversy. Cook's claim was later discredited. His photos were apparently faked, and his Inuit companions said that he had stopped hundreds of miles south of the pole.

For many years afterward, Peary was widely considered to have been the first person to reach the North Pole. In the 1980s, however, doubts arose as to whether he had actually reached his goal. His expedition diary and newly released documents were examined. They suggested that he had made navigational mistakes and record-keeping errors. Peary may actually have advanced only to a point 30–60 miles (50–100 kilometers) short of the pole, an impressive achievement in any case. The truth remains uncertain.

Flying to the Pole. The first expedition that definitely reached the North Pole was an aerial one. It flew over the pole in 1926. The first attempt to fly to the pole had been made in 1897. In that year the Swedish scientist Salomon August Andrée and two companions left Spitsbergen in a balloon. They never returned.

In 1925 the Norwegian explorer Roald Amundsen and the American explorer Lincoln Ellsworth made an attempt in seaplanes. They reached as far as 87°44′ N. They had to make an emergency landing without radio and were given up for lost. With 30 days of grim effort, however, they carved out a takeoff field on the polar ice pack. They then flew safely to Svalbard.

On May 9, 1926, the U.S. naval officer Richard E. Byrd and the American pilot Floyd Bennett flew north from Svalbard. They claimed to have reached the North Pole. After the flight, the two became national heroes and were awarded the U.S. Congressional Medal of Honor. In the 1990s, however, Byrd's diary was discovered, and

The airship **Norge** *floats above Spitsbergen in 1926 before Roald Amundsen's expedition to the North Pole. Amundsen, Umberto Nobile (the pilot and designer of the airship), and Lincoln Ellsworth would fly from Spitsbergen to Alaska, becoming the first people to definitely reach the North Pole.*

AP

their claim was cast into serious doubt. The diary suggests that the airplane was still about 150 miles (240 kilometers) short of the North Pole when Byrd decided to turn back because the plane had an oil leak.

Three days after Byrd and Bennett's supposed success, three other explorers flew to the pole. On May 12, 1926, Amundsen, Ellsworth, and the Italian aeronautical engineer Umberto Nobile set off from Svalbard. They flew across the North Pole to Alaska in the *Norge*, a semirigid airship. They are now recognized as the first explorers to have definitely reached the pole. In 1928 Nobile tried to make the flight again, but after reaching the pole, his airship crashed near Svalbard. While flying to rescue Nobile, Amundsen was killed; Nobile was later saved by another plane.

The first landing made by an aircraft at (or near) the North Pole was by the Soviet pilot Mikhail Vasilevich Vodopyanov in 1937. He deposited Soviet scientists so that they could establish the first floating scientific station on an ice floe. It was the first of several such floating Soviet research stations.

Other "firsts." The first surface expedition confirmed as having reached the North Pole was an American effort led by Ralph Plaisted. The explorers reached the pole from northern Ellesmere Island by snowmobile in 1968.

The following year the British Transarctic Expedition became the first to reach the pole by dogsled. It was

Wally Herbert photographed his dogsled team trekking across Antarctica in the early 1960s. Herbert later made a surface crossing of the frozen Arctic Ocean, becoming the first person known for certain to have reached the North Pole by foot.

Robert Harding Picture Library/Alamy

Ann Bancroft

The first woman to reach the North Pole by land was the American explorer Ann Bancroft. She also reached the South Pole and skied across Antarctica.

Bancroft was born on Sept. 29, 1955, in St. Paul, Minn. She grew up in rural Minnesota in what she described as a family of risk takers. Although she struggled with a learning disability, she graduated from St. Paul Academy. She became a gym teacher, coach, and wilderness instructor in the Saint Paul area.

When an opportunity arose to participate in the 1986 Steger International North Pole Expedition, Bancroft resigned her teaching position. After 56 days she and five other team members arrived at the North Pole by dogsled without benefit of resupply. She thus became the first woman to reach the North Pole by sled and on foot. (Louise Boyd was the first woman to fly across the North Pole, in 1955.) In 1992 Bancroft became the first woman to ski across Greenland.

Bancroft then turned to Antarctic exploration. In 1992–93 she led three other women on the American Women's Expedition to the South Pole. They traveled for 67 days across 660 miles (1,060 kilometers), becoming the first women's team to reach the South Pole on skis. In 2001 Bancroft and the Norwegian explorer Liv Arnesen became the first women to cross Antarctica on foot. They were both in their mid-40s. On their 94-day trek across the continent, the pair skied more than 1,700 miles (2,750 kilometers). Bancroft has received many honors, including induction into the U.S. National Women's Hall of Fame.

led by Wally Herbert. He left Point Barrow, Alaska, in February 1968 with three colleagues, four sleds, and 40 dogs. They reached the pole in April of the following year and continued on to Spitsbergen. By that time, they had walked more than 3,600 miles (5,800 kilometers).

The first ships to visit the pole were the U.S. nuclear submarines *Nautilus* (1958), which remained submerged, and *Skate* (1959), which surfaced through the ice. The first surface vessel to reach the pole was the Soviet nuclear icebreaker *Arktika*, in 1977. It approached the pole from the direction of the New Siberian Islands.

ANTARCTICA

A great many countries, large and small, played important roles in the discovery and exploration of Antarctica. Who first saw the continent is controversial. Three separate European expeditions claim to have sighted it first in 1820. Long before that, in about AD 650, Maori legend tells of a voyage that sailed at least as far south as the frozen ocean. It was made in a New Zealand Polynesian war canoe, under the command of Ui-te-Rangiora.

Starting in about the 12th century, many European geographers thought that there must be an enormous southern continent to balance out the land in the Northern Hemisphere. They called this mythical continent Terra Australis Incognita, which means "Unknown Southern Continent." Numerous explorers sought to discover this vast land. Along the way, they found the much smaller continent of Australia. In 1772–75 the British explorer James Cook sailed completely around the globe in the far south but found no great continent. He proved that Terra Australis Incognita, if it existed at all, could not be enormous. It would have to lie somewhere beyond the ice packs that he discovered between about 60° and 70° S. In the 19th century Europeans discovered Antarctica, the ice-covered seventh continent. There was no vast southern land after all. (*See also* Australia and the Pacific Islands.)

> *" The risk one runs in exploring a coast, in these unknown and icy seas, is so very great, that I can be bold though to say that no man will ever venture further than I have done; and that the lands which may lie to the south will never be explored. "*
>
> —James Cook, 1775

Early Exploration

From the 1760s until about 1900 sealers and whalers dominated the exploration of the southern seas. They were particularly active along Scotia Ridge, in the South Atlantic. Sealing vessels hunted the southern fur seal to near extinction in order to obtain their pelts. The whaling industry reached its peak following World War I, after the decline of sealing.

First sightings. A few expeditions of the period explored the southern waters for the purpose of geographic and scientific discovery. These voyages led to the first confirmed sightings of Antarctica. The Russian explorer Fabian von Bellingshausen and the British naval officer Edward Bransfield both claimed to have seen the continent first in 1820. So, too did the American sealer Nathaniel Palmer.

Bellingshausen led the first expedition to closely circle Antarctica, in 1819–21. He discovered two of the South Sandwich Islands in what were the first sightings of land within the Antarctic Circle. Earlier, in January 1820, Bellingshausen had sighted a shelf edge of the continental ice, in the region of Antarctica south of Africa. A few days later, Bransfield caught sight of snow-covered mountains on the Antarctic Peninsula, in the west. He became the first person to chart a portion of Antarctica. In November, Palmer also sighted land on the Antarctic Peninsula. Today, the southern part of the peninsula is named Palmer Land.

The deep bay along the eastern coast of the Antarctic Peninsula is named the Weddell Sea. It is the southernmost part of the Atlantic Ocean. The Weddell Sea is usually heavily iced, a factor that severely hindered early ship exploration. Bransfield made one of the first attempts to sail into the sea in February 1820. He was stopped by ice off the peninsula's northeast coast. In the same year pack ice stopped Bellingshausen just south of the South Sandwich Islands. On Feb. 20, 1823, James Weddell, a British explorer and sealer, found an unusually open route southeastward from the South Orkney Islands. He sailed into the sea that now bears his name, reaching as far as 74°15' S.

Dumont d'Urville. The French navigator Jules-Sébastien-César Dumont d'Urville hoped to sail farther south in the Weddell Sea than Weddell. He had already completed an extensive charting mission in the South Pacific. In September 1837 he set sail for Antarctica. His ships reached the pack ice at 63°29' S., but they were ill-equipped for ice navigation. Unable to penetrate the pack ice, they coasted it for 300 miles (480 kilometers) to the east. Heading westward, the explorers visited the South Orkney and South Shetland islands. After the crew became ill with scurvy, the ships had to stop in Chile.

The explorers later returned to Antarctica. They hoped to discover the south magnetic pole in the unexplored sector between 120° and 160° E., south of Australia. In January 1840 they landed on the Antarctic coast in this sector. Dumont d'Urville claimed part of the coast for France, naming it Adélie Land after his wife. The expedition returned to France late in 1841.

Wilkes. The U.S. naval officer Charles Wilkes explored a large section of the East Antarctic coast. From 1838 to 1842 he commanded an exploring and surveying expedition that ultimately took him into the southern

An engraving based on a sketch by Charles Wilkes shows his men on the Antarctic ice.
The Granger Collection, New York

Indian Ocean. He reported land at a number of points in the region of Antarctica now known as Wilkes Land (which includes Adélie Land). He also explored parts of South America, visited islands in the Pacific, and explored the West Coast of the United States. He then recrossed the Pacific to New York, having sailed completely around the world.

Ross. The British naval officer James Clark Ross explored Antarctica on an expedition in 1839–43. He wanted to find the south magnetic pole, having already located the north magnetic pole on his earlier Arctic journeys. On his Antarctic voyage, he commanded the *Erebus* and *Terror*, the ships that John Franklin would later take on his fatal voyage.

On Jan. 5, 1841, Ross discovered what is now called the Ross Sea, an extension of the South Pacific Ocean. Like the Weddell Sea, the Ross Sea is in many places covered by ice shelves—sheets of ice floating on the sea. At the head of the Ross Sea, the Ross expedition discovered what is now called the Ross Ice Shelf. It is the world's largest body of floating ice. The Ross Ice Shelf later served as an important gateway for expeditions to the Antarctic interior. Ross also sighted part of the Antarctic coast just west of Wilkes Land; he named it Victoria Land after the British queen.

Ross found that it was impossible to reach the south magnetic pole by ship. The way was blocked by the Ross Ice Shelf. The expedition wintered at Tasmania, Australia, and in November 1841 sailed again for Antarctica. Ross charted part of the coast of the northern Antarctic Peninsula and sailed around the Weddell Sea ice.

First landing. In 1895 Leonard Christensen, captain of a Norwegian whaler, landed a party at Cape Adare, in Victoria Land. He and his men became the first to set foot on Antarctica. Other expeditions soon began exploring inland.

The "Heroic Era" of Exploration

The first two decades of the 20th century are commonly called the "heroic era" of Antarctic exploration. During this period, great advances were made in not only geographic but also scientific knowledge of the continent. The British explorers Robert F. Scott and Ernest Henry Shackleton led three expeditions from 1901 to 1913 that pioneered routes into the interior. They also made important discoveries about Antarctic geology, glaciers, and weather. These discoveries provided a firm foundation for present-day scientific programs.

Earlier, it was thought that explorers might not be able to survive an Antarctic winter. The "heroic era" was preceded by two events that proved that people could successfully spend the winter in the region. First, the explorers of the Belgian ship *Belgica* involuntarily became the first people to winter in Antarctic waters. From March 1898 to March 1899, their ship was trapped in the pack ice of the Bellingshausen Sea. The expedition's leader was Adrien de Gerlache, and its mate was Roald Amundsen. Frederick A. Cook was the expedition's surgeon. The crew nearly died of scurvy,

but they recovered after eating seal meat, at Cook's insistence.

Second, a British scientific expedition under Carsten E. Borchgrevink intentionally spent the next winter camped at Cape Adare. After becoming the first people to successfully winter on Antarctica, they began exploring the interior.

The goal of many subsequent Antarctic expeditions was to reach the South Pole. Attaining the pole would bring glory to the successful explorers and to their country. In the early 1900s many expeditions also wanted to study Antarctica scientifically and to claim territory for their countries.

Scott and Shackleton explore the interior. Scott and Shackleton led sledge probes deep into the interior in attempts to reach the South Pole. Scott, in the *Discovery*, commanded the British National Antarctic Expedition in 1901–04. Shackleton was his third lieutenant. The explorers reached the Ross Sea in early 1902 and set up a base camp on Ross Island, at McMurdo Sound at the northern edge of the Ross Ice Shelf. Scott went aloft in a hydrogen balloon tied to the ship for aerial reconnaissance, presaging the aerial age of Antarctic exploration.

In the spring the men began exploring the ice shelf, the coast of Victoria Land, and Ross Island, gathering geographic and scientific data. Scott, Shackleton, and the zoologist Edward A. Wilson set off on a dog sledge journey southward across the Ross Ice Shelf. The dogs were underfed, and many of them died or were killed along the way to feed the other dogs. The men often had to haul the sledges themselves. On Dec. 30, 1902, they reached 82°17′ S., farther south than anyone had been before them. However, they were still more than 500 miles (800 kilometers) from the South Pole.

Sick with scurvy and short on provisions, they traveled back to the base camp. Shackleton's health remained poor, and he was sent back home on a supply ship in early 1903. Scott and the others continued their exploration until early 1904.

Ernest Shackleton
Library of Congress, Washington, D.C. (neg. no. LC-DIG-ggbain-04778)

Shackleton was determined to resume his explorations and to reach the South Pole. He nearly succeeded. In 1907 he returned in the *Nimrod* as leader of the British Antarctic Expedition. Shackleton proved to be an excellent leader. The explorers reached the Ross Sea in early 1908 and wintered on Ross Island. There, three of the men—the Australian geologists T.W. Edgeworth David and David Mawson and the British physician Alistair MacKay—became the first people to climb Mount Erebus, an active volcano.

The explorers had brought dogs and hardy Manchurian ponies to pull the sledges, as well as an automobile equipped with skies. The expedition formed smaller exploring parties. David, Mawson, and MacKay set off on a quest for the south magnetic pole using the automobile. They soon gave up on the vehicle, which was not useful in the snow. The three men had to pull their own heavy sledge. On Jan. 16, 1909, they became the first people to reach the south magnetic pole, on the ice plateau of Victoria Land.

" I thought you'd rather have a live donkey than a dead lion. "

—Ernest Shackleton, explaining to his wife why he turned back after having nearly reached the South Pole in 1909

Meanwhile, Shackleton led a party toward the South Pole (the pole of Earth's rotation). Besides Shackleton, the party consisted of Frank Wild, Jameson Adams, and Eric Marshall. Four ponies pulled their sledges. The explorers crossed the Ross Ice Shelf and climbed the great Beardmore Glacier, which ascends about 7,200 feet (2,200 meters). They continued on across the polar plateau. The explorers began to shoot and eat their ponies one by one; the last of the ponies fell into a deep crack in the ice. Finally, on Jan. 9, 1909, the explorers reached 88°23′ S., a new record and only about 112 miles (180 kilometers) from the South Pole. They were extremely short on food, however, and Shackleton decided to turn back. He and his men trekked back half-starving to the base camp. Shackleton returned to England to great acclaim for his brilliant expedition. His experimental use of the ponies and pioneering of a route up Beardmore Glacier paved the way for Scott's epic sledging trip in 1911–12 to the South Pole.

Amundsen and Scott race to the South Pole. In June 1910 two rival expeditions set off for Antarctica hoping to reach the pole first. Roald Amundsen led a Norwegian expedition, and Robert Franklin Scott commanded a British one. Scott sought to gather scientific information about the Ross Sea area, as well as to reach the South Pole.

Amundsen had originally planned to journey to the Arctic. He wanted to be the first to reach the North Pole, planning to drift across it in Fridtjof Nansen's old ship, the *Fram*. However, as Amundsen prepared for his expedition, he learned that Robert E. Peary had already reached the North Pole. Amundsen continued his preparations. When he left Norway, no one but his brother knew that he was heading for the South Pole

Roald Amundsen, 1923
AP

instead of the North. He did not even tell his crew until they stopped in the Madeira Islands. There, Amundsen also sent a telegram to Scott announcing his plans. At the time, Scott was in Australia, on his way to Antarctica.

Amundsen sailed the *Fram* directly to the Bay of Whales, Antarctica, along the Ross Sea. The base he set up there was 60 miles (100 kilometers) closer to the pole than was Scott's base. An experienced polar traveler, Amundsen prepared carefully for the coming journey.

Oscar Wisting, a member of Roald Amundsen's expedition, stands at the South Pole with his dog team in 1911.

Library of Congress, Washington, D.C.

He made a preliminary trip to deposit food supplies along the first part of his route.

On Oct. 19, 1911, Amundsen set out with four other explorers, 52 dogs, and four sledges. After encountering good weather, he arrived at the South Pole on December 14. The explorers recorded scientific data at the pole before beginning the return journey on December 17. They safely reached their base at the Bay of Whales on Jan. 25, 1912. Amundsen estimated that they had trekked about 1,860 miles (3,000 kilometers) round-trip.

Meanwhile, Scott had reached Antarctica in the *Terra Nova* in January 1911. He established a base at Cape Evans, on Ross Island. Like Amundsen, Scott first established food depots along part of his route. Scott and 11 others then set out for the pole on October 24. They were equipped with motor sledges, ponies, and dogs. The motors soon broke down, however, in the extreme cold. The ponies became exhausted, and the explorers shot them for food before reaching 83°30' S. From there they also sent the dog teams back.

On December 10 the party began to ascend Beardmore Glacier with three man-hauled sledges. By December 31 seven men had been sent back to the base. The remaining polar party—Scott, Edward A. Wilson, H.R. Bowers, L.E.G. Oates, and Edgar Evans—reached the pole on Jan. 18, 1912. Exhausted by their 81-day trek, they were bitterly disappointed to find evidence that Amundsen had beaten them to the pole by about a month.

The weather on the return journey was exceptionally bad. Evans died at Beardmore. Food and fuel supplies

Robert F. Scott writes in his diary during his final expedition to the South Pole, at his base at Cape Evans, on Ross Island, Antarctica.

ran low, and the explorers suffered from scurvy. Oates became disabled with severe frostbite on his feet. Hoping to aid his companions by his own disappearance, he crawled out into a blizzard on March 17. Unfortunately, his sacrifice did not save the others. The three survivors struggled on for 10 miles (16 kilometers) but then were trapped in their tent by another blizzard. The blizzard lasted for nine days. With quiet fortitude they awaited their death—only 11 miles from their destination. On March 29, Scott wrote the final entry in his diary:

"Every day we have been ready to start for our depot 11 miles away but outside the door of the tent it remains a scene of whirling drift.... We shall stick it out to the end, but we are getting weaker, of course, and the end cannot be far. It seems a pity, but I do not think I can write more."

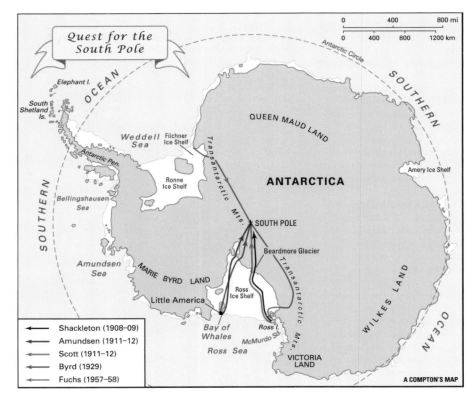

Quest for the South Pole

0 — 400 — 800 mi
0 — 400 — 800 — 1200 km

Antarctic Circle

SOUTHERN OCEAN

Elephant I.
South Shetland Is.
Antarctic Pen.
Weddell Sea
Filchner Ice Shelf
Ronne Ice Shelf
Bellingshausen Sea
QUEEN MAUD LAND
Amery Ice Shelf
Transantarctic Mts.
ANTARCTICA
SOUTH POLE
Beardmore Glacier
Amundsen Sea
MARIE BYRD LAND
Little America
Ross Ice Shelf
Transantarctic Mts.
WILKES LAND
OCEAN
Bay of Whales
Ross I.
McMurdo
Ross Sea
VICTORIA LAND

→ Shackleton (1908–09)
→ Amundsen (1911–12)
→ Scott (1911–12)
→ Byrd (1929)
→ Fuchs (1957–58)

A COMPTON'S MAP

Members of Robert F. Scott's last expedition haul a heavy sledge laden with supplies.
Library of Congress, Washington, D.C. (neg. no. LC-USZ62-8744)

On Nov. 12, 1912, searchers found the tent with the three explorers' frozen bodies. They also recovered Scott's records and diaries and geological specimens the explorers had collected. After his death Scott was regarded as a national hero in Britain for his courage and patriotism.

Shackleton and the *Endurance*. After Amundsen and Scott reached the South Pole, the idea that particularly haunted people's minds was that of an overland crossing of Antarctica. Shackleton returned to the continent in 1914 to lead a British attempt. He planned to cross Antarctica from a base on the Weddell Sea to McMurdo Sound, passing over the South Pole on the way. He sailed from England in the *Endurance* on Aug. 8, 1914, with a crew of 27 men. The *Endurance* headed toward the Weddell Sea, while the *Aurora* sailed to the Ross Sea on the other side of Antarctica. It carried supply teams who were to lay down food and equipment along the route for Shackleton's men.

Shackleton had difficulty landing because of the ice conditions in the Weddell Sea. On Jan. 19, 1915, the *Endurance* became trapped in the ice. The ship drifted for several months. After it began leaking in October, the men took their provisions and the ship's three small boats and set up camp on an ice floe. The following month the *Endurance* was crushed in the ice and sank.

The explorers drifted on a series of ice floes for several months. In April they finally escaped in the boats to Elephant Island, in the South Shetland Islands. However, they were unlikely to be rescued on this remote island. To seek aid, Shackleton, Frank Worsley, and four others set out in one of the small boats. In an impressive feat of navigation, Worsley guided them across 800 miles (1,300 kilometers) of rough seas to the island of South Georgia.

They landed on an uninhabited part of the island. After completing this miserable journey, three of them—Shackleton, Worsley, and Thomas Crean—set out on foot for a whaling station on the other side of the island. In order to reach the station, they had to climb high mountains and glaciers. They became the first people to cross South Georgia. The whalers sent a steamship to pick up the three explorers left on the other side of South Georgia, but there were still 22 men left on Elephant Island. Shackleton led three relief expeditions that were foiled by ice. He finally succeeded in rescuing the remaining men in August 1916. Remarkably, not one of Shackleton's men died.

The Ross Sea party, led by A.E. Mackintosh, had laid supply depots on Antarctica for the use of Shackleton's men. Three of this party died on the return journey.

Ernest Shackleton's ship the Endurance *sinks in the ice of the Weddell Sea in November 1915, while a team of sled dogs looks on.*

The Granger Collection, New York

The Aerial and Mechanical Age

The period between World Wars I and II was the beginning of the aerial and mechanical age of Antarctic exploration. The advent of the airplane and motorized vehicles revolutionized exploration techniques. Wartime developments in aircraft, aerial cameras, radios, and motor transport were adapted for polar operation. The first airplane flight in Antarctica was made by the Australian-born British explorer George Hubert Wilkins and the Alaskan bush pilot Carl Ben Eielson. They took off on Nov. 16, 1928, in a monoplane. The pair flew 600 miles (970 kilometers) south from Deception Island, crossing the Antarctic Peninsula. They discovered several new islands.

Byrd's flight over the South Pole. This flight was quickly followed by the four aircraft expeditions of the U.S. naval officer Richard E. Byrd. He made use of new technologies and gathered a wealth of new information about Antarctica. He made increasing use of ski-planes to transport men and equipment. He also used aerial photography for mapping and reconnaissance.

Byrd's first expedition, in 1928–30, was the largest and best-equipped expedition that had yet set out for Antarctica. He established a well-supplied base, called Little America, on the Ross Ice Shelf. From this base, the explorers flew over the Antarctic interior. On Nov. 29, 1929, Byrd became the first person to fly over the South Pole; he had earlier claimed to have been the first to have flown over the North Pole. He and three companions flew from their base to the South Pole and back in 19 hours. They discovered a large region of Antarctica bordering the South Pacific. Byrd named it Marie Byrd Land, after his wife.

In 1933–35 Byrd led a second Antarctic expedition with the aim of mapping land around the South Pole. The explorers used aircraft, several tractors, and other motorized vehicles. During the winter of 1934 Byrd spent five months alone in a hut at a weather station buried beneath the ice shelf face. He had to endure temperatures between –58° and –76° F (–50° and –60° C) and sometimes much lower. Byrd was finally rescued in a desperately sick condition, suffering from frostbite and carbon monoxide poisoning, caused by fumes from a clogged chimney.

On his third expedition, in 1939–41, Byrd discovered the southern limit of the Pacific Ocean. His fourth expedition, called "Operation High Jump," in the summer of 1946–47, was sponsored by the U.S. government. It was the most massive sea and air expedition theretofore attempted in Antarctica. The operation involved 4,700 men, 25 airplanes, and 13 ships, including two seaplane tenders and an aircraft carrier. The ship- and land-based aircraft mapped and photographed about 60 percent of the Antarctic coast, nearly a quarter of which had been previously unseen. Innovations by Byrd included the use of six helicopters.

Crossing the continent. Meanwhile, the American explorer Lincoln Ellsworth and the Canadian pilot Herbert Hollick-Kenyon had completed the first aerial crossing of the continent. They flew from the Antarctic Peninsula to the Little America base on the Ross Ice Shelf from Nov. 23 to Dec. 5, 1935. Their courageous flight took them across vast uncharted lands and ice fields. They had to complete the journey on foot after having run out of fuel. This expedition clearly demonstrated the feasibility of aircraft landings and takeoffs for inland exploration.

The British geologist and explorer Vivian Fuchs led the first overland journey across Antarctica. Using tracked vehicles and aided by aerial flights, the party left from the Filchner Ice Shelf, at the head of the Weddell Sea, on Nov. 24, 1957. Passing over the South Pole, they reached Ross Island on March 2, 1958. The expedition's other team established supply bases for Fuchs and his party. The supply team was led by the New Zealand explorer Edmund Hillary, who had earlier been the first person to climb Mount Everest, along with Tenzing Norgay (*see* Eurasia).

Richard E. Byrd, left, sits with fellow explorers at the Little America base on the Ross Ice Shelf, in about 1930.
The Granger Collection, New York

Territorial claims and scientific research. The beginning of the aerial and mechanical age overlapped with the colonial age of Antarctic history. Between 1908 and 1942, seven countries claimed control of pie-shaped sectors of the continent. Most other countries do not recognize these claims.

This unsettled situation might have continued had it not been for a surge of scientific interest in Antarctica in the mid-1950s. At that time scientists of 12 countries decided to make research in Antarctica a major portion of a large investigation, the International Geophysical Year. The 12 countries were Argentina, Australia, Belgium, Chile, France, Japan, New Zealand, Norway, South Africa, the Soviet Union, the United Kingdom, and the United States. When the program was completed in 1958, these countries decided to continue their research programs in Antarctica. In 1959 they signed a treaty that reserves the continent for peaceful purposes, especially scientific research. The treaty does not recognize or dispute the territorial claims of any country, but it also does not allow any new claims to be made. Many other countries subsequently signed this treaty.

Every year about 25 countries send scientists to Antarctica to do research. In the Antarctic summer about 4,000 people are in the region for this work. They run research stations and camps scattered across the continent and operate ships for resupply and oceanic research. In winter about 1,000 people remain to operate more than 35 research stations. The winter inhabitants

Kyodo/Landov

Japanese scientists study Adélie penguins in Antarctica.

are isolated for several months at a time because the weather prevents anyone from getting to them, even in airplanes. Biologists, geologists, oceanographers, geophysicists, astronomers, glaciologists, and meteorologists conduct experiments here that cannot be duplicated anywhere else.

International Polar Years

An important secondary motive in much of the great polar exploration was pure scientific curiosity—the desire to add to the general store of the world's knowledge. Numerous other Arctic and Antarctic expeditions have been conducted solely for the purpose of scientific study.

The importance of coordinating polar science efforts was recognized in the late 19th century. The German explorer Karl Weyprecht made an important proposal for international cooperation in collecting scientific data. His suggestion led to the establishment of the first International Polar Year, in 1882–83. As part of this program, 11 countries set up polar research stations—12 stations in the better-known Arctic and two in the Antarctic. Scientists took observations at the stations and then pooled the results. It was decided that similar international polar research programs would be organized every 50 years.

The second International Polar Year took place in 1932–33. Its emphasis was on studying polar weather systems, especially as they related to the recently discovered jet stream. This time 40 countries set up 40 research stations in the Arctic. Many of these stations are still in use. Richard Byrd's second Antarctic expedition was also part of this International Polar Year. The weather station he established was the first inland research station in Antarctica.

Rather than wait another 50 years, scientists wanted to hold another international program on the 25th anniversary of the last polar year. They proposed to take advantage of increasing technological developments and interest in the polar regions.

They also wanted to study the Sun. Sunspot activity was expected to reach a maximum in 1957–58, whereas the last polar year had been a time of minimum sunspot activity.

The idea grew quickly. The International Geophysical Year (IGY) was held in 1957–58. The program included much polar study, but its scope encompassed scientific study of the whole Earth. Scientists from more than 70 countries conducted research around the globe as well as in space.

The IGY led to a multitude of discoveries. Many of them revolutionized concepts of Earth and its oceans, landmasses, glaciers, and atmosphere. The IGY pioneered in the use of rocketry to conduct studies of the upper atmosphere. Several of the earliest artificial satellites launched in the late 1950s were used to gather data for the IGY. The discovery of the Van Allen radiation belts surrounding Earth was another major achievement. The IGY also confirmed that a system of underwater mountains, called the mid-oceanic ridges, circles the globe. This important discovery led to the development of the theory of plate tectonics in the 1970s. The IGY also led to the signing of the Antarctic Treaty, which reserved the use of Antarctica for peaceful, scientific purposes.

The next International Polar Year was held 50 years later, in 2007–08. It brought together experts from more than 60 countries to study the Arctic and Antarctic regions. A focus of their research was the role of the polar regions in global warming and other climate processes. For the first time, the program placed a priority on involving Inuit and other people who lived in the Arctic, making use of their knowledge of the region.

World Explorers at a Glance

Amundsen, Roald (1872–1928?). Norwegian explorer, born on July 16, 1872, in Borge, Norway. In 1897–99 he participated in a Belgian expedition that was the first to winter in the Antarctic. In 1903–06 he was the first to navigate the Northwest Passage. He also led the first expedition to reach the South Pole, arriving in December 1911, about a month before Robert F. Scott. Amundsen returned to Norway and established a successful shipping business. In 1926 Amundsen, Umberto Nobile, and Lincoln Ellsworth flew over the North Pole in an airship, becoming the first people known for certain to have reached that pole. Amundsen disappeared on June 18, 1928, while flying over the Arctic Ocean to rescue Nobile from an airship crash.

Baffin, William (1584?–1622). English navigator. He searched for the Northwest Passage in the Canadian Arctic in 1612, 1615, and 1616, exploring Hudson Strait and what is now named Baffin Bay. In service to the East India Company, he made surveys of the Red Sea and the Persian Gulf. In 1622, during his final voyage to the Persian Gulf, he was killed in an Anglo-Persian attack on Qeshm (now in Iran) on Jan. 23, 1622. Canada's Baffin Island is also named in his honor.

Baker, Samuel White (1821–93). English explorer, born on June 8, 1821, in London. He lived on what are now Mauritius and Sri Lanka before traveling through the Balkans and the Middle East in 1856–60. At a slave market in the Balkans he purchased Florence von Sass, whom he later married. In 1861–65 he and von Sass searched for the source of the Nile River in eastern Africa. Baker discovered and named Lake Albert in 1864. He was knighted in 1866. In 1869 Baker commanded a military expedition in Egypt. There he helped to put down the slave trade, annexed territories, and served as their governor-general for four years. He died on Dec. 30, 1893, in Sanford Orleigh, England.

Balboa, Vasco Núñez de (1475–1519). Spanish conquistador and explorer, born in Jerez de los Caballeros, Spain. In 1500 he explored the coast of Colombia, and then settled in Hispaniola. Forced to flee creditors, he joined an expedition to a colony in Colombia. He persuaded the settlers to move to Darién (Panama), where in 1511 they founded the first stable settlement in Central America. In 1513 he became the first European to see the Pacific Ocean. A rival, Pedro Arias Dávila, had him charged with treason and beheaded, on Jan. 12, 1519, in Acla, Panama.

Barents, Willem (1550?–97). Dutch navigator. On three voyages (1594–97) he searched for the Northeast Passage. In 1596 he rediscovered Svalbard, which had been lost to Europeans since the days of the Vikings. He died in the Arctic on June 20, 1597. Because of his accurate charting and collection of valuable meteorological data, he is regarded as one of the most important early Arctic explorers. The Barents Sea is named after him.

Barth, Heinrich (1821–65). German geographer and explorer, born on Feb. 16, 1821, in Hamburg. After studying at the University of Berlin, he traveled to coastal Tunisia and Libya in 1845–47. He traveled to western Africa in 1850–55, visiting Timbuktu, Mali, and mapping the upper reaches of the Benue River. He published a comprehensive scientific account of the areas he visited. Later travels took him to Turkey, Spain, Italy, and the Alps. He became a professor at the University of Berlin in 1863. He died in Berlin on Nov. 25, 1865.

Bass, George (1771–1803). British naval surgeon and sailor, born on Jan. 30, 1771, in Aswarby, England. With Matthew Flinders, he explored Botany Bay, Australia, in 1795. The following year they unsuccessfully sought a river south of Botany Bay and discovered Port Hocking. In 1797 Bass explored the coast south of Sydney and confirmed reports of coal there. He then discovered a strait—now Bass Strait—between New South Wales and Tasmania. In 1803 he died at sea en route from Australia to South America.

Bellingshausen, Fabian Gottlieb von (1778–1852). Russian explorer, born on Aug. 18, 1778, in Ösel (now Saaremaa), Estonia. He entered the Russian navy at age 10; by the time of his death he had become an admiral and the governor of Kronshtadt, Russia. In 1819–21 he led the second expedition to circumnavigate Antarctica. He may have been the first person to sight the continent, in 1820. He died on Jan. 13, 1852, in Kronshtadt. The Bellingshausen Sea was named for him.

Bering, Vitus (1681–1741). Russian navigator, born in Horsens, Denmark. After joining the fleet of the Russian tsar Peter I, he was appointed leader of an expedition to determine whether Asia and North America are connected by land. In 1728 he set sail from the Kamchatka Peninsula of Siberia and passed through what would later be named the Bering Strait. His plan for a second expedition was expanded into Russia's Great Northern Expedition (1733–43), which mapped much of the Arctic coast of Siberia. After exploring the Alaskan coast, he fell ill from scurvy. After his ship was wrecked, he died on Dec. 19, 1741, on Bering Island.

Bougainville, Louis-Antoine de (1729–1811). French navigator, born on Nov. 11, 1729, in Paris. In 1764 he established a colony for France in the Falkland Islands. He led an official French expedition that circled the globe in 1766–69. After touching Samoa and the New Hebrides, he continued west into waters not previously navigated by any European. He later was secretary to King Louis XV (1772), led the French fleet in support of the American Revolution, and was named to the Legion of Honor by Napoleon. He died on Aug. 3, 1811, in Paris. The plant genus *Bougainvillea* is named for him.

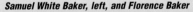
Samuel White Baker, left, and Florence Baker

Bransfield, Edward (1785?–1852). English naval officer. He sailed to the recently discovered South Shetland Islands in January 1820 and took formal possession of King George Island for Britain. Later that month he sighted the Antarctic Peninsula; he may have been the first to see the continent. He then became the first person to chart a portion of the Antarctic coast.

Bruce, James (1730–94). Scottish explorer, born on Dec. 14, 1730, in Larbert, Scotland. As British consul in Algeria (from 1763), he studied antiquities in North Africa, recording what he saw in fine drawings. Starting in 1765 he traveled widely in the Mediterranean region, notably in Syria. He arrived in Egypt in 1768. Intent on reaching the source of the Nile River, he left Cairo on an arduous journey to Ethiopia. He reached Lake Tana, where the Blue Nile rises, in 1770. He returned to Europe in 1774. He died on April 27, 1794, in Larbert.

Burckhardt, Johann Ludwig (1784–1817). Swiss traveler, born on Nov. 24, 1784, in Lausanne, Switzerland. He studied in England at Cambridge University. In 1809 he visited Syria to learn Arabic. During his travels through the Middle East, he took a Muslim name and often wore Muslim clothing. He became the first European in modern times to visit Petra (in Jordan) and the temple of Abu Simbel (in Egypt). He also journeyed to Arabia, visiting Mecca. He died in Cairo, Egypt, on Oct. 15, 1817.

Burke, Robert O'Hara (1820/21–1861). Australian police officer and explorer, born in St. Clerah's, Ireland, possibly on May 6, 1820 or 1821. He served in the Austrian army and later the Irish Mounted Constabulary. After moving to Victoria, Australia, in 1853, he worked for the police force. In 1860–61 he led the Burke and Wills expedition, the first to try to cross Australia from south to north. The explorers nearly reached the north coast, but on the return trip both Burke and his second in command, William Wills, died in late June 1861.

Burton, Richard (1821–90). English scholar-explorer, born on March 19, 1821, in Torquay, England. Expelled from Oxford in 1842, he served in the army in India. There he disguised himself as a Muslim and wrote reports on bazaars and brothels. He later traveled to Arabia, again disguised as a Muslim, and entered the forbidden holy cities. In 1857–58 he and John Speke searched for the source of the Nile River in Africa and became the first Europeans to reach Lake Tanganyika. Burton learned 25 languages and many dialects, wrote 43 books about his travels, and completed some 30 volumes of translations, including a translation of *The Arabian Nights*. He died on Oct. 20, 1890, in Trieste (now in Italy).

Navy Department/National Archives, Washington, D.C.
Richard Evelyn Byrd

Byrd, Richard Evelyn (1888–1957). U.S. naval officer, aviator, and explorer, born on Oct. 25, 1888, in Winchester, Va. After serving in World War I, he worked developing navigational aids for aircraft. In 1926 he and Floyd Bennett claimed to have reached the North Pole by airplane, but the claim was later called into question. In 1928–30 Byrd led his first expedition to Antarctica. In 1929 he and three companions became the first to fly over the South Pole, and Byrd was made a rear admiral. He led subsequent expeditions that discovered and mapped large areas of Antarctica. He died on March 11, 1957, in Boston, Mass. His brother Harry F. Byrd served as a U.S. senator from Virginia.

Robert O'Hara Burke, left, and William Wills

The Art Archive/Picture Desk

World Explorers at a Glance—Continued

Cabot, John (1450?–99?). Italian explorer, born perhaps in Genoa. In the 1470s he became a skilled navigator in travels to the eastern Mediterranean. He later moved to England and in 1497 led an English expedition to find trade routes to Asia. He instead landed somewhere in North America, possibly southern Labrador or Cape Breton Island. He took possession of the land for the British king and explored the coastline. On a second expedition in 1498, he may have reached America but probably was lost at sea. His voyages helped lay the groundwork for the later British claim to Canada. The explorer Sebastian Cabot was his son.

Cabrillo, Juan Rodríguez (died 1543?). Explorer in the service of Spain and the European discoverer of California. Little is known of his early life, though he may have been born in Portugal. In 1520 he accompanied Spanish explorers to Mexico. He later helped conquer Guatemala. In 1542 he left Mexico and sailed along the California coast, entering San Diego and Monterey bays. He landed on several islands off the coast; he apparently died (on Jan. 3, 1543?) after breaking his leg on one such landing.

Champlain, Samuel de (1567–1635). French explorer, born in Brouage, France. He made several expeditions to North America before founding Quebec, Canada, in 1608. He joined with northern Indian tribes to defeat Iroquois marauders and promoted the fur trade. He discovered Lake Champlain in 1609 and explored the Ottawa River and the eastern Great Lakes. When English privateers besieged Quebec in 1628, he was captured and imprisoned in England until 1632. The following year he made his last voyage to Quebec, where he lived until his death on Dec. 25, 1635.

Clark, William (1770–1838). American explorer and soldier, born on Aug. 1, 1770, in Caroline county, Va. He was the brother of George Rogers Clark, one of the military heroes of the American Revolution. William Clark joined the army and participated in Indian campaigns. He was recruited by his former army friend Meriwether Lewis to help lead the first overland expedition to the Pacific coast and back. Clark proved a daring and resourceful leader of the famed Lewis and Clark Expedition (1804–06). He also served as its mapmaker and artist. Later, as governor of the

Missouri Territory (1813–21), he became known for his diplomacy with the Indians. He died on Sept. 1, 1838, in St. Louis, Mo.

Columbus, Christopher (1451–1506). Italian navigator and explorer whose transatlantic voyages opened the way for European exploration, exploitation, and colonization of the Americas. He was born probably in Genoa, Italy, between Aug. 26 and Oct. 31, 1451. In 1492 he obtained the sponsorship of the Spanish monarchs Ferdinand II and Isabella I for an attempt to reach Asia by sailing westward over what was presumed to be open sea. He instead "discovered" the Americas, exploring the Caribbean in 1492–93. He led three more expeditions to the Caribbean, South America, and Central America (1493–96, 1498–1500, 1502–04). He died on May 20, 1506, in Valladolid, Spain.

Cook, James (1728–79). British sailor and explorer, born on Oct. 27, 1728, in Marton-in-Cleveland, England. He joined the Royal Navy in 1755 and in 1763–67 surveyed the St. Lawrence River and the coast of Newfoundland (Canada). In 1768–71 he led the first scientific expedition to the Pacific, charting all of New Zealand and exploring the east coast of Australia. His second voyage (1772–75) ranks as one of the greatest of all sailing-ship voyages; he successfully completed the first west-east circumnavigation of the globe in high latitudes. On a third voyage (1776–79) in search of a Northwest Passage around Canada and Alaska, he was killed by Hawaiians on Feb. 14, 1779, at Kealakekua Bay, Hawaii.

Coronado, Francisco Vázquez de (1510?–54). Spanish explorer of the North American Southwest, born in Salamanca, Spain. Appointed governor of a province in western Mexico, he was sent north in 1540 with a large force to capture the legendary Seven Cities of Cíbola, reported to be fabulously wealthy. He was disillusioned to discover instead the poor Zuni pueblos of New Mexico. His explorers were the first Europeans to view the Grand Canyon, and he extended Spanish territory over huge areas of North America. He died in Mexico on Sept. 22, 1554.

Cortés, Hernán (1485–1547). Spanish conquistador who won Mexico for Spain. Born in Medellín, Spain, he left for the Americas at age 19, joining in the conquest of Cuba in 1511. He overthrew the Aztec Empire of Mexico in 1519–21. The absolute ruler of a

Christopher Columbus

James Cook

Hernán Cortés

huge territory, he was forced to retire after a disastrous expedition in 1524 to the Honduran jungles. He died on Dec. 2, 1547, in Castilleja de la Cuesta, Spain.

Dampier, William (1651–1715). English explorer, born in August 1651, in East Coker, England. A pirate in his early years, in 1699–1701 he explored the coasts of Australia, New Guinea, and New Britain for the British Admiralty. He was court-martialed for his cruelty but later led a privateering expedition to the South Seas (1703–07). He was a keen observer of natural phenomena. One of his ship's logs contains the earliest known European description of a typhoon. He died in London in March 1715.

Davis, John (1550?–1605). English navigator, born in Sandridge, England. On three voyages (1585–87) he searched for the Northwest Passage in the Canadian Arctic. He seems to have commanded the *Black Dog* against the Spanish Armada (1588), and he sailed with Thomas Cavendish on his last voyage (1591). In seeking a passage through the Strait of Magellan, Davis discovered the Falkland Islands (1592). He sailed with Walter Raleigh to the Azores (1596–97) and accompanied expeditions to the East Indies (1598, 1601). He was killed by Japanese pirates on Dec. 29 or 30, 1605, off Bintan Island, near Singapore. He invented the backstaff (or Davis quadrant), which was used until the 18th century for determining latitude.

Dias, Bartolomeu (1450?–1500). Portuguese navigator and explorer. In 1487 he set sail on an expedition to determine the southern limit of Africa. He sailed farther south than previous explorers and in 1488 became the first European to round the Cape of Good Hope. His voyage opened the sea route to Asia via the Atlantic and Indian oceans. He later commanded a ship in the expedition under Pedro Álvares Cabral that discovered Brazil; Dias was lost at sea when they reached the Cape.

Doughty, Charles Montagu (1843–1926). English traveler, born on Aug. 19, 1843, in Leiston, England. After attending Cambridge University, he traveled extensively in Europe, Egypt, the Holy Land, and Syria. He is widely regarded as one of the greatest of all Western travelers in Arabia, where he made observations on geography, geology, archaeology, and anthropology. He wrote an account of his travels, as well as epic and dramatic poetry. He died on Jan. 20, 1926, in Sissinghurst, England.

Drake, Francis (1540/43?–1596). English admiral, the most renowned seaman of the Elizabethan Age. He was born in Devonshire, England. He became an outstanding navigator and grew wealthy by raiding and plundering Spanish colonies. He became the second captain to circumnavigate the globe, in 1577–80. In 1581 he was knighted. Appointed vice admiral in 1588, he destroyed ships and supplies destined for the Spanish Armada and delayed the Spanish attack for a year. He died on Jan. 28, 1596, at sea, off Portobelo, Panama.

Dumont d'Urville, Jules-Sébastien-César (1790–1842). French navigator, born on May 23, 1790, in Condé-sur-Noireau, France. In 1820, while on a charting survey of the eastern Mediterranean, he helped France gain possession of the Venus de Milo sculpture. In 1822–25 he served on a sea voyage around the world. His exploration of the South Pacific (1826–29) resulted in extensive revision of charts of South Sea waters. In 1830 he conveyed the exiled king Charles X to England. He sailed for Antarctica in 1837; though unable to penetrate the pack ice, his expedition surveyed the Straits of Magellan and sighted the Adélie coast (named for Dumont's wife) before returning in 1840. He died on May 8, 1842, near Meudon, France.

Eriksson, Leif (11th century). Norse explorer, probably the first European to reach North America. A Viking, he was the second son of Erik the Red and accompanied him on an expedition to Greenland. After learning of a land to the southwest from a man who had accidentally sailed there, Leif set out to explore this land in 1001. He landed in North America, probably in what is now Newfoundland and Labrador, Canada. He and his party traveled south to a place he called Vinland (probably southeastern Canada or the southern United States). According to a different account, Leif reached North America inadvertently after having sailed off course from Greenland.

Erik the Red (10th century). Norse explorer. A Viking from Norway, he grew up in Iceland after his father was exiled from Norway for manslaughter. Erik was himself exiled from Iceland for manslaughter in about 980. He set sail and landed on Greenland, later returning with colonists and founding the first European settlement there. Leif Eriksson was his son.

Flinders, Matthew (1774–1814). British navigator, born on March 16, 1774, in Donington, England. He entered the Royal Navy in 1789. In two expeditions (1795–99, 1801–03) he sailed completely around Australia and Tasmania, charting their coasts and waters. He was imprisoned by the French on Mauritius in 1803–10, when England and France were at war. He died in London on July 19, 1814. His name was given to several geographic features in Australia. The archaeologist Flinders Petrie was his grandson.

Franklin, John (1786–1847). British rear admiral and explorer, born on April 16, 1786, in Spilsby, England. He entered the Royal Navy at the age of 14, accompanied Matthew Flinders on an expedition to Australia (1801–03), and served in the battles of Trafalgar (1805) and New Orleans (1814). He commanded a ship on David Buchan's Arctic expedition of 1818. Franklin conducted two overland expeditions (1819–22, 1825–27) to the Arctic, exploring part of the northwest coast of North America. Knighted in 1829, he served as governor of Tasmania (1836–43). In 1845 he set sail to search for the Northwest Passage but soon disappeared. Numerous expeditions searched for Franklin and his men. It was found that Franklin died on June 11, 1847, near King William Island.

Gama, Vasco da (1460?–1524). Portuguese navigator. His first voyage to India (1497–99) opened the sea route from western Europe to Asia. He traveled around the Cape of Good Hope, visiting trading cities in eastern Africa en route. In 1502 he returned to India as admiral of a fleet of 20 ships, forcing allegiance to Portugal from local rulers along the way and attacking Arab shipping. In 1524 he was appointed Portuguese viceroy in India, but he died shortly after arriving there, on December 24, in Cochin (now Kochi).

Vasco da Gama

World Explorers at a Glance—Continued

Gilbert, Humphrey (1539?–83). English soldier and navigator. The half brother of Walter Raleigh, he proposed in his *Discourse* (1566) a voyage in search of the Northwest Passage. Queen Elizabeth I instead sent him to Ireland (1567–70), where he ruthlessly suppressed an uprising; for this service he was knighted. In 1578 he set out with seven ships, intending to colonize North America. Through his poor leadership some ships returned to England and others turned to piracy. He sailed again in 1583, arriving in Newfoundland, Canada, which he claimed for England. He died at sea on the return journey, in September 1583, near the Azores.

Grant, James Augustus (1827–92). Scottish soldier and explorer, born on April 11, 1827, in Nairn, Scotland. Commissioned in the British army in 1846, Grant saw action in India in his Sikh Wars and the Indian Mutiny of 1857. In India he befriended his fellow officer John Speke. In 1860 Grant joined Speke's second expedition to eastern Africa, which found the outlet of Lake Victoria from which the Nile River issues. In 1868 Grant served in the British intelligence department. He died on Feb. 11, 1892, in Nairn.

Hartog, Dirck (1580–1621). Dutch sea captain, baptized on Oct. 30, 1580, in Amsterdam, Netherlands. In 1616 he set off for Indonesia as captain of a Dutch East India Company ship. After inadvertently sailing off course, he arrived at western Australia in October and made the first recorded exploration of the west coast. He died in 1621 in Amsterdam.

Hillary, Edmund (1919–2008). New Zealand mountain climber and explorer, born on July 20, 1919, in Auckland, New Zealand. He was a professional beekeeper but enjoyed climbing in the New Zealand Alps. In 1951 he joined a New Zealand party to the central Himalayas and then helped in a reconnaissance of the southern flank of Mount Everest. In 1953 he and Tenzing Norgay became the first people known to have reached its summit. Hillary was knighted that same year. In 1958 he participated in the first crossing of Antarctica by vehicle. In 1977 he led the first jet boat expedition up India's Ganges River. From the 1960s he helped build schools and hospitals for the Sherpa people of Nepal. He died on Jan. 11, 2008, in Auckland.

Hudson, Henry (1565?–1611). English navigator and explorer. Sailing three times for the English (1607, 1608, 1610–11) and once for the Dutch (1609), he tried to discover a short route from Europe to Asia through the Arctic Ocean, from both the west and the east. A river, a strait, and a bay in North America are named for him. In 1609 he cruised along the Atlantic coast and up the Hudson River. In 1610 he discovered Hudson Bay. On the homeward voyage the crew mutinied and set him adrift in a small boat, never to be found. He died sometime after June 22, 1611. His discoveries formed the basis for Dutch colonization of the Hudson River and for English claims to much of Canada.

Humboldt, Alexander von (1769–1859). German naturalist and explorer, born on Sept. 14, 1769, in Berlin. In 1792 he joined the mining department of the Prussian government. From 1799 he explored Central and South America and Mexico, traveling in the Amazon jungles and the Andean highlands. He discovered the connection between the Amazon and Orinoco river systems and made a vast amount of scientific observations. He returned to Europe in 1804. In Paris he used his financial resources to help Louis Agassiz and others launch scientific careers. In 1829 he traveled to Russia and explored Central Asia. The last 25 years of his life were spent writing an account of the structure of the universe. He died on May 6, 1859, in Berlin.

Ibn Battutah (1304–1368/69 or 1377). Noted Arab traveler and writer. Born on Feb. 24, 1304, in Tangier, Morocco, he received a traditional legal and literary education. After a pilgrimage to Mecca (1325), he decided to visit as many parts of the world as possible. His 27-year wanderings through Africa, Asia, and Europe covered some 75,000 miles (120,000 kilometers). On his return, he dictated his reminiscences, which became one of the world's most famous travel books, the *Rihlah*.

Idrisi, ash-Sharif al- (1100–1165/66). Arab geographer. Born in Sabtah (now Ceuta, a Spanish exclave in Morocco), he spent much of his early life traveling in North Africa and Spain. His travels also took him to Asia Minor and many parts of western Europe. In 1154, as adviser to Roger II, the Norman king of Sicily, al-Idrisi wrote one of the greatest works of medieval geography. He died in either Sabtah or Sicily.

Jolliet, Louis (1645–1700). French Canadian explorer and cartographer, born before Sept. 21, 1645, probably in Beaupré, near Quebec, Canada. He led an expedition in the Great Lakes region in 1669. In 1673 Jolliet, Jacques Marquette, and five others became the first Europeans to explore the upper Mississippi, traveling down the river to its confluence with the Arkansas. They correctly concluded that the Mississippi flows south to the Gulf of Mexico. After their return, Jolliet explored areas of Hudson Bay and the Labrador coast (in Canada). He died sometime after May 1700, in Quebec province.

La Salle, René-Robert Cavelier, sieur de (1643–87). French explorer, born on Nov. 22, 1643, in Rouen, France. In 1666 he left for North America. He explored the Ohio River region in 1669 and then worked to extend French influence, building new forts. He sailed down the Illinois River and canoed down the Mississippi River to the Gulf of Mexico. There in 1682 he claimed the entire Mississippi Basin for France. In 1684 he sailed from France on a mission to build a fort at the mouth of the Mississippi. He mistakenly landed at Matagorda Bay, Texas. He was killed by mutineers on March 19, 1687, near the Brazos River.

Leichhardt, Ludwig (1813–48?). German explorer and naturalist, born on Oct. 23, 1813, in Trebatsch. After studying at the universities of Berlin and Göttingen, he conducted scientific field work with the English chemist William Nicholson in England, France, Italy, and Switzerland. In 1842 Leichhardt arrived in Australia to explore its interior. He did field work in the Hunter River Valley until 1844. In 1844–45 he led the first expedition to cross northeastern Australia. He set out on another expedition in March 1848 and after April was never seen again. His mysterious disappearance inspired efforts to find him for nearly a century.

Lewis, Meriwether (1774–1809). U.S. explorer, born on Aug. 18, 1774, near Charlottesville, Va. After enlisting in the army, he advanced rapidly, becoming a captain in 1800. In 1801 he became private secretary to Pres. Thomas Jefferson, who selected him to lead the first overland expedition to the Pacific Northwest. At Lewis' request, William Clark was appointed to share the command. The success of the Lewis and Clark Expedition (1804–06) was greatly due to Lewis' preparation and skill. Lewis was named governor of the Territory of Upper Louisiana in 1808. He died from gunshot wounds on Oct. 11, 1809, at an inn near Hohenwald, Tenn.; he either was murdered or committed suicide.

Livingstone, David (1813–73). Scottish explorer, born on March 19, 1813, in Blantyre, Scotland. He studied theology and medicine in Glasgow before being ordained (1840) and deciding to work as a missionary in Africa. He was the first European to reach Lake Ngami (1849) and the first to reach Luanda, Angola, from the interior (1854). He encountered and named Victoria Falls (1855), journeyed across the continent to eastern Mozambique (1856, 1862), and explored the Lake Malawi region (1861–63). He ventured farther east of Lake Tanganyika than any previous expedition (1871). His attempt to find the source of the Nile River (1867–71) failed. When he was found by Henry Morton Stanley in 1871, his health was poor, but he refused to leave. His aides found him dead on May 1, 1873, in Chitambo (now in Zambia).

Mackenzie, Alexander (1764–1820). Canadian explorer, born in Stornoway, Isle of Lewis, Scotland. He moved to Canada as a young man, entering a fur-trading firm in 1779. In 1788 he set up a trading post on Lake Athabasca. From there he began an expedition (1789) that followed the Mackenzie River from Great Slave Lake to the Arctic Ocean. In 1792–93 he journeyed through the Rocky Mountains to the Pacific coast, becoming the first European to cross the continent north of Mexico. He died on March 12, 1820, near Dunkeld, Scotland.

The Granger Collection, New York
Ferdinand Magellan

Magellan, Ferdinand (1480?–1521). Portuguese navigator and explorer, born in Sabrosa or Porto, Portugal. After sailing in the service of Portugal in 1505–13, he set out in 1519 for Spain, hoping to reach Asia by sailing westward. He sailed around South America, discovered the Strait of Magellan, and continued across the Pacific Ocean. He was killed on Mactan Island, the Philippines, on April 27, 1521. However, one of his ships continued westward to Spain, becoming the first to circle the globe.

Marquette, Jacques (1637–75). French missionary and explorer, born in Laon, France, on June 1, 1637. Ordained a Jesuit priest, he arrived in Quebec in 1666 to preach among the Ottawa. He helped found missions at Sault Ste. Marie and St. Ignace, Mich. In 1673 he accompanied Louis Jolliet on his exploration of the Mississippi River. In 1674 Marquette set out to found a mission among the Illinois Indians, reaching the site of what is now Chicago. He died on May 18, 1675, at Ludington, Mich.

Nansen, Fridtjof (1861–1930). Norwegian explorer and statesman, born on Oct. 10, 1861, in Store-Frøen, Norway. In 1888 he led the first expedition to cross the ice fields of Greenland. In 1893–96 he led the *Fram* expedition and attempted to ski to the North Pole. He then engaged in scientific research and led oceanographic expeditions in the North Atlantic. He undertook diplomatic missions as Norway's first minister to Britain (1906–08) and as head of Norway's delegation to the new League of Nations (1920). He directed the repatriation from Russia of over 400,000 prisoners of war and organized famine relief. In 1922 he was awarded the Nobel peace prize. He died on May 13, 1930, in Lysaker, Norway.

Palmer, Nathaniel (1799–1877). American sea captain and explorer, born on Aug. 8, 1799, in Stonington, Conn. He went to sea at the age of 14, and in the War of 1812 he served as a sailor on a blockade runner. He later became a sealer, exploring the Southern Ocean in search of seal rookeries. In 1820 he sighted Antarctica, possibly becoming the first to do so. He later discovered the South Orkney Islands. From 1822 to 1826 he engaged in trade and helped transport troops to Simón Bolívar during the war of South American independence. Palmer died on June 21, 1877, in San Francisco, Calif. Palmer Land in Antarctica is named for him.

Park, Mungo (1771–1806). Scottish explorer, born on Sept. 10, 1771, in Fowlshiels, Scotland. A trained surgeon, in 1792 he traveled as a medical officer on a trade ship to Sumatra (now in Indonesia), where he studied the plants and animals. In 1795–97 he led an expedition to find the source of the Niger River. He reached the Niger at Ségou (now in Mali) but not the river's source. On a second expedition (1805–06) he reached Bamako (now in Mali) but was killed on the return trip, in about January 1806, near Bussa (now in Nigeria).

Peary, Robert Edwin (1856–1920). American explorer, born on May 6, 1856, in Cresson, Pa. He joined the U.S. Navy in 1881 but was granted leaves of absence to pursue his Arctic expeditions. He explored Greenland by dog sled in 1886 and 1891 and returned there on three trips to transport meteorites to the United States. He made several attempts to reach the North Pole between 1898 and 1905. In 1909, accompanied by Matthew Henson and four Inuit, he reached what he thought was the pole. In 1911 Peary retired from the Navy with the rank of rear admiral. He died on Feb. 20, 1920, in Washington, D.C. Examination of his expedition diary later suggested that he may have inadvertently stopped short of the pole.

Philby, H. Saint John (1885–1960). British diplomat and explorer, born on April 3, 1885, in Badula (now in Sri Lanka). In 1917 he was sent on a diplomatic mission to the future king of Saudi Arabia. He then crossed the Arabian Desert. He succeeded T.E. Lawrence as chief British representative in what is now Jordan (1921–24), converted to Islam in 1930, and was an unofficial adviser to the Saudi king. After an unsuccessful foray into politics in England in 1939, he was briefly imprisoned because of his antiwar views. He returned to Arabia in 1945 but was expelled 10 years later for having publicly criticized the Saudi regime. He died on Sept. 30, 1960, in Beirut, Lebanon. His son, Kim Philby, became a Soviet agent within the British intelligence service.

Pike, Zebulon Montgomery (1779–1813). American explorer, born on Jan. 5, 1779, in Lamberton, N.J. He joined the army at age 15. In 1805 he led an expedition to find the headwaters of the Mississippi River. In 1806 he was sent to the Southwest to explore the Arkansas and Red rivers. Passing through Colorado, he tried

Robert Edwin Peary

Encyclopædia Britannica, Inc.

World Explorers at a Glance—Continued

unsuccessfully to climb the mountain later named Pikes Peak. His party continued into northern New Mexico (1807); his report on the Santa Fe region encouraged later expansion into the Southwest. In the War of 1812 he was killed in the attack on York (Toronto), Canada, on April 27, 1813.

Pizarro, Francisco (1475?–1541). Spanish conqueror of the Inca Empire, born in Trujillo, Spain. In 1510 he joined an expedition to the Americas and three years later joined Balboa on the expedition that discovered the Pacific Ocean. He made two voyages of discovery down the Colombian coast (1524–25, 1526–28) and continued to Peru. After overthrowing the Inca in 1531–33, he spent the rest of his life consolidating Spain's hold on Peru. In 1535 he founded the city of Lima. He was killed there on June 26, 1541, by fellow Spaniards he had betrayed.

Polo, Marco (1254?–1324). Venetian traveler who journeyed from Europe to Asia. Born into a Venetian merchant family, he joined his father and uncle on a journey to China in 1271, traveling along the Silk Road and reaching the court of Kublai Khan in about 1274. The Polos remained in China for about 17 years, and Kublai sent Marco on several fact-finding missions to distant lands. Soon after the Polos returned to Venice in 1295, Marco was captured by the Genoese. In prison, he dictated an account of his travels, *Il milione*. He died in Venice on Jan. 8, 1324.

Ponce de León, Juan (1460–1521). Spanish explorer, born in Tierra de Campos Palencia, Spain. He may have accompanied Christopher Columbus' expedition in 1493 and later fought in the West Indies (1502), becoming governor of eastern Hispaniola. He colonized Puerto Rico (1508–09) and founded the island's oldest settlement, near what is now San Juan. While searching for the mythical fountain of youth, he discovered Florida in 1513. He sailed again to colonize Florida in 1521 but was wounded in an Indian attack and died in Havana, Cuba.

Przhevalsky, Nikolay Mikhaylovich (1839–88). Russian soldier and traveler, born on April 6, 1839, in Smolensk, Russia. After serving in the Russian army, he began exploring Asia, hoping to reach Lhasa, Tibet. In two voyages (1870–76) he traveled from Siberia across the Gobi to China, and then crossed the Tien Shan (mountains) and Takla Makan (desert). His third journey brought him within 170 miles (270 kilometers) of Lhasa, but he was forbidden to proceed. In 1883 he set out from Mongolia, traveling to what is now Kyrgyzstan. He died there, at Karakol, on Nov. 1, 1888. Through his explorations and plant and animal collections, he added vastly to geographic knowledge of east-central Asia.

Marco Polo

iStockphoto/Thinkstock

Mansell Collection—Time Life Pictures/Getty Images

Walter Raleigh

Raleigh, Walter (1554?–1618). English adventurer, born in Hayes Barton, England. He joined his half brother Humphrey Gilbert on a piratical expedition against the Spanish (1578) and then fought against the Irish rebels in Munster (1580). He was a favorite of Queen Elizabeth I until about 1596. In 1584 he sent an expedition to establish a colony in Virginia, but the colony failed. He was knighted in 1585. Ten years later he led an expedition up the Orinoco River of South America in search of gold. In 1603 he was accused of plotting to depose the British king and was imprisoned until 1616. He then led an unsuccessful expedition to search for gold in Guyana. His men burned a Spanish settlement there, and he was executed, on Oct. 29, 1618, in London.

Ross, James Clark (1800–62). British naval officer, born on April 15, 1800, in London. He accompanied the expedition of his uncle, John Ross, in search of the Northwest Passage (1818) and William Parry's Arctic voyages (1819–27). On his uncle's second Arctic expedition, he located the north magnetic pole in 1831. On his own Antarctic expedition (1839–43), he carried out important magnetic surveys and tried to reach the south magnetic pole. He discovered the Ross Sea and Victoria Land, Antarctica, in 1841. He died on April 3, 1862, in Aylesbury, England.

Scott, Robert Falcon (1868–1912). English explorer, born on June 6, 1868, in Devonport, England. He joined the Royal Navy in 1880, led an Antarctic expedition (1901–04), and was promoted to captain. In 1910 he embarked on a second expedition, and in October 1911 his party started overland for the South Pole. In January 1912 he and four others reached the pole, only to find that Roald Amundsen had preceded them by about a month. Exhausted and beset by bad weather and insufficient supplies, the men died on the return trip; Scott died on about March 29, 1912.

Shackleton, Ernest Henry (1874–1922). Anglo-Irish explorer, born on Feb. 15, 1874, in Kilkea, Ireland. He joined the merchant marine at age 16. He participated (1901–04) in Robert F. Scott's first expedition to the Antarctic. He led his own expedition in 1907–09 and almost reached the South Pole by sledge. In 1914 he led an expedition that aimed to cross Antarctica, but his ship was caught in pack ice and was crushed 10 months later. He and his crew drifted on ice floes for several months and then reached Elephant Island in the ship's boats. He and five others then sailed to South Georgia Island to get help. He led relief expeditions to rescue his men, all of whom survived. Shackleton died on Jan. 5, 1922, in Grytviken, South Georgia, at the outset of another Antarctic expedition.

Soto, Hernando de (1496/97?–1542). Spanish explorer, born in Jerez de los Caballeros, Spain. He joined the 1514 expedition of Pedro Arias Dávila to the West Indies. By 1520 he had gained a small fortune through slave trading in Nicaragua and Panama. He joined Francisco Pizarro on an expedition to conquer Peru in 1532. In 1539–42 he explored what is now the southeastern United States, becoming the first European to travel on the Mississippi River. He died on May 21, 1542, along the river in Louisiana.

Speke, John Hanning (1827–64). English explorer, born on May 3, 1827, in Bideford, England. He fought in the British army in India and traveled in the Himalayas and Tibet. In 1857–58 he and Richard Burton led an expedition to eastern Africa, and they became the first Europeans to reach Lake Tanganyika. On the return trip Speke struck out alone, reaching and naming Lake Victoria. His claim that it was the source of the Nile River was questioned, but on a second expedition (1860–63) with James Grant, Speke found the Nile's exit from the lake. He was killed by his own gun while hunting near Corsham, England, on Sept. 15, 1864.

Stanley, Henry Morton (1841–1904). British American explorer, born as John Rowlands on Jan. 28, 1841, in Denbigh, Wales. After growing up partly in a British workhouse, in 1859 he sailed to the United States as a cabin boy. He became a journalist for the *New York Herald* in 1867. In 1871 he set off on a journey to locate the missing explorer David Livingstone, whom he found at Ujiji on Lake Tanganyika. Stanley further explored central Africa for extended periods between 1874 and 1884, paving the way for the colonization of the Congo region. In 1888 he escorted Mehmed Emin Pasha, who had been cut off by a revolt in Sudan, and 1,500 others to the east coast. Stanley wrote many popular books about his travels. He died on May 10, 1904, in London, England.

Stuart, John McDouall (1815–66). Australian explorer, born on Sept. 7, 1815, in Dysart (now Kirkcaldy), Scotland. He moved to Australia in 1838 and worked as a surveyor for the South Australian government. He joined Charles Sturt on his 1844–46 expedition into the Australian interior. Starting in 1860, Stuart led a series of expeditions in the attempt to cross Australia from south to north. In 1862 he successfully reached the Indian Ocean but became ill and nearly blind on the return trip. He went to London, England, to recover but died there on June 5, 1866.

Sturt, Charles (1795–1869). Australian explorer, born on April 28, 1795, in Bengal, India. Educated in England, he entered the British Army at the age of 18. For the next 13 years he saw service in Spain, Canada, France, and Ireland. In 1827 he became military secretary to the governor of New South Wales, Australia. His expedition

John MacDouall Stuart

The Art Archive/Picture Desk

down the Murrumbidgee and Murray rivers (1829–30) is considered one of the greatest explorations in Australian history. He also led an expedition north from Adelaide to the edge of Simpson Desert (1844–46). He settled in England in 1853 and died in Cheltenham on June 16, 1869.

Tasman, Abel Janszoon (1603?–59?). Dutch navigator, born in Lutjegast, Netherlands. For the Dutch East India Company, he made exploratory and trading voyages to East and Southeast Asia (1634–39). In 1642 he sailed in search of the hypothetical southern continent of the Pacific. He discovered Tasmania and then sailed along the coast of New Zealand. He also discovered Tonga and the Fiji Islands. On his next voyage (1644) he sailed along the north and west coasts of Australia. He died probably before Oct. 22, 1659, but certainly before Feb. 5, 1661.

Thompson, David (1770–1857). English explorer and geographer, born on April 30, 1770, in London. He led exploring expeditions for fur-trading companies in northwestern North America. In 1798 he discovered Turtle Lake, one of the headwaters of the Mississippi River. In 1807 he crossed the Rocky Mountains and built the first trading post on the Columbia River. He descended (1811) and mapped the entire length of that river. He helped chart the border between Canada and the United States in 1818–26. He died on Feb. 10, 1857, in Longueil, Canada.

Vancouver, George (1757–98). English navigator, born on June 22, 1757, in King's Lynn, England. He entered the Royal Navy at age 13 and sailed with James Cook on his second and third voyages (1772–75, 1776–79) to the Pacific. In 1791 he explored the coasts of Australia, New Zealand, Tahiti, and Hawaii before reaching the Pacific coast of North America in 1792. Over the next two years he mapped a major portion of the coast. He died on May 10, 1798, in Richmond, England.

Verrazzano, Giovanni da (1485–1528). Italian navigator and explorer for France. Born in Tuscany, he moved to Dieppe, France, where he entered the maritime service. In 1524 he was sent to find a westward passage to Asia and instead reached North America. He explored the eastern coast from Cape Fear northward and became the first European to explore the sites of New York Harbor and Narragansett Bay. He later led expeditions to Brazil (1527) and to the Caribbean, where he was killed and eaten by cannibals.

Wilkes, Charles (1798–1877). U.S. naval officer and explorer, born on April 3, 1798, in New York City. He joined the Navy in 1818. From 1838 to 1842 he commanded an exploring and surveying expedition that circled the globe. Along the way, he reached Antarctica, where he reported land at points in the region now known as Wilkes Land. He also visited islands in the Pacific and explored the U.S. West Coast. He wrote several volumes about his expedition and then served in the U.S. Civil War (1861–65). He was court-martialed in 1864, partly for insubordination. He was commissioned rear admiral, retired, in 1866. He died on Feb. 8, 1877, in Washington, D.C.

Xuanzang (602–664). Chinese Buddhist monk and traveler, born in Guoshi, China. He received a classical Confucian education before converting to Buddhism. He left on a pilgrimage to India in 629 to study the religion at its source. He traveled by foot across Central Asia and reached India in 633. After study at the famous Nalanda monastery, he returned home in 645 to a hero's welcome, bringing back hundreds of Buddhist texts, which he spent the rest of his life translating. He established the Weishi ("Ideation Only") school of Buddhism, which won many followers in Japan as the Hosso school. He died in Chang'an, China. The classic novel *Xiyou ji* was inspired by his life.

Zheng He (1371?–1433). Chinese admiral and diplomat. He was born Ma Sanbao in Kunyang, China, to a family of Chinese Muslims. As a young man, he was made a eunuch and sent into the army. The Chinese emperor later named him commander in chief of missions to the "Western Oceans." Zheng made seven sea voyages from 1405 to 1433, visiting many places in South Asia, Southeast Asia, the Middle East, and Africa. He helped to extend Chinese maritime and commercial influence throughout the regions bordering the Indian Ocean. He died in 1433 in what is now Kozhikode, India.

FURTHER RESOURCES

General

Baker, Daniel B., ed. Explorers and Discoverers of the World (Gale, 1993).

Buisseret, David. The Oxford Companion to World Exploration (Oxford Univ. Press, 2007).

Explorers and Exploration, 11 vols. (Marshall Cavendish, 2005).

Ganeria, Anita, and Mills, Andrea. Atlas of Exploration (DK, 2008).

George Philip & Son. Atlas of Exploration (Oxford Univ. Press, 2008).

Konstam, Angus. Historical Atlas of Exploration: 1492–1600 (Mercury, 2006).

Netzley, P.D. Encyclopedia of Women's Travel and Exploration (Oryx, 2001).

Ross, Val. The Road to There: Mapmakers and Their Stories (Tundra, 2009).

Stefoff, Rebecca. The Accidental Explorers; Scientific Explorers (Oxford Univ. Press, 2009).

Waldman, Carl, and Wexler, Alan. Encyclopedia of Exploration (Facts on File, 2004).

Eurasia

Bowman, J.S. Exploration in the World of the Ancients, rev. ed. (Chelsea House, 2010).

Currie, Stephen. The Himalayas (Lucent, 2005).

Galloway, Priscilla, and Hunter, Dawn. Adventures on the Ancient Silk Road (Annick, 2009).

Harvey, Gill. Desert Adventures (Usborne, 2008).

Simon, Charnan. Explorers of the Ancient World (Childrens, 1990).

White, Pamela. Exploration in the World of the Middle Ages, 500–1500, rev. ed. (Chelsea House, 2010).

The Americas

Cothran, Helen. Early American Civilization and Exploration (Greenhaven, 2003).

Cox, Caroline, and Albala, Ken. Opening up North America, 1497–1800, rev. ed. (Chelsea House, 2010).

Edwards, Judith. Lewis and Clark's Journey of Discovery in American History (Enslow, 1999).

Faber, Harold. The Discoverers of America (Scribner, 1992).

Freedman, Russell. Who Was First?: Discovering the Americas (Clarion, 2007).

Smith, Tom. Discovery of the Americas, 1492–1800, rev. ed. (Chelsea House, 2010).

Australia and the Pacific Islands

Coupe, Robert. Australian Explorers: Unlocking the Great South Land (New Holland, 1998).

Currie, Stephen. Australia and the Pacific Islands (Lucent, 2005).

Lace, W.W. Captain James Cook (Chelsea House, 2009).

Nicholson, John. Fishing for Islands: Traditional Boats and Seafarers of the Pacific (Allen & Unwin, 1999).

Vail, Martha. Exploring the Pacific, rev. ed. (Chelsea House, 2010).

Africa

Currie, Stephen. West Africa (Lucent, 2005).

Otfinoski, Steven. David Livingstone: Deep in the Heart of Africa (Marshall Cavendish Benchmark, 2007).

Sherman, Steven. Henry Stanley and the European Explorers of Africa (Chelsea, 1993).

Simon, Charnan. Henry the Navigator (Childrens Press, 1993).

Stefoff, Rebecca. Vasco da Gama and the Portuguese Explorers (Chelsea, 1993).

Young, Serinity. Richard Francis Burton: Explorer, Scholar, Spy (Marshall Cavendish Benchmark, 2007).

The Polar Regions

Anderson, H.S. Exploring the Polar Regions, rev. ed. (Chelsea House, 2010).

Armstrong, Jennifer. Shipwreck at the Bottom of the World: The Extraordinary True Story of Shackleton and the Endurance (Paw Prints, 2008).

Calvert, Patricia. Robert E. Peary: To the Top of the World (Benchmark/Marshall Cavendish, 2002).

Delgado, J.P. Across the Top of the World: The Quest for the Northwest Passage (British Museum, 1999).

Gogerly, Liz. Amundsen and Scott's Race to the South Pole (Heinemann, 2008).

Myers, W.D. Antarctica: Journeys to the South Pole (Scholastic, 2005).

Quotation Sources

Atlas of Exploration (Oxford Univ. Press, 1997)—p. 18; Burton, Rosemary, and others, *Journeys of the Great Explorers* (AA Publishing, 1992)—p. 69; Ch'en, Kenneth K.S., *Buddhism in China: A Historical Survey* (Princeton Univ. Press, 1964)—p. 6; Cook, James, *The Journals of Captain Cook* (Penguin, 1999)—p. 57; Fleming, Fergus, *Off the Map: Tales of Endurance and Exploration* (Grove Press, 2004)—pp. 33, 64, 86; Hanbury-Tenison, Robert, ed., *The Oxford Book of Exploration* (Oxford Univ. Press, 1993)—pp. 9, 24, 36, 59, 70, 76, 85, 89; Moss, Sarah, *The Frozen Ship: The Histories and Tales of Polar Exploration* (BlueBridge, 2006)—p. 91; Ryan, Simon, *The Cartographic Eye: How Explorers Saw Australia* (Cambridge Univ. Press, 1996)—p. 61

INDEX

Page numbers in **bold** indicate main subject references; page numbers in *italics* indicate illustrations.

Page numbers in **bold** indicate main subject references; page numbers in *italics* indicate illustrations.